Urban Regeneration & Social Sustainability

Best practice from European cities

The intersection of urban regeneration and sustainability has long been separated at birth, with much of the research, policy and practice focused on linking the two through a greater understanding of environmental sustainability. Yet social sustainability, especially in an urban regeneration context, remains underdeveloped, theoretical and oversimplified when compared to the progress of the environmental movement. In their new book, the authors now look to break down more silos and explore the social sustainability side of urban regeneration.

The book highlights a range of best practice from the efforts of governments of major European cities to those of private investors such as igloo, and is honest about the challenges of isolating impact and developing indicators that measure the all-important 'soft stuff.' I am thrilled that the authors throw the lid open on the difficulties of past efforts which tried to apply a simplified triple bottom line framework to urban regeneration. They clearly highlight the need for a more sophisticated approach that understands the socio-economic needs and complexities of people, cities and investment.

**Bill Boler, Director, Investment and Physical
Regeneration Business in the Community, UK**

The 21st century will hold huge challenges for cities from cultural and social perspectives. Using case studies from across the EU, this book is an essential reference point for those seeking to understand the issues which need to be addressed.

**Pooran Desai OBE, Co-founder, BioRegional
and Sustainability Director, BioRegional Quintain Ltd**

This is a big book which raises big questions on a big subject – the challenge of achieving socially sustainable regeneration in European cities. It provides much important analytical discussion of – as well as empirical evidence about – this big idea at a European level based on good studies in five European cities – Barcelona, Leipzig, Turin, Rotterdam, and Cardiff. It clearly outlines the development of European thinking and policy about the issue. It also has important things to say about how to measure the elusive ideas implied in the concept as well as the principles and practices of delivery vehicles. Importantly it brings in the roles, contribution and views of the private sector – a critical player, but often absent in the discussions of these issues. The EIB has helped to fill an important gap in a crucial field. So has this book.

**Michael Parkinson, Director of European Institute for Urban Affairs
and Author of *State of the English Cities, Competitive European Cities:
Where Does the UK Stand?* and *The Credit Crunch
and Regeneration: Impact and Implications***

Social sustainability is often treated as the poor cousin in evaluating the success or failure of urban renewal projects. This volume offers a comprehensive, systematic and authoritative overview of the scholarly literature and the practice models relevant to the topic. An illuminating overview of experiences with Europe's Structural Funds and Cohesion Funds provides essential background to five carefully chosen case studies from which "best practice" conclusions are drawn. The book is essential reading for scholars and practitioners alike.

**Steve Rayner, James Martin Professor of Science and Civilization,
University of Oxford and Director, Oxford Programme for the Future of Cities**

Regeneration is a difficult task with multiple ambitions and multiple problems. This book manages successfully to draw from a series of case studies to bring out lessons for the slippery concept of social sustainability which will help guide practitioners both in setting up programmes and in monitoring their success.

**Bridget Rosewell, Chairman, Volterra Consulting,
Chief Economic Adviser, Greater London Authority**

Urban Regeneration
& Social Sustainability

Best practice from European cities

Andrea Colantonio

Research Coordinator at LSE Cities
London School of Economics and Political Sciences
UK

Tim Dixon

Director of the Oxford Institute of Sustainable Development (OISD)
Professor of Real Estate in the Department of Real Estate
and Construction at Oxford Brookes University
UK

WILEY-BLACKWELL

A John Wiley & Sons, Ltd., Publication

Library of Congress Cataloging-in-Publication Data

Colantonio, Andrea.
    Urban regeneration & social sustainability : best practice from European cities / Andrea Colantonio and Tim Dixon.
      p.   cm. – (RICS research series)
    Includes bibliographical references and index.
    ISBN 978-1-4051-9419-8 (alk. paper)
1. Urban renewal–Europe.   2. City planning–Europe.   3. Sustainable urban development–Europe.   I. Dixon, Timothy J., 1958–   II. Title.   III. Title: Urban regeneration and social sustainability.
    HT178.E8C59 2011
    307.3'416094–dc22

                                        2010029194

This book is published in the following electronic formats: ePDF [9781444329452]; Wiley Online Library [9781444329445]; ePub [9781444329469].

A catalogue record for this book is available from the British Library.

Set in 10/13pt TrumpMediaeval by SPi Publisher Services, Pondicherry, India
Printed in Singapore by Ho Printing Singapore Pte Ltd

1   2011

Acknowledgements

A significant part of the work presented in this volume was carried out during the EIBURS (European Investment Bank University Research Sponsorship) project entitled 'Measuring the Social Dimension of Social Sustainability' during the period from January 2007 to September 2009. In respect of the conduct of the work we owe a considerable debt to the European Investment Bank (EIB) for *de facto* making the publication of this book possible, and particularly Mateo Turro (former associate director at Projects Directorate, EIB) and his team for their support during the duration of the EIBURS programme. We also would like to thank the numerous project participants from the municipalities examined as part of this book for sharing their experiences of urban regeneration with us. In addition we wish to thank Professor John Glasson (OISD) for his valuable suggestions concerning sustainability assessment and monitoring indicators. We are also grateful to Dr Juliet Carpenter, Dr Robin Ganser, Austine Ng'ombe (OISD) and Venere Sanna, University of Rome, for their contributions to important chapters of this book.

At the more personal level, Andrea would like to thank his parents for their consistent and unconditional support, which they have given over the last few years. Further appreciation is expressed to Federica for the patience shown during the writing process of this volume. Tim would also like to thank his family for their love and support.

Finally, both authors would also like to thank their colleagues for their support during the process of writing the book.

The material in this book is based on research conducted by the authors during 2007–2009 in the Oxford Institute for Sustainable Development (OISD), School of the Built Environment, Oxford Brookes University.

The research was funded under the European Investment Bank's EIBURS research programme, which the authors would like to gratefully acknowledge. Further details of this research can be found at: http://www.brookes.ac.uk/schools/be/oisd/sustainable_communities/index.html

Andrea Colantonio
and Tim Dixon

The Royal Institution of Chartered Surveyors is the mark of property professionalism worldwide, promoting best practice, regulation and consumer protection for business and the community. It is the home of property related knowledge and is an impartial advisor to governments and global organisations. It is committed to the promotion of research in support of the efficient and effective operation of land and property markets worldwide.

Real Estate Issues

Series Managing Editors

Stephen Brown Head of Research, Royal Institution of Chartered Surveyors

John Henneberry Department of Town & Regional Planning, University of Sheffield

K.W. Chau Chair Professor, Department of Real Estate and Construction, The University of Hong Kong

Elaine Worzala Professor, Director of the Accelerated MSRE, Edward St. John Department of Real Estate, Johns Hopkins University

Real Estate Issues is an international book series presenting the latest thinking into how real estate markets operate. The books have a strong theoretical basis – providing the underpinning for the development of new ideas.

The books are inclusive in nature, drawing both upon established techniques for real estate market analysis and on those from other academic disciplines as appropriate. The series embraces a comparative approach, allowing theory and practice to be put forward and tested for their applicability and relevance to the understanding of new situations. It does not seek to impose solutions, but rather provides a more effective means by which solutions can be found. It will not make any presumptions as to the importance of real estate markets but will uncover and present, through the clarity of the thinking, the real significance of the operation of real estate markets.

Books in the series

Greenfields, Brownfields & Housing Development
Adams & Watkins
97806320063871

Planning, Public Policy & Property Markets
Edited by Adams, Watkins & White
9781405124300

Housing & Welfare in Southern Europe
Allen, Barlow, Léal, Maloutas & Padovani
9781405103077

Markets & Institutions in Real Estate & Construction
Ball
978140510990

Building Cycles: Growth & Instability
Barras
9781405130011

Neighbourhood Renewal & Housing Markets
Edited by Beider
9781405134101

Mortgage Markets Worldwide
Ben-Shahar, Leung & Ong
9781405132107

The Cost of Land Use Decisions
Buitelaar
9781405151238

Urban Regeneration & Social Sustainability
Colantonio & Dixon
9781405194198

Urban Regeneration in Europe
Couch, Fraser & Percy
9780632058412

Urban Sprawl
Couch, Leontidou & Petschel-Held
9781405151238

Real Estate & the New Economy
Dixon, McAllister, Marston & Snow
9781405117784

Economics & Land Use Planning
Evans
9781405118613

Economics, Real Estate & the Supply of Land
Evans
9781405118620

Management of Privatised Housing: International Policies & Practice
Gruis, Tsenkova & Nieboer
9781405181884

Development & Developers
Guy & Henneberry
9780632058426

The Right to Buy
Jones & Murie
9781405131971

Housing Markets & Planning Policy
Jones & Watkins
9781405175203

Mass Appraisal Methods
Kauko & d'Amato
9781405180979

Economics of the Mortgage Market
Leece
9781405114615

Towers of Capital: Office Markets & International Financial Services
Lizieri
9781405156721

Making Housing More Affordable: The Role of Intermediate Tenures
Monk & Whitehead
9781405147149

Global Trends in Real Estate Finance
Newell & Sieracki
9781405151283

Housing Economics & Public Policy
O'Sullivan & Gibb
9780632064618

International Real Estate
Seabrooke, Kent & How
9781405103084

British Housebuilders
Wellings
9781405149181

Forthcoming

Transforming Private Landlords
Crook & Kemp
9781405184151

Housing Stock Transfer
Taylor
9781405170321

Urban Design in the Real Estate Development Process
Tiesdell & Adams
9781405192194

Real Estate Finance in the New Economic World
Tiwari & White
9781405158718

To my parents, Bernardo and Chiara
AC

To my mother and to my wife (Rachel)
and son (Sam) for all their love and support.
TD

Contents

All chapters authored by Andrea Colantonio and Tim Dixon unless otherwise stated

The Authors

Andrea Colantonio is Research Coordinator at LSE Cities, London School of Economics and Political Sciences, London, UK. He is an urban geographer and economist who specialises in the investigation of the complex linkages between urban growth, sustainability and the geographies of development in both developing and developed countries. He has worked and researched in numerous international universities, and he is main author of 'Urban Tourism and Development in the Socialist State. Havana during the "Special Period"' (2006).

Tim Dixon is Director of the Oxford Institute of Sustainable Development (OISD) and Professor of Real Estate in the Department of Real Estate and Construction at Oxford Brookes University. With more than 25 years' experience of research, education and professional practice in the built environment he is a qualified fellow of the RICS and of the Higher Education Academy, a former member of SEEDA's South East Excellence Advisory Board, as well as the editorial boards of five leading international real-estate journals. He has worked on funded collaborative research projects with UK and overseas academics and practitioners and his personal research interests revolve around (i) the sustainability agenda and its impact on property development, investment and occupation, and (ii) the impact of ICT on commercial property and real-estate markets. The research is based on a strong interdisciplinary approach, which incorporates policy and practice impacts, and futures thinking. He is also a member of the CORENET Sustainability Working Group, and a member of the Steering Group for the 'Future of Cities' Research programme, based in the James Martin 21st Century School at Oxford University. In 2009 he was awarded Honorary Fellow status of the Institute of Green Professionals.

Contributing Authors

Juliet Carpenter is Senior Research Fellow at the Oxford Institute of Sustainable Development (OISD) at Oxford Brookes University. She is a specialist in urban regeneration, in particular the evaluation of EU Structural Funds related to sustainable development and regeneration. Her particular research interests lie in the application of a holistic approach to regeneration, and its contribution to sustainable communities.

Robin Ganser is Professor in Spatial Planning at the University of Applied Sciences, Luebeck, Germany, and former Senior Lecturer in Spatial Planning at Oxford Brookes University. He has worked on funded interdisciplinary research projects mainly in the UK and in Germany but also with partners in the USA and in China. His research interests include urban and rural regeneration, brownfield development and spatial planning for sustainable development – the latter with a particular focus on planning instruments and management of planning processes.

Austine Ng'ombe is Research Assistant in the Department of Real Estate and Construction at Oxford Brookes University. Austine is a Land Economist and before joining Oxford Brookes he worked as a Provincial Lands Officer in the Department of Lands in Zambia. His research preoccupation is an exploration of the dynamics of land tenure in both developed and developing countries, informed by the emerging science of complexity.

Venere Stefania Sanna is Visiting Researcher at the Oxford Institute for Sustainable Development (OISD) of the Oxford Brookes University. In addition to her expertise in Geographical Information Systems (GIS) and spatial statistics, her research interests include regional and local economic development issues, regional and urban competitiveness and theories and methods for socioeconomic research.

Foreword

Sustainability is arguably one of the most over and inappropriately used words in the English language, the net result of which has been a dilution of the sustainability concept. Multiple interpretations of sustainability by authors, researchers, policy makers, journalists and other commentators prevail and while broad consensus may appear to exist there is considerable debate on the objectives, goals and instruments to be used in advancing the sustainability agenda. Politically, sustainability is perceived to be good, though, in reality, policy action to advance the sustainability agenda frequently lags both the evidence base and public opinion.

The fusing of urban regeneration with sustainability to produce the hybrid concept of sustainable urban regeneration reflects the evolutionary journey and different phases of regeneration. This is well illustrated in the UK, where over thirty years of urban policy has produced an evolving and changing definition of regeneration. There is increasing recognition that regeneration, if it is to be sustainable, must adopt a long-term multi-faceted approach, addressing unemployment, enhancing educational attainment, and reducing crime as well as transforming the urban fabric through infrastructure provision, improved housing and the redevelopment of derelict land and buildings. The focus on sustainable regeneration does not, however, mean that all previous regeneration policies and tools were unsustainable. Indeed, the contrary may be apparent with schemes initially considered to be merely property driven or development-led regeneration meeting sustainability objectives in terms of investment performance, employment locations and wider goals. Output evaluations suggest the attainments of regeneration initiatives have been considerable, though the question remains as to how these outputs contribute in achieving sustainable regeneration. Regeneration initiatives have often been highly successful in realising their objectives but very often failed to understand or tackle the root causes of deprivation.

The major criticism of regeneration has been the failure to close the socio-economic gap between the poorest neighbourhoods and the national average. Despite a multiplicity of innovations and attempts to address the components of urban decline, a combination of poor investment and inadequacies in urban policy have consolidated symptoms of social polarisation, economic hardship and environmental deprivation in many inner-city areas. This has led to a refocus upon social issues in regeneration which are sometimes perceived to be the 'softer' or less tangible side of regeneration and which require new metrics in the assessment and measurement of objectives. Scale is important, with social sustainability frequently interpreted at the neighbourhood level and based on limited goals. For instance, while it is recognised that well-designed mixed-use developments on brownfield sites are fundamental to the creation of sustainable communities and the realisation of housing targets, there has been a tendency to over simplify the interpretation of mixed use, resulting in pockets of schemes rather than regenerating areas.

Arguably, for social sustainability to be achieved, regeneration needs to be bolder and encompass larger swathes of cities and embrace not only employment and environmental issues but the wider provision of hospitals/medical centres, schools and leisure facilities. This requires a new understanding of regeneration and partnership delivery vehicles. In a post-recessionary environment, the challenges are immense and will require new structures between the equally constrained public and private sectors. For the latter the need to show its socially responsible investment credentials and the search for alternative asset classes, as interest in the traditional sectors of retail and office property wane, socially sustainable regeneration may look increasingly attractive but appropriate policies are required and the private sector will want assurances of sufficiently attractive risk-adjusted returns.

The social-sustainability agenda is complex and will be instrumental in shaping the future development of our cities and towns over the coming decades. This book, in drawing together the knowledge base on the subject, through generic considerations and best-practice examples, is a major contribution in raising the level of debate on the understanding and interpretation of social sustainability.

Professor Stanley McGreal
Director of the Built Environment Research Institute,
University of Ulster, April 2010

Part I

Social Sustainability and Urban Regeneration

1

Introduction

Background and context

In 2007, for the first time in history the majority of the people in the world lived in cities (EC, 2007). This is the direct result of the rapid growth not only of the world's largest cities (where conurbations of more than 10 million people predominate), but also the growth of smaller and medium-sized cities (UN Habitat, 2006).

In the wider global context of accelerating urbanisation Europe's cities are amongst some of the oldest in the world, and today more than 60% of people live in urban areas with a population of more than 50 000. However, with the exception of London and Paris, Europe is also characterised by a unique polycentric structure of large, medium-sized and small cities (EC, 2006).

If cities are to succeed as engines of economic growth then it is important that policies founded on economic, social and environmental issues are fully integrated. In other words that there should be a balance between promoting economic competitiveness and social cohesion and tackling environmental issues, because it is generally agreed that these, alongside other issues relating to inadequate governance and leadership, are the most pressing challenges to the economic performance, attractiveness and competitiveness of cities (EC, 2006; European Institute for Urban Affairs, 2007).

Today cities face change brought about by a series of structural forces, including globalisation, economic restructuring, increasing competition from other cities and restructuring of the welfare state (European Institute for Urban Affairs, 2007). Furthermore, by their very nature, of course, cities are often characterised by substantial spatial and/or group polarisation in economic and social opportunities, and, moreover, these differences can be even more extreme between neighbourhoods in the same city than between cities. The challenges faced within our cities can also vary significantly ranging from increasing population, through to rising house prices, lack of development land or a poorly resourced public sector. In some cities depopulation, dereliction, lack of jobs or poor quality of life may be problematic, while in others urban sprawl and suburbanisation may be an issue. At an urban scale, therefore, tackling transport, accessibility and mobility; improving access to services and amenities; improving the physical and natural environments and developing a city's cultural focus are key to improving its attractiveness (EC, 2006).

Set in this recent context of an integrated approach to cohesion policy, previous research on sustainability has, sadly, often been limited to environmental and economic concerns. However, in recent years, social sustainability has gained increased recognition as a fundamental component of sustainable development, and has begun to receive political and institutional endorsement within the sustainable development agenda, and the sustainable urban regeneration discourse.

In the 1980s, urban regeneration projects focused mainly on the physical and economic renewal of degraded inner-city areas. However, since the 1990s across the EU, this approach to urban regeneration, which emphasised the environmental and economic spheres of regeneration, has been replaced by a more integrated approach to urban redevelopment, which links the stimulation of economic activities and environmental improvements to wider social and cultural elements.

There has therefore been a shift in emphasis from 'urban renaissance' to 'city competitiveness'. Essentially the key drivers for urban competitiveness include (EC, 2006; European Institute for Urban Affairs, 2007):

- Innovation in processes and products;
- economic diversity;
- skilled people;
- connectivity and communications;
- place quality; and
- strategic capacity (or decision making, political processes and leadership).

Barcelona is a key example of this change in emphasis. During the 1990s, the city's strategy was founded on urban regeneration that focused on infrastructure, the physical environment, city centre, waterfront and key projects like the Olympics. However, the limits of this hitherto successful approach were recognised as its GDP growth and knowledge base lay relatively undernourished. More recently, therefore, the city has focused on the promotion of the knowledge sector, and developing a much stronger innovation base to underpin job creation (European Institute for Urban Affairs, 2007).

The emergence of 'community' as a focal point for the delivery of sustainable urban development has also moved to the heart of European urban policy. For example, in 1998 the report 'Urban Sustainable Development in the EU: A Framework for Action' (CEC, 1998) combined the twin themes of sustainable development and urban governance, and encouraged and promoted partnerships between the public and private sectors. Moreover, in 2005 the 'Bristol Accord', which focused on the theme of sustainable communities, was approved amongst member states (ODPM, 2006). The Accord set out what is meant by a 'sustainable community' and highlighted eight characteristics of such places, which are discussed in more detail in Chapter 2 of this book.

Sustainable development was in fact enshrined in the EU's *Sustainable Development Strategy*, where it was seen as being (EU, 2006: 2):

> ... about safeguarding the earth's capacity to support life in all its diversity. It is based on the principles of democracy and the rule of law and respect for fundamental rights including freedom and equal opportunities for all. It brings about solidarity within and between generations. It seeks to promote a dynamic economy with a high level of employment and education, of health protection, of social and territorial cohesion and of environmental protection in a peaceful and secure world, respecting cultural diversity.

This effectively underpinned and linked with key objectives at an urban level in the EU, which sought to promote economic prosperity, social equity and cohesion and environmental protection.

There was also a strong feeling that integrated strategies and co-ordinated actions were needed at an urban level in Europe (EC, 2009). More recently, therefore, building on the Bristol Accord, in May 2007 European Ministers signed the 'Leipzig Charter on Sustainable European Cities' (EU Ministers, 2007), which itself built on the 'Urban Acquis' of 2004 (Ministry of Kingdom and Interior Relations, 2005) (see Chapter 12).[1] For the first time, therefore, all of the 27 member states outlined an ideal model for the 'European city of the 21st century', and agreed on common principles and strategies for policy

---

[1] Essentially the Rotterdam Urban Acquis of 2004 promoted the concept of 'integrated sustainable urban development" (ISUD), which is a system of interlinked actions seeking to bring about a lasting improvement in the economic, physical, social and environmental conditions of a city or an area within a city. The key to the process is 'integration', meaning that all policies, projects and proposals are considered in relation to one another (URBACT, 2010; EIB, 2010).

related to urban development. The Leipzig Charter lays the foundation for a new integrated urban policy in Europe, focusing on addressing urban challenges related to social exclusion, structural change, ageing, climate change and mobility.

The broad approach to urban policy promoted recently at EU level has also advocated integrated area-based regeneration initiatives which combine economic, social, cultural and environmental aspects, and are managed through partnerships with strong civic involvement. As a result, the concept of 'partnership' has been woven into recent EU urban initiatives such as URBAN I and URBAN II, with proposals for good practice based on partnerships involving the public, private and voluntary sectors. This has also encouraged the establishment of an increasing number of Public Private Partnerships (PPPs) in urban regeneration programmes, which are one facet of the drive towards sustainable financing for cities and the development of a complex array of investment vehicles, involving local authorities, institutional investors, private developers and banks, for example.

There has therefore been a changing emphasis from a 'compartmentalised' approach to urban regeneration in Europe to a more 'integrated' approach that brings together the physical, economic and social dimensions of urban development and ties it strongly into the sustainable development agenda (URBACT, 2009). Key to this is the concept of a long-term consistent vision for urban areas. As the European Commission suggest (EC, 2006: 26):

> Cities should have a long term, consistent plan for all the different factors promoting sustainable growth and jobs in urban areas. Actions in one field must be consistent with those in another. Notably, economic measures must be sustainable in social and environmental terms. Monitoring and evaluation systems should be in place to verify results on the ground.

This integrated approach focuses on the following elements therefore (Franke *et al.*, 2007):

- Identifying the strengths and weaknesses of the city and of particular neighbourhoods.
- Formulating realistic goals for particular areas.
- Increasing the impact of public intervention measures through early co-ordination and pooling of public–private funds.
- Integrating planning for particular areas, sectors and technical support.
- Empowering citizens and promoting corporate social responsibility.
- Supporting inter-municipal co-ordination to harmonise and link the city's development aims with its hinterland.

Many areas that are the focus of regeneration include some of Europe's most deprived neighbourhoods, which have entered a spiral of decline often through forces of globalisation and structural change. These may, for example, be areas that have been previously characterised by manufacturing industry and are now brownfield sites (Dixon *et al.*, 2007); inner city areas with stagnating economies; residential neighbourhoods with defunct urban structures; or residential areas that have concentrated social and economic problems (LUDA, 2003; Franke *et al.*, 2007).

The emphasis given to urban policy issues, however, varies among EU member states and there is a wide variation in policies at a national level. Nonetheless, eight policy challenges also continue to hold true at a national and city level (Franke *et al.*, 2007):

- Developing the labour market for all sections of the population;
- ensuring adequate income and wealth for all;
- overcoming educational disadvantage;
- fostering family cohesion and equal rights for men and women;
- guaranteeing adequate housing for all; and
- promoting equal rights of access to services.

There is also a perception amongst many commentators that the need for urban investment is greater than ever if cities are to become more 'investable' and 'investment-ready' (Clark, 2007). Innovative forms of partnership financing (public private partnerships or PPPs) and joint ventures between the public and private sector are therefore becoming of paramount importance. Indeed, this is even more important in the current economic recession, which began towards the end of 2007, and is likely to trigger a broad process of financial restructuring that will prompt cities to explore and test additional financial tools and revenue-raising options (IPF, 2009; APUDG, 2009; ULI, 2009).

Nonetheless, despite these recent developments in the policy and practice of urban regeneration, our understanding of the social dimension of sustainable urban regeneration is still limited, especially from an assessment and measurement point of view. There is therefore a clear need for further research in this field.

Urban regeneration and social sustainability

A variety of definitions of the term 'regeneration' exist depending on particular perspectives (IPF, 2006). In the UK the government has defined regeneration as a set of activities that reverse economic, social and physical decline in areas where the market will not resolve this without government support (CLG, 2009). An alternative and perhaps broader definition of urban regeneration, is provided by Roberts (2000: 17) who provides an initial definition of urban regeneration as: 'a comprehensive and integrated vision and action which leads to the resolution of urban problems and which seeks to bring about a lasting improvement in the economic, physical, social and environmental conditions of an area that has been subject to change'.

However, recent policy initiatives in the UK have also sought to highlight the distinction between 'economic development' and 'regeneration' (CLG, 2008). For example, whilst development is seen as focusing on profit and being commercially viable in its focus, regeneration should also incorporate elements of social and economic diversity to benefit existing communities (IPF, 2009).[2]

Broadly speaking, according to key commentators, the main thematic narratives (although not necessarily mutually exclusive) to area-based regeneration and renewal, have included the following:

- Property-led physical approach, where, for example, a major retail-led or mixed-use scheme is expected to have multiplier effects in the local economy (for example, Dixon & Marston, 2003; DTZ, 2009).
- Business-driven approach, which highlights the importance of 'underserved markets' particularly in inner-city areas as important foci for regeneration through business investment (for example, Porter, 1995).
- Urban form and design perspective, which highlights the importance of the relationship between sustainable development (SD) and urban form (for example, Burton *et al.*, 1997).
- Cultural industries approach, which stresses the importance of creative and cultural media industries as vehicles for regeneration (for example, Florida, 2004).
- Health and well-being perspective, which highlights the role that well-designed spaces can have on neighbourhood health and liveability (for example, Barton *et al.*, 2003).
- Community-based, social economy approach, which highlights the importance of involving local communities in decision making and developing social capital networks (for example, Thomas & Duncan, 2000).

Throughout these perspectives there has been a 'social' dimension to the regeneration, but the exact strength and positioning of this varies depending on the perspective adopted. Thus, some have pointed out the gentrification and displacement effect of regeneration on local residents and activities

---

[2]   These and related issues are explored in more detail in Chapter 4 of this book.

(Scarpaci, 2000), the exacerbation of social exclusion of particular groups within local communities (Gosling, 2008), and the generation of low-skill retail jobs for local residents (Law, 2002), whilst others have critically examined the potential positive social effects of urban regeneration, including the role of social capital in regeneration (Cento Bull & Jones, 2006); the reduction of local social problems and increased engagement and participation of residents (Hemphill *et al.*, 2006); the improved image of the local community (Pratt, 2009), and the reduction of crime and illegal activities (Raco, 2003). It can be argued, however, that a comprehensive study of urban regeneration from a social-sustainability perspective is still missing from the literature.

As pointed out earlier, it is important to highlight how, since the 1990s, regeneration programmes in the EU have increasingly linked the stimulation of economic activities and environmental improvements with social and cultural vitality. In this new sustainability-oriented approach to urban regeneration, the concepts of 'community' and 'neighbourhood' have become the central focus of the analysis. This new model emphasises practices of consultation and participation, especially through so-called 'community partnerships' and the involvement of the voluntary or third sector. Further, it seeks to transform the state into an enabling partner (Bevir & Rhodes, 2003) and identifies the 'community' and the local level as the main arenas for the achievement of sustainability.

More importantly the concept of social sustainability has become vitally important to consider. In this sense we suggest in this book that social sustainability concerns how individuals, communities and societies live with each other and set out to achieve the objectives of development models that they have chosen for themselves, also taking into account the physical boundaries of their places and planet earth as a whole (see Chapter 2 for a more detailed discussion of this). This book therefore examines social sustainability as an independent and equally recognised dimension of sustainable urban development through an integrated approach to the analysis of sustainability.

Aims and objectives

This book examines how sustainable urban regeneration is being approached by local governments, developers and the construction industry, funding bodies and investors from a social perspective. The book is based on a programme of research that was funded under the EIBURS (European Investment Bank University Research Sponsorship) Programme in 2006. The study was carried out between January 2007 and August 2009 by a team from the Oxford Institute for Sustainable Development

(OISD), School of the Built Environment, Oxford Brookes University (Colantonio & Dixon, 2009).

The main aim of this book is to identify and examine socially sustainable urban regeneration models and vehicles, and best practice measurement systems across European cities, including exemplar and innovative social sustainability metrics and tools.

The objectives of the book are to:

- Define social sustainability and explore the main themes and dimensions at the heart of this concept, in the context of EU cities and regeneration policies;
- examine to what extent, and in what ways, social sustainability is incorporated within urban regeneration projects funded by national initiatives and the EU;
- investigate how lenders and investors approach social sustainability;
- examine approaches to social sustainability and urban regeneration in five EU cities, including Cardiff (UK), Rotterdam (NL), Turin (IT), Sant Adriá de Besós (ES) and Leipzig (DE);
- critically review governance models and vehicles, which seek to deliver socially sustainable communities in urban areas, with a particular emphasis on Public Private Partnerships (PPPs);
- analyse the current sustainability indicators and tools used by the public, private and Non-Governmental Organisation sectors to deliver social sustainability in the case study cities; and
- examine and identify best practice to measure and monitor socially sustainable urban regeneration.

Linked to these research objectives, the book also addresses the following related questions:

- What are the main ingredients required to deliver socially sustainable urban regeneration?
- Is the social aspect of sustainable development receiving adequate recognition at the EU level, together with environmental and economic priorities?
- What has been the impact of EU-funded urban regeneration programmes (e.g. URBAN, URBACT) on social sustainability and its monitoring?
- How is Corporate Social Responsibility (CSR) and Socially Responsible Investing (SRI) impacting on the delivery of sustainable communities?
- What are the best assessment methods and monitoring systems currently used to monitor the social sustainability of urban regeneration in European cities?
- What can we learn from current practice to deliver socially sustainable urban regeneration?

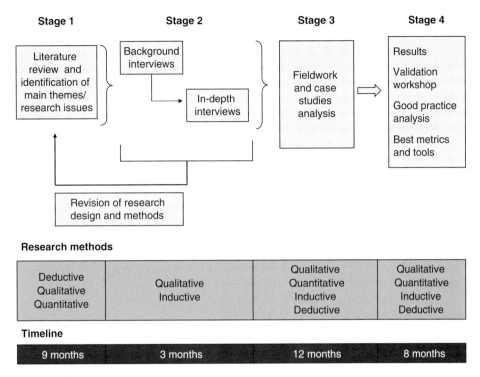

Figure 1.1   Research, methods and stages.

Methodology for the research

The research methodology, which is summarised in Figure 1.1, included a literature review, background and in-depth interviews, fieldwork in selected cities participating in the research, and a workshop to validate preliminary results. These elements of the research will be briefly reviewed in the remainder of this section of the book.

Literature review   At the beginning of the research process an extensive literature review was conducted in order to explore the concept of social sustainability and critically examine the main assessment methods and metrics established to 'measure' its nature. The scoping of literature on social sustainability and assessment methods was conducted until 'theoretical saturation' was reached and no new themes, assessment methods, metrics and relationships emerged from the review. This was subsequently linked with a parallel review of literature on the relationships between urban regeneration, EU policy, Public Private Partnerships and social sustainability.

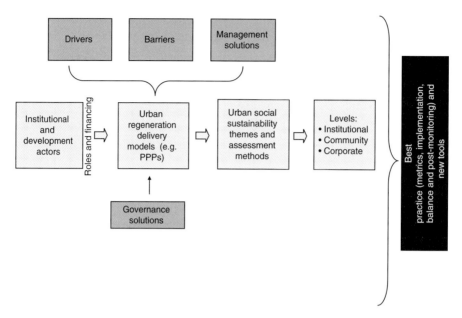

Figure 1.2   Theoretical research framework.

During this phase of the research, the main approaches and models of social sustainability were identified and the provisional theoretical research framework was designed.

Background and in-depth interviews   At the end of the literature review, a series of interviews was conducted (see Appendix 1) with private sector investors, developers and construction companies mainly based in the UK. The main objective of these was to ascertain how and to what extent the theoretical issues identified in the literature were taken into account, and dealt with at the practical level, by key actors involved in regeneration. The interviews were important in helping design the data gathering for the case studies and refining the theoretical framework of the research, which is illustrated in Figure 1.2.

Fieldwork   The fieldwork was conducted during the second year of the research. A template for data gathering in each case study was designed following the literature review and interview phase in order to collect information on the following elements:

- Approach adopted for urban regeneration, including objectives, policies, plans, programmes and the themes and dimensions adopted within the selected case studies.

- Management, which focused on the key actors involved in the regeneration process; governance and partnership solutions, and funding arrangements.
- Social sustainability, including the examination of a variety of themes and dimensions, social impacts, indicators, tools and initiatives.
- Outputs and outcomes of each case study, which endeavoured to provide an overview of the post-project monitoring arrangements and the lessons learned.

Case study selection

The case studies were selected after an in-depth review of over 50 urban regeneration projects across the EU. It was felt that they could provide examples of best practice or exemplify the lessons learned from an integrated approach to regeneration and the related measurement of social sustainability.

The case studies selected as part of the research included the following (in alphabetical order; see also Figure 1.3):

La Mina neighbourhood is located in Sant Adriá de Besós, Spain, a Catalan municipality bordering Barcelona's Eastern outskirts. This residential area of 20 tower blocks was built in the 1960s, as a social housing neighbourhood. It was designed to rehouse a local Roma community and inhabitants of Barcelona's shanty towns. The aim was to eradicate these particularly conflictive places and communities from the city with their serious problems of exclusion, marginality and delinquency. This, however, led to a high concentration of illegal activities and lack of community cohesion in the area. In 2000 a consortium of public administrations and departments was set up to regenerate the area, capitalising on EU funding and development opportunities provided by the eastward urban expansion of Barcelona, which was prompted by the 1992 Olympics.

Leipziger Osten, Leipzig, Germany, encompasses several suburbs to the east of Leipzig's city centre. This mainly residential area is characterised by dense, late nineteenth-century block structures and large-panel construction development, which is generally of comparatively low structural quality. These suburbs had been characterised by the degrading of both the social and built environment for several years and were included in the *Soziale Stadt* (Socially Integrated City) programme implemented by the German government in late 1990s and early 2000s.

Porta Palazzo is an inner city area of Turin, Italy. Before the urban renewal process started the area was a decaying inner city neighbourhood, characterised by an informal economy, inadequate social services, low cultural integration of international immigrants, a highly mobile and transient population, a myriad of short lived micro-enterprises, and a reputation

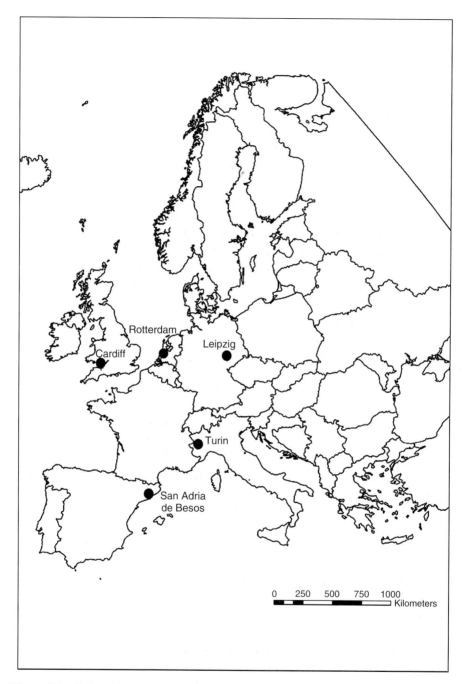

Figure 1.3   Selected case studies. *Source*: Re-drawn by Colantonio (2010).

linked to crime and illegal immigrants. The regeneration of the area gained initial momentum after receiving EU funding through the Urban Pilot Projects and URBAN programme during the second half of the 1990s and has continued since.

Roath Basin, Cardiff, Wales, United Kingdom, is part of a new approach to the sustainable regeneration of Cardiff Bay. The site is the last major derelict area in the inner harbour to be regenerated and was granted out-line planning permission for the regeneration programme in 2006. The regeneration of the basin will be carried out through a scheme based on a Public Private Partnership between the Welsh Government, local authori-ties and a private developer with an innovative Socially Responsible Investment policy.

Rotterdam South Pact (Pact op Zuid) comprises five sub-municipalities located in South Rotterdam, The Netherlands. Traditionally, this city area has been characterised by high unemployment, a poor image, and low edu-cational achievement, which made it difficult to attract private investment or middle–high income people to these neighbourhoods. The latter have also received little benefits from major waterfront redevelopment projects, such as *Kop van Zuid*, implemented in Rotterdam since the 1980s. *Pact op Zuid*, which involves several important private and public sector actors, including Housing Corporations, Rotterdam City and five sub-municipalities, will run between 2006 and 2015. It is forecast that participant stakeholders will jointly invest one billion euros in Rotterdam South throughout the duration of the Pact, in addition to normal investment programmes.

It is important to highlight that the case studies were selected in order to provide the widest possible spatial, temporal and institutional coverage of how social sustainability had been incorporated and monitored in urban regeneration schemes at varying development stages, diverging urban scales and in the context of different institutional arrangements. The ultimate selection of the case studies was therefore carried out taking into account three main criteria, which are illustrated in Figure 1.3. These included:

- Governance model and partnership;
- spatial scale; and
- development stage.

Figure 1.4 shows how, from a governance perspective, the selected projects range from fully public regeneration agencies to public-private-partnership. The spatial scale of regeneration schemes ranges from small neighbourhood to city-wide projects. Similarly, some of the projects are still in their plan-ning stages whilst others are close to completion or have been completed. In this context, it should be stressed that the case studies were selected not in order to develop entirely new tools, but rather to:

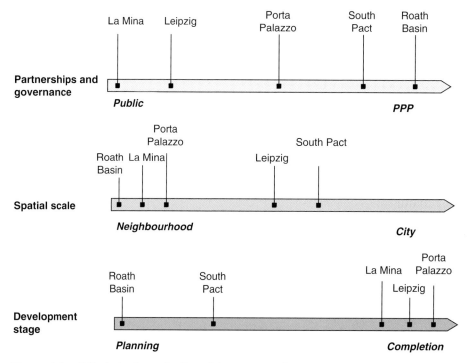

Figure 1.4   Criteria for the selection of the case studies.

- review the existing metrics and tools currently being used to assess, measure and monitor key aspects of social sustainability;
- highlight tools that are not necessarily known about, but are found to be used and seen by users as working well; and
- suggest 'improved tools', where there are deficiencies and room for improvement, and devise a comprehensive social sustainability assessment framework.

Finally, it is important to highlight that the fieldwork was designed and conducted before the current economic crisis took hold. The book therefore does not focus on this issue per se, but does attempt to draw conclusions set in the context of a very different current economic environment while also looking to the future. It is also worth pointing out that although the present recession may change the emphasis of current regeneration practices and delivery vehicles over the next few years across Europe, equally there can be little doubt that the validity of the basic principles and 'best practice' monitoring systems analysed in the case studies will transcend macro-economic cycles and economic fluctuations, although they are likely to affected by decreasing financial resources available for regeneration.

Outline of the book

This book is divided in three main parts.

Part I, comprising Chapters 1 to 4, addresses the context of the research and reviews the literature concerning urban regeneration, social sustainability and delivery vehicles. Further, it establishes the theoretical framework for the analysis of best practice in the case studies. The present chapter has set the context of the study by introducing the relationship between urban regeneration and social sustainability, and illustrating the main aims, objectives and methodology of the book. Chapters 2 and 3 endeavour to deconstruct the concept of social sustainability and to explore its evolutionary meaning, together with the development of emerging assessment methodologies, which are being applied to measure and appraise the complexity inherent in the notion of social sustainability. Chapter 4 examines the nature of urban regeneration together with the growth of corporate responsibility and responsible investment agendas and how, linked to the rise of the sustainability agenda, these have driven and been linked with an increasing trend towards institutional involvement in urban regeneration. The diversity of partnership models, which have been developed to deliver urban regeneration projects, are examined, together with the emergence of more recent urban development fund models, such as JESSICA and local asset-backed vehicles. The chapter concludes by summarising how attempts have been made to measure social sustainability in the context of urban regeneration.

Part II of the book, comprising Chapters 5 to 10, provides an overview of urban regeneration policy at the EU level and reports the main findings of the case-study analysis and the lessons learned from each case in terms of themes, assessment methods and monitoring systems of social sustainability. Most specifically, Chapter 5 provides the European policy context, setting out the EU's involvement in urban regeneration policy, in particular exploring the role of the Structural Funds in promoting sustainable urban development. The remaining chapters of Part II, focus on the case study of urban regeneration and social sustainability in Roath Basin in Cardiff (Chapter 6), La Mina – Sant Adriá de Besós (Chapter 7), Porta Palazzo in Turin (Chapter 8), South Pact in Rotterdam (Chapter 9) and Leipziger Osten (Chapter 10).

The main findings of Parts I and II, will be discussed in Part III of the book, which comprises Chapters 11 and 12. Most specifically, Chapter 11 illustrates our social sustainability assessment framework, which draws upon the case-study analysis and literature review, and was developed as part of the research process. Chapter 12 summarises the main conclusions of the study and suggests recommendations to enhance the measurement of social sustainability in the context of the regeneration in EU cities.

2

Social Sustainability and Sustainable Communities: Towards a Conceptual Framework

Introduction

In recent years the social dimension (or 'social sustainability') has gained increased recognition as a fundamental component of sustainable development, becoming increasingly entwined with the delivery of the sustainable communities and the urban sustainability discourses. Initially environmental and economic issues dominated the sustainable development debate (Nijkamp & Frits, 1988; Hardoy *et al.*, 1992) and it was only in the late 1990s that social issues began to be seriously taken into account within the sustainability agenda (Hediger, 2000). Although this growing recognition has spurred an emerging body of literature on social sustainability, our understanding of this concept is still fuzzy and limited by theoretical and methodological constraints, which stem from its context and disciplinary-dependent definitions and measurements. As Sachs (1999) put it, at a fundamental level, it is still unclear whether the concept of social sustainability means the social preconditions for sustainable development, or the need to sustain specific structures and customs in communities and societies.

The aim of this chapter is therefore twofold. First, it endeavours to deconstruct the concept of social sustainability and to explore its evolutionary meaning, highlighting the shift from the analysis of traditional 'hard' social policy areas towards emerging 'softer' research and policy-making themes. It is important to clarify that this chapter does not seek to provide operational definitions of, or normative prescriptions for, social sustainability,

Urban Regeneration & Social Sustainability: Best Practice from European Cities, by Andrea Colantonio and Tim Dixon   © 2011 Andrea Colantonio and Tim Dixon

which will be addressed within the context of the assessment framework presented in Chapter 11. Rather, it debates alternative meanings of social sustainability in the light of past, present and possible future interpretations of this concept. The chapter also aims to examine the theoretical and methodological approaches to (social) sustainability assessment within the context of the ongoing debate regarding the level of integration of assessment techniques, themes and metrics, which will be reviewed in Chapter 3.

The chapter is divided in four main parts. The first part presents an overview of the main interpretations of social sustainability, with a special focus on the urban environment, and illustrates how different worldviews amongst social scientists have so far prevented an unequivocal and widespread acceptance of the themes at the heart of this notion. The second part argues that the traditional 'hard' social sustainability themes such as employment and poverty alleviation have increasingly been complemented or replaced by emerging 'soft' and less measurable concepts such as happiness, social mixing and sense of place. Within this context, and as an example of 'best practice', the chapter also looks at how Vancouver City's local authorities have approached urban social sustainability and discusses the importance of the selection of sustainability principles, objectives and themes. The third part illustrates how community space has re-emerged as a focal point for the delivery of sustainable development, moving to the heart of the European urban policy in 2005 when the Bristol Accord on the sustainable communities agenda was approved (ODPM, 2006). The chapter concludes with an examination of possible future directions within the social sustainability debate and the main challenges for the assessment of this concept.

What is social sustainability?

The term, 'sustainable development' (or 'sustainability') has evolved through the powerful lobbying of the environmental movement over the last 30 years. Publications such as 'Limits to Growth' (Meadows *et al.*, 1972) and the Worldwatch Institute reports raised awareness of sustainable development as a concept at a global level (Kearns & Turok, 2003). Brundtland's definition of sustainable development has come to be widely used (Brundtland Commission, 1987): 'Development that meets the needs of the present without compromising the ability of future generations to meet their own needs'.

Building on this concept, Elkington (1994, 1997) developed what is often referred to as the 'Triple Bottom Line' approach to sustainable development, which attempts to rationalise development that promotes economic growth, but maintains social inclusion and minimises environmental impact. O'Riordan *et al.* (2001) and Lutzkendorf and Lorenz (2005) outlined two alternative models of this approach. In the 'Three Pillars' model, sustainability is

seen as the merging of economic enterprise, social well-being and environmental integrity, but in the alternative model, often referred to as the 'Russian
Doll', economic capital is placed at the centre as the basis of wealth creation,
which drives the development engine (O'Riordan *et al.*, 2001), but at the
same time is constrained by environmental and social considerations. Over
time these concepts have also become enshrined within national policy
(Dixon, 2007). For example, in 1994, the UK Government became the first to
produce a national strategy on sustainable development, which was followed
in 1999 by the outline of how it would deliver this in the report, 'A Better
Quality of Life' (DETR, 1999). This laid out how the government envisaged
achieving economic, social and environmental outcomes set against a series
of headline indicators. More recently, this approach has been developed further with policy guidance ('Securing the Future'), which seeks to set a new
framework goal for sustainable development (HM Government, 2005).

However, there is general agreement that the different dimensions of sustainable development (e.g. social, economic, environmental and institutional) have not been equally prioritised by policy makers within the
sustainability discourse (Drakakis Smith, 1995). This is not only because
sustainable development was born out of the synergy between the emerging
environmental movement of the 1960s and the 'basic need' advocates of the
1970s, but also because assessing the intangible nature of the social aspects
of development presents measurement quandaries, which will be discussed
later. As a result, there is a limited literature that focuses on social sustainability to the extent that a comprehensive study of this concept is still missing. Indeed, Littig and Grießler (2005) argued that approaches to the social
sustainability concept have not been grounded on theory but rather on a
practical understanding of plausibility and current political agendas. In addition, a study by the OECD (2001) points out that social sustainability is
currently dealt with in connection with the social implications of environmental politics rather than as an equally constitutive component of sustainable development.

These fragmented approaches to social sustainability were also criticised
by Metzner (2000) who contended that social sciences and social policy
research have developed a plethora of social objective strategies and measurement instruments, but with little regard for the sustainability perspective. Therefore, while there exist abundant social research studies and policy
documents, these have rarely been approached from a sustainability perspective, which could offer the potential to integrate sustainable development
dimensions and incorporate equity considerations (intra-generational and
inter-generational) whilst engaging the public in the research process. Even
when cross-discipline approaches have been attempted, covering for example
the environmental and the social dimensions of sustainable development
within the 'ecological footprint' concept (Wackernagel & Rees, 1996), it can

Table 2.1 Examples of definitions of social sustainability.

Definition	Reference
A strong definition of social sustainability must rest on the basic values of equity and democracy, the latter meant as the effective appropriation of all human rights – political, civil, economic, social and cultural – by all people.	Sachs (1999: 27)
… a quality of societies. It signifies the nature–society relationships, mediated by work, as well as relationships within the society. Social sustainability is given, if work within a society and the related institutional arrangements satisfy an extended set of human needs [and] are shaped in a way that nature and its reproductive capabilities are preserved over a long period of time and the normative claims of social justice, human dignity and participation are fulfilled.	Littig and Grießler (2005: 72)
[Sustainability] aims to determine the minimal social requirements for long-term development (sometimes called critical social capital) and to identify the challenges to the very functioning of society in the long run.	Biart (2002: 6)
Development (and/or growth) that is compatible with harmonious evolution of civil society, fostering an environment conducive to the compatible cohabitation of culturally and socially diverse groups while at the same time encouraging social integration, with improvements in the quality of life for all segments of the population.	Polese and Stren (2000: 15–16)

be argued that such endeavours have only been partially framed within an integrated approach to sustainability.

In addition, the concept of social sustainability has been under-theorised or often oversimplified in existing theoretical constructs, and there have been very few attempts to define social sustainability as an independent dimension of sustainable development. For these reasons, the relationships between the different dimensions of sustainable development or indeed between 'sustainabilities' are still very unclear. For example, Assefa and Frostell, (2007) contended that social sustainability is the finality of development whilst economic and environmental sustainabilities are both the goals of sustainable development and instruments to its achievement.

Furthermore, no consensus seems to exist on what criteria and perspectives should be adopted in defining social sustainability. Each author or policy maker derives their own definition according to discipline-specific criteria or the particular study perspective, making a generalised definition difficult to achieve. The relatively few definitions suggested to date are reported in Table 2.1. It can be seen, for example, how in Sachs' (1999) view socioeconomic development is an open ended historical process, which partially depends on human imagination, projects and decisions subject to the constraints of the natural environment and the burden of the living past. Thus, social sustainability can be interpreted as a socio-historical process rather than an end state. From this perspective, the understanding of social sustainability cannot be reduced to a static 'zero-one' situation, where zero suggests an unsustainable situation and one indicates presence of sustainability.

From a strictly sociological standpoint Littig and Grießler (2005: 72) emphasised the importance of both the concept of 'work', which is a traditional anchor concept in the German sustainability discourse, and 'needs' as defined by the Bruntdland Commission (1987). Similarly, Biart (2002: 6) highlighted the importance of the social requirements for the sustainable development of societies. Despite the confusion over the meaning of social capital, his approach emphasises the importance of 'time-frames' and 'social conditions' for the long-term functioning of societal systems. However, in his analysis there is no reference to the physical environment, allowing for the traditional criticism that sociology has often suffered from a neglect of the physical and non-social realm (Omann & Spangenberg, 2002).

A more comprehensive definition of social sustainability with a special focus on urban environments was provided by Polese and Stren (2000: 15–16). They emphasised the economic (development) and social (civil society, cultural diversity and social integration) dimensions of sustainability, highlighting the tensions and trade-offs between development and social disintegration, which is intrinsic to the concept of sustainable development. However, they also acknowledged the importance of the physical environment (e.g. housing, urban design and public spaces) within the urban sustainability debate.

Similarly, from a housing and built-environment perspective, Chiu (2003) identified three main approaches to the interpretation of social sustainability. The first interpretation equates social sustainability with environmental sustainability. As a result, the social sustainability of an activity depends upon specific social relations, customs, structure and value, representing the social limits and constraints of development. The second interpretation, which she labelled 'environment-oriented', refers to the social preconditions required to achieve environmental sustainability. According to this interpretation, social structures, values and norms can be changed in order to carry out human activities within the physical limits of the planet. Lastly, the third 'people-oriented' interpretation refers to improving the well-being of people and the equitable distribution of resources whilst reducing social exclusions and destructive conflict. In her study of the social sustainability of housing, Chiu (2003) adopted the second and third approaches to demonstrate how social preconditions, social relations, housing quality and equitable distribution of housing resources and assets are key components of sustainable housing development.

Other authors do not provide a general definition of social sustainability but suggest the main key themes which form the basis of the operationalisation of this notion. A number of these key themes are listed in Table 2.2,

Table 2.2 Key themes for the operationalisation of social sustainability.

Feature	Reference
Livelihood Equity Capability of withstanding external pressures Safety nets	Chambers and Conway (1992)
Inclusion Equity Poverty Livelihood	DFID (1999)
Equity Democracy Human rights Social homogeneity Equitable income distribution Employment Equitable access to resources and social services	Sachs (1999)
Paid and voluntary work Basic needs Social security Equal opportunities to participate in a democratic society Enabling of social innovation	Hans-Böckler-Foundation (2001)
Social justice Solidarity Participation Security	Thin *et al.* (2002)
Education Skills Experience Consumption Income Employment Participation	Omann and Spangenberg (2002)
Basic needs Personal disability Needs of future generations Social capital Equity Cultural and community diversity Empowerment and participation	Baines and Morgan (2004); Sinner *et al.* (2004)
Interactions in the community/social networks Community participation Pride and sense of place Community stability Security (crime)	Bramley *et al.* (2006)

which shows how basic needs and equity are consistently being held as fundamental pillars of social sustainability. These concepts are deemed necessary for the physiological and social survival of human beings and communities as a whole. This is because, at a basic level there can be little doubt that shelter, food, clean water and employment are essential requirements for the sustainability of individuals and communities. Similarly, equity is considered a crucial component of social sustainability because of the increasing evidence that societies with lower levels of disparity have longer life expectancies, fewer homicides and less crime, stronger patterns of civic engagement and more robust economic vitality (GVRD, 2004a).

For the purpose of this book, as mentioned in the previous chapter, it could be argued that social sustainability concerns how individuals, communities and societies live with each other and set out to achieve the objectives of the development models that they have chosen for themselves, also taking into account the physical boundaries of their places and planet earth as a whole. At a more operational level, social sustainability stems from actions in key thematic areas, encompassing the social realm of individuals and societies, which ranges from capacity building and skills development to environmental and spatial inequalities. In this sense, social sustainability blends traditional social policy areas and principles, such as equity and health, with emerging issues concerning participation, needs, social capital, the economy, the environment, and, more recently, with the notions of happiness, well-being and quality of life.

Traditional and emerging themes and dimensions

The chronological analysis of social sustainability themes also shows how traditional themes, such as equity, poverty reduction and livelihood, have increasingly been complemented or replaced by more intangible and less measurable concepts such as identity, sense of place and the benefits of 'social networks'. Table 2.3 illustrates this shift from 'hard' themes towards 'softer' concepts within the sustainability discourse, which in recent years has spurred a wider debate on the role that governments and policy makers should play in delivering 'soft' objectives. For example, with regard to happiness, Ormerod and Johns (2007) questioned the ability of governments to embark upon happiness-oriented policies whilst they are still struggling to deliver on existing commitments. By contrast, Layard (2007) noted that governments have been interested in happiness at least since the Enlightenment, but only recently have they begun to measure the concept and explain it systematically. Thus, understanding the conditions conducive to human happiness in all their complexity should be the central concern of social science.

Table 2.3 Traditional and emerging social sustainability key themes.

Traditional	Emerging
Basic needs, including housing and environmental health	Demographic change (ageing, migration and mobility)
Education and skills	Social mixing and cohesion
Employment	Identity, sense of place and culture
Equity	Empowerment, participation and access
Human rights and gender issues	Health and Safety
Poverty	Social capital
Social justice	Well-being, happiness and quality of life

Within this context it is worth clarifying that even traditional 'hard' themes such as ageing and migration are increasingly being approached from a more qualitative perspective. For example, the study of migratory flows has moved from the simple analysis of statistical figures to include qualitative profiling of migrants, according to their perceptions, stories, choices and expectations, whenever possible. However, the in-depth analysis of this shift and individual themes and dimensions of social sustainability is outside the scope of this book as a whole. Within the context of this chapter, it is important to briefly review the theoretical foundations of three themes, which have become recurrent policy areas in urban regeneration, as will also be shown in the case studies. These are: participation, social mixing and social capital, and they will be explored in the next three sub-sections of this chapter.

Participation and empowerment

In recent years, participation in interactive governance and public involvement in the planning of development projects have been regarded as fundamental elements of social sustainability and the delivery of sustainable development policies. As Rydin and Pennington (2000: 153) noted, the emphasis on the inherent desirability of public involvement is part of a tradition that seeks to 'open up' planning processes to democratic scrutiny and to expand the scope of public involvement as an integral part of improvements in policy delivery.

The importance of participation for the social sustainability of communities and places can be rationalised following three main arguments. The first argument maintains that participation allows for communities to express their needs and aspirations, which subsequently feed through into policy-making, delivering and monitoring processes. This representation of the community also results in collaborative governance (i.e. the interactive process through which problems of governance are defined, interests constituted, policy agendas identified, and governance programmes followed through; Healey, 1999). The second approach focuses on the democratic right to be involved in the public policy process. This is seen as being an intrinsically 'good' characteristic of societies. The third argument is associated with the greater effectiveness of policy delivery if it is 'more in tune with society's values and preferences' and could thereby result in 'better' policy delivery (Rydin & Pennington, 2000: 155). This efficiency argument is based on the assumption that a more democratic participation in public issues can raise awareness of the cultural and social qualities of localities at the policy-making stage, and therefore avoid conflicts that may emerge in policy implementation later.

Participation in governance has also been conceptualised through institutional theory and has generated a debate on the differences between 'traditional institutionalism' and 'new institutionalism' (Healey, 1999). Indeed, traditional institutionalism envisages institutions in the orthodox way of a formal set of structures and procedures, as in the traditional view of public administration. Within this approach, state, civil society groups and the private sector are often seen as negotiating agents in the policy making–implementing–monitoring process. Governance results from the position and power of the different participating agents, emphasising the importance of 'partnership' and 'empowerment' in the analysis. In the theory of new institutionalism, an institution is not understood as an organisation as such but as an established way of addressing certain issues (Healey, 1999). Here the power redistribution exercise between institutions and civil society, and planners and individuals becomes merged into collaborative action and social communication.

Governance does not stem from the struggle for power, since institutions are already the expression of societal values, beliefs and norms. This allows policies to be locally informed and place based. However, in this context, it is worth pointing out that it would be over simplistic to think of communities as monolithic blocks where all members have the same aspirations or values. Indeed, the latter vary according the socioeconomic and demographic composition of communities.

Social mixing

The concepts of social mixing and mixed communities have become a key component of the sustainable communities agenda since the mid 2000s. For example, the idea of mixed communities has been linked to a number of policy-related goals of the current UK administration, which encompass sustainability, inclusion, cohesion, and the promotion of a balanced housing market (ODPM, 2003; Tunstall & Fenton, 2006). This mixing has been advocated at two different levels. Firstly, places can be, mixed, in terms of buildings, their built form, size, designated uses (e.g. commercial, residential or industrial), market value and rent levels. Secondly, places can be, mixed, in terms of people and their social characteristics such as income and jobs; tenure; households; age; density ethnicity and life stages (Tunstall & Fenton, 2006).

Despite the recent promotion of social mixing, the theoretical rationale underpinning the UK Government's endeavours to promote socialmixing policies and their empirical benefits for sustainability has been absent from research and policy documents. However, a research document written for English Partnerships, The Joseph Rowntree Foundation and the Housing Corporation by Tunstall and Fenton (2006), identified specific ways in which mixed communities may be more sustainable than others. In their analysis, they noted (Tunstall & Fenton 2006: 21):

> that a neighbourhood with a mix of housing sizes, types and tenures may be more able to meet the changing needs and aspirations of those who live in it through changing life stages, household shapes and sizes or changes in income. Mixed tenure has enabled higher-income social housing ten-ants to buy without leaving the area. If parents separate or divorce, the inclusion of private rental in the tenure mix has enabled the parent with-out primary custody to remain close to their children after the breakdown of the relationship. Tenure mix may have a role in preserving age balance in rural communities.

Despite these arguments in favour of mixed communities, an approach that is seen as automatically establishing a direct and unidirectional link between mixing and sustainability has been criticised in recent writing because of a perceived lack of empirical evidence. For example, Butler (2003) noted that housing mix does not necessarily translate into social mixing between resi-dents. Similarly, Bramley *et al.* (2006) noted that social sustainability is not achieved by simply mixing people with different characteristics but also by ensuring that they actually personally interact. It has also been pointed out that social mixing could potentially generate negative rather than positive interaction between residents. This is because the mix of too many diverse groups may undermine the existing social networks present in disadvan-taged areas. It is therefore crucial to establish adequate 'levels' or thresholds of mix, the scale of the mix and the socioeconomic and demographic char-acteristics of the new people moving into a neighbourhood (Tunstall & Fenton 2006).

In addition, from a different perspective, and with a special focus on the sustainability of city centres, Bromley *et al.* (2005) provided empirical evi-dence that the contribution of individuals or groups of individuals to sus-tainability varies according to the sociodemographic characteristics and behavioural patterns of residents. They demonstrated, for example, that younger and older adults are more likely to walk to city centre facilities or work. This in turn reduces the car usage and generates less environmental pollution. They also challenged the mixed-community policy that aims to expand the number of families with children in order to produce a fully balanced community (ODPM, 2005). Indeed, their analysis reached a para-doxical conclusion that a family population is the least appropriate to achieve sustainability goals because of their reliance on car travel (e.g. to reach essential facilities such as schools). As a result, '... for sustainability, this more balanced approach should embrace a mix of younger and older adult age-groups, and not be pursued to the extent of a fully balanced com-munity which includes children (Bromley *et al.*, 2005: 2425).

Social mixing has also become a main goal of restructuring policies of other European governments and has been criticised for being a potential manipulating tool in the hands of local and national authorities.

For example, Uitermark (2003) provided a critical and comprehensive analy-sis of how the Dutch urban-regeneration policy of the 1990s aimed to improve the management of disadvantaged neighbourhoods through social mixing. This policy endeavoured to stabilise the socioeconomic status of designated neighbourhoods by ensuring the presence of a minimum number of affluent households because of four main justifications. First, the presence of affluent households was expected to benefit the less-well-off households in the neigh-bourhood because, for example, children of deprived parents were seen as ben-efiting from the presence of more privileged peers when they attend school. Second, in communities with higher social diversity, problems associated with a high share of poor or ethnic households were to some degree dispersed over a larger territory, which also reduces the burden on institutions operating in disadvantaged neighbourhoods. Third, affluent ethnic households were expected to help their communities in terms of 'socialisation' because of their function as intermediaries between state institutions and the ethnic commu-nities. Fourth, and finally, affluent households were believed to play a proac-tive role within disadvantaged neighbourhoods in terms of building the stock of social capital. However, in Uitermark's (2003) views, this type of social mixing may help hide covert political agendas because residents are partici-pants of governance networks. Thus, central governments can, in theory, manipulate the composition of the groups of actors and stakeholders taking part in governance processes through social mixing. For this reason, he argued that current research on social mixing is focused mainly on the interests and needs of neighbourhood residents, overlooking the broader issues concerning the interrelations between social policy and governance.

Social capital

A growing amount of literature has highlighted the role that 'social capital' plays in the social sustainability of places and communities. Social capital is increasingly being deemed an essential ingredient of sustainability and a tool capable of improving the situation of deprived communities in social, economic and political terms to the extent that it is often considered the distinguishing element between successful and unsuccessful communities (Middleton *et al.*, 2005). The original usage of the term social capital is normally attributed to Coleman (1988), whose broad definition was refined by subsequent writers (see Rydin & Pennington, 2000; Adler & Kwon, 2002, for reviews).

Broadly speaking social capital encompasses the set of social norms of conduct, knowledge, mutual obligations and expectations, reciprocity and trust that are widespread within a given region or community. The level of social capital determines the 'thickness' of a locality in terms of both the cohesion and mutual understanding existing among its members. Furthermore, it enhances self-reliance, collective actions and collective decision making within a community. These qualities are essential to avoid 'free rider behaviour'. Moreover, they allow a community to develop norma-tive plans of action and strategies to be acknowledged as a counterpart in interactive governance. More recently, the concept has also become inter-linked with communication theories and social network analysis, which interpret communities and societies as composed of social networks that overlap and intersect in complex ways. In this sense many people operate in several networks at once which link multiple social and economic worlds (Healey, 1999).

Social capital is often regarded as a pre-condition, a *sine qua non*, of build-ing community participation, and insufficient social capital has often been offered as a justification for technocratic approaches to governance. Technocratic–bureaucratic system-led thinking by some social scientists has therefore held that communities or regions are often unable to articulate their shared values and needs. Thus, it is a professional's task to deduce societal values and preferences and feed these into the policy process. There is little doubt that this practice poses obvious problems of representation that have been extensively explored in the literature (see Brohman, 1996).

In addition to this criticism, the desirability of social capital as a policy objective has also been questioned. For example, with reference to the nature and goals of community networks, it has been argued that networks can be isolated, patronage-based or work against society's collective interests (e.g. gangs and drug cartels), giving social capital a negative connotation or an unproductive purpose (Putnam, 1993, Levy 1996; Portes & Landolt 1996; Hogget, 1997; Rubio 1997). Further, Coleman (1990) contended that social capital is transitory because it consists of relations among persons and it may decrease if the affluence of a given community or official sources of support grow over time. In his view, networks and relationships are created and strengthened by adverse circumstances, but public participation declines as key problems are resolved in deprived communities. According to this analysis, social capital created artificially in deprived communities by poli-cymakers may not be sustainable in the long term if well-being improves. For this reason Middleton *et al.* (2005) questioned the policy perspective according to which the ability of deprived communities to respond to oppor-tunities for regeneration and renewal improve if we increase social capital in those communities.

Another recurrent criticism of the use of the promotion of social capital as a policy tool argues that there is, so far, insufficient empirical evidence that has tested the precepts of social capital theory. For example, because of the dearth of data and the lack of a well-established methodology, Temple (2000) highlighted how recent empirical work has employed the extent of trust in a society as an indicator of its underlying social capital, but there can be little doubt that this is an imperfect and over-simplistic way of cap-turing the ideas behind social capital, which overlooks the complexity of this concept. Furthermore, another recent study carried out by Middleton *et al.* (2005) in the Bournville Village Trust estate in Birmingham claimed that some of the untested assumptions about social capital are incorrect. This is because, for example, the authors demonstrate that: (i) there are dif-ferent types of social capital (bonding, bridging and linking) according to the distinct social, economic, demographic and physical attributes of the diverse parts of the village; and (ii) social capital is a product of wealth and demo-graphics, rather than something that can be artificially increased and sus-tained by policy prescriptions.

Sustainable cities and communities

Since the 1990s, sustainable development has become interlinked with the term 'sustainable cities'. The latter has increasingly been used within the sustainable development discourse and has generated a debate on whether cities contribute to the achievement of sustainable development goals in light of their specific characteristics, or whether sustainability can be achieved in urban environments more easily than in non-urban areas (Satterthwaite, 1997). On the one hand, increasing worldwide urbanisation has created severe environmental problems, and a development model that is often regarded as unsustainable in the long term, but, on the other hand, cities have proved to be effective vehicles for the inclusive provision of health services, sanitation, shelter and other infrastructure that are essential to sat-isfy the basic needs of a substantial proportion of the world's population.

Another important part of the urban sustainability debate has revolved around spatial, ecological, and to a lesser extent, social issues. Research has predominantly investigated the relationship between urban form and sus-tainability with perhaps density being the urban form element that has received most attention in the literature (Bramley *et al.*, 2006). Most of the work has focused on the 'compact city' versus 'urban sprawl' debate, and several studies have claimed that the higher density of compact cities can enhance public transport systems, improve access to facilities and services and reduce social segregation (Burton, 2000). Compact cities can also entail shorter travel to work and fewer car journeys, which in turn reduce pollution, congestion and noise levels. From a sociological perspective, density is also able to impact on social interactions amongst city dwellers with uncertain results on the social sustainability of urban areas. Some authors argue that higher density can facilitate social interactions (Talen, 1999) whilst others contend that social ties and a sense of community may be reduced in high-density areas (Freeman, 2001).

In recent years, the sustainable urban development agenda has been broadened and incorporated into planning practices and governments' policies for urban-regeneration projects. In the 1980s, regeneration projects focused mainly on the physical and economic renewal of degraded areas. However, since the 1990s, especially in Britain, regeneration programmes have combined the stimulation of economic activities and environmental improvements with social and cultural vitality (see Chapter 4). In this new sustainability-oriented approach to urban regeneration, the concepts of 'community' and 'neighbourhood' have become the central focus of the analysis. With reference to the UK, Cento Bull and Jones (2006: 767) noted that the New Labour Government had developed an urban-regeneration policy framework which emphasised the need for strong communities, active citizenship and enhanced political participation. According to their analysis, these goals were to be achieved by building and strengthening networks and norms of reciprocity and trust, that is, social capital, but also by promoting the notion of governance. This approach to sustainability emphasises practices of consultation and participation, especially through so-called community partnerships and the involvement of the voluntary or third sector. Furthermore, it seeks to transform the state into an enabling partner (Bevir & Rhodes, 2003) and identifies the community space as the main arena for the achievement of sustainability (Raco, 2007).

The shift from government to governance has been concisely reviewed by Wollmann (2006) in his analysis of the rise and fall of the local community in a European historical perspective. He argued that in the 1980s, the neo-Liberal attack against the centralised and interventionist Welfare State policies of the 1960s and 1970s, which called for progressive market liberalisation and privatisation, has meant the re-emergence of local community as focal point of political decision making and development processes. Indeed, it is at the community level that networks of actors from the private and public sector have reconverged and generated the shift towards the governance paradigm. As he suggests (Wollmann, 2006: 1431):

... while varying between the countries, local community space has seen the convergent development of two causally interrelated trends. On the one hand, local government has retreated from and abandoned the previous quasi-monopoly-type delivery and production of traditional functions, while, on the other hand, the involvement of private economic enterprises and private as well as voluntary service providers has expanded and multiplied resulting in the 'economic and social communities' regaining ground.

According to the new governance paradigm, different types of communities have the task of releasing a wide array of political, societal and economic resources whilst the local government has the crucial mission of advocating the common good, transparency and political accountability.

'Local Community', as a focal point for the delivery of sustainable development, also moved to the heart of the European urban policy in 2005, when the Bristol Accord on the sustainable communities agenda was approved (ODPM, 2006). This new urban development agenda drew mainly from the UK Office of the Deputy Prime Minister's (ODPM) Five Year Plans 'Homes for All' and 'People, Places and Prosperity'. The former focused on promoting more choice and affordability in the housing market and the latter broadened out the government's approach to sustainable communities through the promotion of better governance, strong leadership and the revitalisation of neighbourhoods. According to ODPM (2006: 9–10) the concept of sustainable communities (see also Box 2.1 and Chapter 5) can be considered to be:

... a framework or unifying set of principles to be applied across all towns and cities .... The core components of sustainable communities present a vision which has gained the commitment of many stakeholders. However, turning the vision into reality raises key questions of delivery. The success of Sustainable Communities policies will depend on the effective interaction of spatial planning, transportation, the economy, the environment and a number of other policy interventions.

Community space has also become central to experimental social sustainability frameworks implemented by cities at international level. For example, Vancouver (in Canada) municipal authorities enacted a Social Development Plan (SDP) in 2005 (City of Vancouver, 2005) for the city and developed an ad hoc Social Sustainability Framework. The latter is the first of its kind to be applied in practice at city level, and so it has been selected as an example of best practice in this chapter. However, it is important to point out that, within the context of this chapter, the social sustainability assessment framework of Vancouver is not examined from an empirical point of view, that is, through the investigation of its operational and practical implications. Rather, the main aim of the analysis of the framework is to

Box 2.1   The sustainable community approach to sustainability of the Bristol accord

Definition of a 'sustainable community'

Sustainable communities are places where people want to live and work, now and in the future. They meet the diverse needs of existing and future residents, are sensitive to their environment, and contribute to a high quality of life. They are safe and inclusive, well planned, built and run, and offer equality of opportunity and good services for all.

The components of a 'sustainable community'

Sustainable communities embody the principles of sustainable development. They do this by:

- Balancing and integrating the social, economic and environmental components of their community;
- meeting the needs of existing and future generations; and
- respecting the needs of other communities in the wider region or internationally to make their own communities sustainable.

Eight key characteristics of sustainable communities

1   **Active, inclusive and safe** – *Fair, tolerant and cohesive with a strong local culture and other shared community activities.*
2   **Well run** – *with effective and inclusive participation, representation and leadership.*
3   **Environmentally sensitive** – *providing places for people to live that are considerate of the environment.*
4   **Well designed and built** – *featuring quality built and natural environment.*
5   **Well connected** – *with good transport services and communication linking people to jobs, schools, health and other services.*
6   **Thriving** – *with a flourishing and diverse local economy.*
7   **Well served** – *with public, private, community and voluntary services that are appropriate to people's needs and accessible to all.*
8   **Fair for everyone** – *including those in other communities, now and in the future.*

Source: ODPM (2006).

highlight the main methodological and theoretical issues involved in the implementation of social sustainability at city level.

In Vancouver's SDP, social sustainability is defined as follows (City of Vancouver, 2005: 12):

For a community to function and be sustainable, the basic needs of its residents must be met. A socially sustainable community must have the ability to maintain and build on its own resources and have the resiliency to prevent and/or address problems in the future.

According to the plan, the main components of social sustainability are basic needs, individual capacity and social capacity. Individual capabilities are linked to education, skills, health, values and leadership whilst community capabilities stem from relationships, networks and norms facilitating collective action.

Figure 2.1 illustrates how the pursuit of these overarching milestones of social sustainability is guided by four principles and policy actions in seven areas or themes. The principles include equity, inclusion, adaptability and security More specifically 'equity' is taken as being access to sufficient resources to participate fully in community life and as sufficient opportunities for personal development and advancement; 'inclusion and interaction' encompasses involvement in setting and working towards collective community goals, which is fostered by ensuring that individuals have both the right and the opportunity to participate in and enjoy all aspects of community life; and 'adaptability' is intended as the resiliency for both individuals and communities and the ability to respond appropriately and creatively to change. Finally, 'security' allows individuals and communities to have economic security and have confidence that they live in safe, supportive and healthy environments (City of Vancouver, 2005).

In addition, Figure 2.1 shows how these four overarching principles provide guidelines to achieve sustainability in seven themes or dimensions, ranging from 'living' to 'moving', which are divided into several sub-themes. Indeed, a guide to the implementation of the framework (GVRD, 2004b),

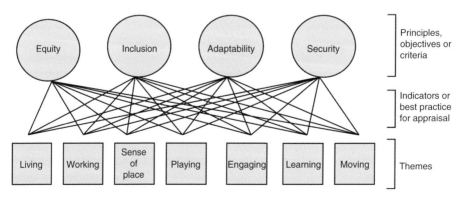

Figure 2.1 Framework for social sustainability assessment in Vancouver. *Source*: Elaborated from GVRD (2004a, b) and City of Vancouver (2005).

identifies the characteristics required to 'live', 'work', 'play' and so on in an equitable, inclusive, safe and adaptable way. Although an in-depth analysis of these is outside the scope of this chapter it is clear that the Vancouver SDP pinpoints the fundamental guiding role played by principles and themes in social sustainability frameworks and the importance of the selection of social sustainability indicators.

The interrelationships between principles and themes, underpinning the progress towards a socially sustainable Vancouver, are monitored through a set of urban and regional sustainability indicators that draw upon expert-based and citizen-based recommendations, which are gathered also through the work of the Regional Vancouver Urban Observatory initiative (Holden, 2006). The selection of sustainability indicators, however, is still a work in progress although it is expected to build mainly on Quality of Life of Indicators developed by the Federation of Canadian Municipalities, which are summarised in Appendix 2. From a local authority perspective, quality of life indicators provide an overview of changes and trends in society and can therefore offer a unique insight into its sustainable development (City of Vancouver, 2005). The analysis of social sustainability indicators will be examined in more detail in the next chapter.

Conclusions

This chapter has shown how new 'soft' themes, such as happiness, well-being and social capital, are becoming central to the social sustainability debate, together with more traditional 'hard' concepts, which include basic needs, equity and employment. On the one hand, this 'sophistication' mirrors the changing social needs of individuals and communities, but, on the other hand, it is adding complexity to the interpretation and measurement of social sustainability. Indeed, at present, there is disagreement concerning the main underlying themes and objectives of social sustainability in light of diverging worldviews, study perspectives and discipline-specific criteria amongst social scientists, which have been briefly introduced in this chapter.

The taxonomic division between 'traditional' and 'emergent' social sustainability themes and indicators proposed in this chapter underpins and reinforces the view that the shift toward the analysis of more elusive concepts in the social sustainability debate may continue for the foreseeable future as many of the larger sectors of communities and societies become more affluent and relatively less concerned about the satisfaction of basic needs.

Nonetheless, due to the speculative nature of social sciences, and the emerging mix of hard and soft themes in the social policy debate, it may prove difficult not only to understand the interrelationships between these themes in a rigorously scientific way but also to identify the optimal social targets and objectives to be pursued in order to deliver socially sustainable places. Indeed, the multiple combinations of hard and soft themes, and the disagreement over their meanings, hinder the scientific identification of what is socially sustainable and what is not.

Future research therefore needs to focus on unravelling the underlying linkages between social sustainability themes (for example, equity and happiness or well-being and identity), and their principles and objectives. Furthermore, this research will also need to investigate how these can be 'quantified' using simple and user-friendly methods capable of deconstructing and monitoring these elements without losing the richness of information that is embedded within them. The next chapter explores some of these ideas in more detail.

3

Metrics and Tools for Social Sustainability

Introduction

This chapter examines the main assessment methods, metrics and tools used to assess and monitor key underlying themes of social sustainability. The chapter builds upon the recent 'reductionist' versus 'integrated' sustainability assessment debate and contends that there is a paucity of social sustainability assessment methodologies and tools.

Building on the taxonomic categorisation proposed in Chapter 2, this chapter maintains that the development of new sustainability indicators is increasingly focused on measuring 'emerging' themes rather than on improving the assessment of more 'traditional' concepts such as equity and fairness. Indeed, the latter continue to be measured mainly in terms of income distribution and other monetary variables, hampering meaningful progress in the ultimate goal of assessing social sustainability.

The current chapter argues that a new breed of indicators focusing on individual perceptions rather than factual data and values is increasingly being suggested for sustainability policy prescriptions. In this context, the chapter also pinpoints the main differences between 'traditional' and emerging 'sustainability' indicators, suggesting a set of characteristics for the latter, and reviewing the main methodological and practical hurdles to their full implementation.

Thus, the aim of this chapter is twofold. First, it endeavours to examine the theoretical and methodological approaches to (social) sustainability assessment in the context of the ongoing debate on the appropriate level of integration of assessment techniques, themes and metrics. The second main

Urban Regeneration & Social Sustainability: Best Practice from European Cities, by Andrea Colantonio and Tim Dixon © 2011 Andrea Colantonio and Tim Dixon

objective is to demonstrate how, at a practical level, social sustainability assessment is often conducted: (i) through social impact assessment (SIA), which is extended to incorporate biophysical and economical variables, and (ii) by broadening the definition of 'environment' and hence the thematic coverage of theme-specific assessment techniques such as SIA.

The chapter is therefore divided into three main parts. It begins with an analysis of how impact assessment is evolving into sustainability assessment (SA), and new appraisal methods and metrics are emerging in the sustainability literature. The second part provides an overview of the recent evolution of sustainability indicators and how these are increasingly being deployed at a local level through a new set of hybrid indicators, which take into account local actors and residents' perceptions as part of the overall measurement process. In this context, the analysis highlights the main differences between 'traditional' and emerging 'sustainability' indicators, suggesting a set of characteristics for the latter. The third part proposes a taxonomical distinction between 'traditional' and 'emerging' (social) sustainability indicators, which is linked to the categorisation suggested in Chapter 2. Lastly, the chapter concludes with a short commentary on the complexity and uncertainty that the measurement of social sustainability will need to address in the future.

Impact assessment and social sustainability assessment

Sustainability Assessment (SA) is a key element connecting social sustainability research and evidence-based policies. Broadly speaking, sustainability appraisal is a form of assessment[1] which aims to inform and improve strategic decision making (Sheate *et al.*, 2008). The assessment relies on the application of a variety of methods of enquiry and argument to produce policy-relevant information, and this is then utilised to evaluate the consequences of human actions against the normative goal of sustainable development (Stagl, 2007: 9). Indeed, as Gasparatos *et al.* (2008) suggested, sustainability assessments ought to:

- Integrate economic, environmental, social and increasingly institutional issues as well as consider their interdependencies;
- consider the consequences of present actions well into the future;
- acknowledge the existence of uncertainties concerning the result of our present actions;
- act with a precautionary bias;

---

[1] The terms 'assessment' and 'appraisal' are used interchangeably throughout this chapter.

- engage the public; and
- include equity considerations (intragenerational and intergenerational).

Sustainability assessment builds on Environmental Impact Assessment (EIA) and Strategic Environmental Assessment (SEA) and despite being a less mature assessment framework than its predecessors, there is general agreement that the assessment is characterised by four main features. These include: (i) an emphasis on integration of techniques and themes; (ii) the call for multi-criteria approaches; (iii) the importance of objectives and principles setting; and (iv) stakeholders' participation in the assessment itself. An in-depth analysis on these aspects is outside the scope of this chapter but a brief overview is now provided.

1 Integration of techniques and themes   Many of the approaches to sustainability assessment can be said to be examples of 'integrated assessment' derived from EIA and SEA, which have been extended to incorporate social and economic considerations as well as environmental ones (Pope *et al.*, 2004; Dalal-Clayton & Sadler, 2005). For example, Pope (2007) argued that sustainability assessment can be seen as the 'third generation' of impact assessment processes, following project EIA and the SEA of policies, plans and programmes. From this perspective, EIA-based integrated assessment has been adopted as a sustainability appraisal method by simply replicating the one-dimensional form of assessment in the three-pillar model of sustainable development. This allows for the discrete assessment of the potential environmental, social and economic changes of a proposal and reflects a systemic 'triple bottom line' approach to sustainability (Elkington, 1994).

2 Multi-criteria approach   There have also been increasing calls to use a multi-criteria approach in sustainability appraisal, because of the multifaceted nature of a concept that amalgamates social, environmental and economic matters into what is essentially a new independent entity. For example, in the field of decision making, Multi-Criteria Decision Analysis is an emerging method for sustainability appraisal. It consists of a set of methods using dissimilar criteria, which are combined together by using scores and weightings in order to aid decision making in order to choose between and resolve conflicting evaluations, options and interests. Examples of these methods are Analytic Hierarchy Process, Goal Programming and the Novel Approach to Imprecise Assessment and Decision Environments. These appraisal methods acknowledge a pluralist view of society (Glasson *et al.*, 2003) and render the decision-making process more transparent (Stewart, 2001). Furthermore, because of the social learning and the reflexive participatory process involved in such an assessment, these techniques can help in the evaluation of projects or proposals the impacts of which are not well understood and would therefore benefit from a participatory and multi-disciplinary approach (Stagl, 2007).

3 Importance of objectives and principles setting Sustainability appraisal is a form of strategic assessment linked to guiding principles and the achievement of policy objectives. Within this context, Pope *et al.* (2004) distinguished an objective-led appraisal and a principle-based assessment approach to sustainability. The former is similar in nature to SEA, in which the assessment is carried out to achieve specific policy goals within an explicit framework encompassing environmental, social and economic objectives. The latter is led by objectives derived from broader sustainability principles. In their view, the objective-led appraisal focuses on the appraisal of the 'direction to target', which is usually indicated with '+' '0' or '−' for a positive, neutral and negative move toward the sustainability target. Conversely, the principle-based assessment goes beyond the mere establishment of a 'direction to target' and endeavours to establish the 'distance from target', or the extent of progress toward sustainability.

4 Stakeholders' participation in the assessment There has been an increasing call for more participation in the sustainability assessment process because the latter is often wrongly grounded on the traditional assessor – client relationship (Cavanagh *et al.*, 2007). For example, this form of assessment often fails to understand how specific issues are perceived differently by a plethora of actors with a stake in the project, process or objective. Stagl (2007) pointed out that this traditional technical-rational model of appraisal, in which 'objective assessment' by an assessor is assumed to lead automatically to better decisions, has proved theoretically, politically and practically inadequate. In his view, the type of assessment can influence its outcome, or, in other words, the choice of appraisal method and criteria is not a wholly technical question, but an 'institutionalising social choice' (Stagl, 2007: 3), in which participation is likely to engender a greater sense of ownership of the appraisal process itself (Keogh & Blahna, 2006).

However, despite the rapid ascent of sustainability assessment techniques in the international arena, this form of assessment has also been subject to criticisms. For example, the current integrated assessment approaches are often regarded as imperfect because they restrict a holistic concept of sustainability to the consideration of separate environmental, economic and social factors by focusing on balancing the trade-offs between these dimensions, rather than exploring the linkages and interdependencies between them (George, 2001). Furthermore, there is no consensus concerning the meaning of integrated assessment. Scrase and Sheate (2002) identified

14 meanings of the word 'integration' whilst Lee (2002: 14) maintained that the term could be used in three general senses. These include: (i) bringing together different types or categories of impacts, such as biophysical and socioeconomic (horizontal integration); (ii) linking together separate assessments undertaken at different levels and/or stages (vertical integration); and (iii) integration of assessments into decision making, for example linking a plan to the policy-making process (Glasson & Gosling 2001).

Another criticism voiced against sustainability assessment is its superficiality and lack of quantification (RCEP, 2002), which is often due to insufficient provision of benchmarks or the difficulty in establishing how and who should set critical threshold levels for non-environmental variables. Indeed, it is not surprising that, in the context of a recent sustainability appraisal project of mountain areas of Europe, Sheate *et al.* (2008) reported how some quantitative ecologists saw the appraisal process as 'unscientific' and highly qualitative rather than quantitative and objective. Similarly, according to their analysis, a number of socioeconomists have expressed scepticism about sustainability assessment because it lacks theoretical grounding in social sciences. These concerns are also echoed by other authors, who maintain that the appraisal process entails subjective judgements concerning integration, win–win solutions and trade-off (Therivel, 2004), making the process not entirely scientific.

Undeniably, sustainability appraisal is as much about assessing and providing strategic guidance as it is about generating a participatory and reflective process in which objectives, principles and assessment criteria are commonly defined through stakeholders' participation. In fact, the significance of sustainability appraisal is to be found not only in its actual *product* but also in the *process* by which the appraisal is developed and conducted (Pope *et al.*, 2004; Gibson *et al.*, 2005). This greater emphasis on *how* impacts are assessed rather than on *which* optimum targets are to be achieved can be rationalised following two different arguments. The first argument focuses on the democratic right to be involved in the assessment procedure if the development being assessed might have a significant direct or indirect impact on the stakeholders themselves. The second argument is associated with the greater effectiveness of the assessment itself if it incorporates stakeholders' or society's values, beliefs and preferences. As Rydin and Pennington (2000) pointed out, a more democratic participation in the planning of future developments can raise awareness of the cultural and social qualities of localities and avoid conflicts that may emerge in policy implementation later.

However, the true participatory nature and efficacy of these processes have been questioned on both practical and theoretical grounds. In practice, stakeholder involvement is often deemed more consultative rather than participative due to the complexity of the overall assessment process and the availability of resources (Sheate *et al.*, 2008). For these reasons, other authors call for stakeholders' participation to go beyond mere consultation or con-sensus building on a series of alternatives (Van de Kerkhof, 2006). Coglianese (1999), for instance, noted that in consensus-building processes the ultimate goal shifts away from reaching a 'quality' decision and moves towards reach-ing an 'agreeable' one. By contrast, stakeholders should actively express the objectives and aspirations that they seek to achieve through the develop-ment project being assessed for it to be truly sustainable.

Recent sustainability assessment legislation in the UK and EU

Over the last few decades, sustainability assessment has gained increased recognition in sustainable development legislation and policy agendas at both national and international level. For example, in the UK, the Planning and Compulsory Purchase Act (UK Government, 2004) enforced a mandatory sustainability appraisal of project proposals to be carried out by local planning authorities. In addition, since the release of the report *A Better Quality of Life, a Strategy for Sustainable Development in the UK* (HM Government, 1999) and *Securing the Future: The UK Sustainable Development Strategy* (HM Government, 2005), the UK Government has published two additional documents providing guidance on sustainability appraisal and evaluation methodologies:

- *The Green Book* (HM Treasury, 2005); and
- *The Sustainability Appraisal of Regional Spatial Strategies and Local Development Document* (ODPM, 2005).

The former describes how the economic, financial, social and environmen-tal assessments of policies, programmes, plans or projects should be com-bined together. The latter provides practical guidance for regional planning bodies and local planning authorities concerning how sustainability princi-ples should be incorporated in development proposals. If read in conjunc-tion, both documents provide the backbone of the sustainability assessment framework endorsed by the UK Government.

Similarly, at EU level, there are four main assessment frameworks related to sustainability aspects that have been legislated since 1985 (Ruddy & Hilty, 2008). These include:

1 *Environmental Impact Assessment*, which has been typically applied to projects on land-use planning at the national level since 1985 through Directives 85/337/EEC and 97/11/EC.
2 *Strategic Environmental Assessment* came into practice in the mid 1990s as a method to assess the impacts of certain policies, plans and pro-grammes at a higher governance level than land planning. In 2001 the

European Council formally adopted the SEA Directive 2001/42/EC that legislates this form of assessment.

3 *Sustainability Impact Assessment*, introduced by Directorate General (DG) trade in 1999 to integrate sustainability into trade policy by informing negotiators of the possible social, environmental and economic consequences of a trade agreement (EC, 2005).

4 *The EU Impact Assessment System* introduced in 2003 by the European Commission to support of the EU's Sustainable Development Strategy and to enhance the quality of the Commission's regulatory activity.

Although these frameworks demonstrate the variety of assessment techniques legislated at policy level they also highlight the confusion over the terminology used to measure sustainability and the piecemeal approach that characterises this field (Colantonio & Dixon, 2009). For example, according to the EU terminology, Sustainability Impact Assessment is a process undertaken before and during a trade negotiation in order to identify the economic, social and environmental impacts of a trade agreement (EC, 2005). Thus it can be argued that sustainability assessment is currently limited to trade agreements rather than to wider policies, plans and programmes. Furthermore, the methodology developed for the assessment draws upon traditional EIA stages, including Screening – Scoping – Preliminary Assessment – Flanking Measures (mitigation and enhancement analysis), but very little is said about the integration criteria and the sustainability principles to be adopted.

To clarify some of the differences and similarities between the main families of assessment techniques, Figure 3.1 provides a succinct overview of EIA, SIA, SEA and SA. The diagram offers snapshots of selected definitions, main characteristics and limitations of these forms of assessment. These are meant to summarise rather than replace the very extensive and comprehensive coverage of assessment-related issues that can be found in the abundant literature in this field.

Conceptual scope and range of social sustainability assessment techniques

From a social sustainability perspective, there is a paucity of specific sustainability assessment methodologies. The assessment is often conducted through social impact assessment (SIA), which is extended to include other sustainability pillars. Indeed, a recent definition by the International Association for Impact Assessment (IAIA, 2003: 2) states that:

Social impact assessment includes the processes of analysing, monitoring and managing the intended and unintended social consequences, both

Increasing integration, strategicness and comprehensiveness of themes and methods

Since	1960s	1970s	1990s	2000s
	EIA	SIA	SEA	SA
Selected definitions and objectives	A public process by which the likely effects of a project on the environment are identified, assessed and then taken into account by the consenting authority in the decision-making process	A systematic, iterative, ex-ante form of assessment that seeks help individuals, groups, organisations and communities understand possible social and cultural, or economic impacts of change or, better still, impacts of proposed change	A form of environmental assessment intended to identify and assess the likely significant effects of a plan, programme or policy on the environment, the results of which are then taken into account in the decision-making process	A form of strategic assessment that integrates environmental, social and economic parameters and relies on the application of a variety of methods of enquiry and argument to produce policy-relevant information in order to evaluate human actions against the normative goals of sustainable development
Main features	• Focus on environmental dimension of sustainable development, though it may include separate social considerations • Physical/quantitative approach to the measurement of selected variables • Selection of objective but contextual targets and thresholds • Limited to project level	• Focus on social dimension • Speculative in nature, does not provide precise, accurate and repeatable results • The selection of targets and thresholds relies on system values and political objectives rather than scientific criteria • Primary, secondary, cumulative and 'dead-weight' effects are difficult to calculate and measure	• Operates at a strategic level • Stresses process rather than detailed technical analysis • Foundations in EIA but by nature more open-ended, consultative and iterative than EIA • No need for sophisticated and expensive data gathering and modelling capacity • Inter-institutional cooperation and public participation key determinants of success	• Integration of sustainable development dimensions • Relies upon principles rather than targets and thresholds • Acknowledges the existence of uncertainties concerning the results of our present actions and acts with a precautionary basis • Engages the public • Includes equity considerations (intra- and inter-generational)
Examples of main limitations	• Ignores politics and models of decision making • Too narrow focus on bio-physical environment	• Quality and availability of data at local level • 'Social engineering' risk	• Environmental effects hard to predict at strategic level • Achieving integration	• Quanlification issues • Trade-offs, aggregation and weights difficulties

EIA= environmental impact assessment; SIA=social impact assessment; SEA=strategic environmental assessment; SA= sustainability assesment

Figure 3.1   Overview of main methods used to assess sustainable development and its dimensions. *Sources*: Barrow (2000); Glasson (2001); European Union (2003); Glasson *et al.* (2003); Imperial College Consultants (2005); Saunders and Therivel (2006); Stagl, (2007); Gasparatos *et al.* (2008); LUC and RTPI (2008); Schmidt *et al.* (2008); Sheate *et al.* (2008).

positive and negative, of planned interventions (policies, programs, plans, projects) and any social change processes invoked by those interventions. Its primary purpose is to bring about a more sustainable and equitable biophysical and human environment.

This interpretation shows how the coverage of social impact assessment is progressively being extended to incorporate biophysical and economical variables. Furthermore, it illustrates how sustainability assessment is increasingly providing a framework for the convergence and amalgamation of diverse impact assessments under a single theoretical umbrella.

Hacking and Guthrie (2007) maintained that the extended coverage of sustainability appraisal is being accommodated by 'stretching' EIA or SEA and broadening the definition of 'environment' and hence the thematic coverage of theme-specific assessment such as SIA. However, they question the real level of integration of these techniques because in their view SIA may be undertaken on its own, as a component of EIA, in parallel with EIA, or as part of an 'integrated' S&EIA. It is also worth pointing out that these diverse impact assessment techniques were not designed for sustainability appraisal per se. As a result, their semantic or substantive integration may not be able to capture, address and suggest solutions for a diverse set of issues that affect stakeholders with different values that span over different spatial and temporal scales (Gasparatos *et al.*, 2007).

Example of recent practices

In a recent study of 20 Environmental Statements (ESs) concerning randomly selected urban regeneration projects implemented in the UK between 1998 and 2007, Glasson and Wood (2008) pointed out that SIA is covered in 80% of the cases, often in a separate chapter. According to their analysis, the scope of SIA content has widened from the 1990s experience to cover population profile and occupational groups; economic and business context; learning and employment; general well-being, health, crime and deprivation; community facilities and services; recreation and public open space; and social inclusion and community integration. Moreover, they argued that there is increasing evidence of best practices in project-based SIA after 2004, partly because of the publication of the Planning and Compulsory Purchase Act (UK Government, 2004) and the Sustainability Appraisal of Regional Spatial Strategies and Local Development Document (ODPM, 2005).

However, they also noted that there is limited evidence of a sustainability approach that set the SIA and ESs within a wider sustainability context. This is, for example, because: (i) only 50% of ESs contain methodological information that goes beyond a bland descriptive review of population and employment baseline; (ii) there is insufficient analysis of the links between socioeconomic components (e.g. between demographic profile and jobs created); (iii) quantification is limited and mainly focused on demographics, employment, services and facilities provision; and (iv) the assessment methods showed limited community engagement and reduced involvement of a wide range of stakeholders.

In addition, it could be argued that at a practical level, the assessment and measurement of social sustainability has been hampered by at least six methodological and practical hurdles. These include:

1 The *social impact assessment* presents several problems. These are linked to: (i) the nature of the impacts, which may make it difficult to isolate a specific impact; (ii) the existence of conflicting impacts (e.g. gain in transport system and displacement effect or gentrification); (iii) difficulties in distinguishing a specific impact of a project from changes that may be generated at a macro-economic level; (iv) cumulative and derived impacts,

because the overall impact of a development plan differs from the sum of the single development projects contained in the plan; and (v) the lack of longitudinal studies, which leads to difficulties in establishing the pre-development condition or obstacles in determining the significance of the change because of the lack of relevant data (Coccossis & Parpairis, 1992; Barrow, 2002; Hughes, 2002).

2 The *concept of social sustainability has been under-theorised* and often oversimplified, or incorporated within existing theoretical constructs and assessment criteria such as the concepts of environmental justice or eco-logical footprints. Further more, there is no clear differentiation between the analytical, normative, and political aspects of social sustainability whereas Littig and Grießler (2004) pointed out that the broad and multi-faceted connotation of the word 'social' has an analytical as well as a normative meaning.

3 There is a *divergence concerning assessment criteria and methods*. This is due to internationally heterogeneous social and cultural conditions, which hamper the universally accepted criteria used to assess social sus-tainability. For example, at the European level, in Germany work and employment have historically formed societal priorities but in the Netherlands consumption, gender aspects and the ageing society have been given more importance. In Italy and Spain, family relationships and religious issues are seen as having important impacts on their respective societies. These divergences are even more evident when comparing com-munities or countries from the North and the South.

4 The *bad experience of the 1960s* makes social scientists hesitant to for-mulate normative targets and objectives. Indeed, there can be little doubt that the social engineering practices of the 1960s have been criticised for promoting ill-conceived social formulations and homogenous lifestyles (Omann & Spangenberg, 2002).

5 *Social objectives* as part of an overall sustainability framework need to be contextualised within different development models. These range from neoliberalist policies to the European social security model and to more eclectic approaches to development adopted by transitional economies and socialist countries (see Colantonio & Potter, 2006).

6 There is *no optimum for indicators* and it is problematic to establish *benchmarks*. Indeed, it proves difficult to establish how and who should set critical threshold values, such as minimal or optimal base level, for the indicators. In addition, the availability of data as well as the source and reliability of that data should also be taken into account when using indicators (UNCSD, 2001).

Despite these hindrances, indicators and tools of sustainability have been developed and these are reviewed in the remainder of this chapter.

A brief overview of sustainability indicators and social sustainability tools

Indicators are fundamental instruments for measuring the progress towards sustainability. The first major step towards the identification of sustainability indicators can be traced back to Agenda 21, a blueprint for sustainability launched at the UN Conference on Environment and Development (Earth Summit) at Rio de Janeiro (UN, 1992). In response to Chapter 40 of Agenda 21, between 1995 and 2000, the UN Commission on Sustainable Development (UNCSD) developed and tested a set 134 indicators in 22 countries in the categories of society, economies, environment and institutions with methodology sheets for each indicator (UN, 2001). This set was subsequently revised twice and finalised in 2006 and consists of a set of 50 core indicators, which are part of a larger set of 98 indicators of sustainable development.

Since this initial attempt by the UNCSD, a plethora of sustainability indicators have been developed. Both a recent study by Therivel (2004) and the Compendium of Sustainable Development Indicator Initiatives, hosted on the website of the International Institute for Sustainable Development (www.iisd.org), report over 600 initiatives concerning leading indicator initiatives worldwide. These initiatives differ in terms of geographic scope; initiative type; initiative goal; issue areas and organisation type. However, two main features would seem to characterise these initiatives. First, the majority of the sustainability indicators concentrate on environmental issues, reflecting different weights of the dimensions of sustainability. Second, indicators are suggested for small-scale, discrete issues accessible to specific methodologies, rather than for holistic approaches to sustainability. This is because of the methodological constraints concerning the setting up of a single composite sustainability index outlined earlier.

Appendix 3 summarises a list of the 11 main indicators developed at governmental and institutional level. Different organisations from the public and private sectors have endeavoured to develop sets of indicators to audit local, national and international development processes with respect to sustainability objectives.

The indicators in Appendix 3 are ordered chronologically and reveal three main features concerning the evolution of the measurement of social aspects of sustainable development. First, different sets of indicators cover specific aspects of social sustainability, although it can be argued that older indices prioritise the 'basic needs' component. In contrast, indicators developed more recently seem to emphasise the importance of governance, representation and institutional factors. Furthermore, in older indices the elements taken into account were weighted together with other dimensions of sustainable development in an attempt to deliver an integrated approach to sustainability. However, some of the later sustainability indicators do not identify the methods used to weight the different components of sustainable development. In fact, the final decision about trade-off is left to 'sound judgement', as well as leadership and communication skills, but rather they look at the long-term trend of the progress of each component toward the sustainability state (Egan, 2004).

Second, the chronological evolution of indicators mirrors the re-emergence of the community as the main spatial and operational space for the pursuit of sustainability. The list contained in Appendix 3 suggests that sustainability is increasingly being sought at the city, neighbourhood and community level. Early attempts by UNCSD aimed to develop indicators that would assist decision makers in measuring progress towards nationally defined goals and objectives of sustainable development (UNEP, 2004). By contrast, indicators proposed more recently focus on the delivery of the sustainable communities agenda at the local level. For example, the Egan Review, a report published for the ODPM, UK, in 2004, concluded that the different dimensions of sustainable development are relevant at different spatial levels. Thus, while economic data are more relevant at regional or sub-regional level, indicators of cleanliness, safety and open space are more likely to be relevant at the neighbourhood level (Egan, 2004: 24).

Third, there has been a shift from purely statistics-based indicators toward hybrid sets of indicators that mix quantitative data and qualitative information. For example, the indicators proposed by the Egan review (2004) include a mixture of objective and subjective data inputs. According to the report, subjective indicators linked to surveys and questionnaires are an essential part of the sustainability assessment and implementation process because they reflect people's perceptions of where they live. Furthermore, the choice of indicators should depend on local circumstances and the needs and priorities of local people. The use of such indicators is a clear step toward more inclusion and representativeness, which also acknowledges place-specific conditions and the importance of subjective values at the policy-making level. However, it can be argued that it poses methodological problems related to the aggregation and comparison of the value of the indicators. For instance, since the choice of indicators can potentially differ from community to community, it may prove difficult to compare the performance of places and communities. In addition, it is uncertain how the performance of local communities should be aggregated to indicate the sustainability progress of cities, regions and nations. Lastly, even if statistic-based indicators are to be used, these may not be available at the local level, as pointed out by Shutt *et al.* (2007).

Alongside indicators and initiatives developed by governmental organisations, the corporate and research sectors have developed several sustainability tools and techniques that can be framed within the CSR and Social Capital initiatives umbrella. The most important initiatives are summarised in Appendix 4 (see also Table 4.5 in Chapter 4), which highlights, for example, how sustainability tools mainly consist of reporting, rating, certification and check-listing procedures. Although this allows for easy and measurable comparison between the performances of companies, these procedures often do not identify the underlying methodologies upon which the individual results are based. Furthermore, as highlighted earlier, standards and certifications schemes are often beyond the financial and technical capabilities of smaller companies.

   In addition, several sustainability assessment tools are based on monetisation and financial accounting techniques, some of which have been considered ethically inadequate to take into account certain environmental and social issues. For example, Gasparatos *et al.* (2007) noted that monetary tools such as the Contingent Valuation Method (CVM) and aggregation tools like Cost-Benefit Analysis (CBA), have the great advantage of strong theoretical foundations in economic theory but they can be inadequate in certain situations as progress towards sustainability should go beyond economic efficiency to include equity considerations. In addition, Cavanagh *et al.* (2007) pointed out that monetisation predominantly relies on assumptions and discount techniques and focuses on absolute figures, which neglects the importance of subjectivity and perception.

   The list of initiatives in Appendix 4 also illustrates how the majority of these initiatives are grounded on the traditional assessor–client relationship. This clearly fails to include the views of a plethora of actors who have a stake in the development project, process or objective being assessed. For example, in the context of the Sustainablity Assessment Model (SAM), Cavanagh *et al.* (2007: 479) noted that:

> There is a need to clarify the process and purpose of SAM to participating stakeholders in order to achieve active stakeholder participation in developing alternative options to what may have originally been proposed. A key aspect in achieving this participation is recognition that the technical and data-intensive aspect of SAM is secondary to its role as presenting a debate into sensitivity of not only what the stakeholder believes to be important, but also the importance of societal externalities that may not have been considered.

Finally, it is worth noting that despite the significant emphasis given to social capital in community development policies, there are only a handful of tools for its assessment, or even its promotion. Indeed, several indicators have been developed for the measurement of different components of social capital but these have only been deployed to design community surveys at the local level or used as proxies to deduce the level of social capital of countries from available national statistics.

This indicates that more empirical work needs to be done on social capital tools if the promotion of this concept is to be included in social sustainability policies. The main hurdles to this empirical work are clearly represented by the difficulties in measuring 'soft' qualities of social relationships (e.g. trust and obedience to social norms) but also in including the impact of technological developments, such as texting and emailing, which lead to shifts in lifestyle and influence the way people relate, in the analysis. It is also important to recognise that the social capital experience within one country is impacted by the events in other countries, for example, through migration and the interaction of differing cultures (Babb, 2005). Furthermore, it can prove challenging to harmonise the measurement of the diversity existing at national and international level due to the varying nature of different communities and societies and their experience of social capital (e.g. interpretation of trust).

Traditional social indicators versus emerging social sustainability indicators

Broadly speaking, the review of recent developments in social sustainability measurement suggests a broad distinction between 'traditional social indicators' and emerging 'social sustainability indicators', which is summarised in Table 3.1. According to this categorisation, it can be argued that traditional social indicators are used for the analysis of measurable variables through specific methodologies, which are often linked to the achievement of predefined targets. They are also often selected by panels of experts in national and regional statistical offices. They focus on targets or outcomes and provide a static analysis of national and regional social phenomena.

By contrast, emerging social sustainability indicators are concerned with the integration of multidimensional and intergenerational issues inherent to the notion of sustainability. Their selection is informed by sustainability principles and objectives, which stem from a deliberative and reiterative

Table 3.1 Characteristics of traditional social indicators and social sustainability indicators.

Traditional social indicators	[Emerging] social sustainability indicators
Static	Intergenerational and incorporating uncertainty
Predominantly quantitative	Hybrid
Product	Process
Descriptive	Strategic
Mono-dimensional	Multi-dimensional
Target oriented	Principles and objective driven
Top-down selection	Deliberative and reiterative selection

participation process involving a wide array of stakeholders and local agents. Moreover, sustainability indicators are *process indicators* in the sense that they analyse the processes through which sustainability principles and objectives are defined, themes agreed and solutions implemented. They allow the monitoring of the actual implementation of a project or a phenomenon and assess the progress towards specific objectives in a more interactive way than traditional social indicators.

To briefly clarify and exemplify these differences we can look, for example, at how poverty would be 'measured' from a 'traditional perspective' as opposed to a 'social sustainability perspective'. The traditional approach to measuring poverty involves establishing an income threshold and calculating how many individuals, families or households fall below it (Townsend & Kennedy, 2004). Poverty is measured in a discrete way and linked, for instance, to a poverty reduction target. By contrast, from a sustainability perspective, poverty would be measured together with its main manifestations – including, for example, ill-health, inadequate housing and limited access to basic services – in a multi-dimensional index that integrates the processes and factors conducive of poverty. These include, for example, marginalisation and inability to access education.

From an operational perspective, however, the aggregation of single indices and dimensions presents several difficulties. For example, current integrative frameworks still do not allow a meaningful aggregation of diverse metrics. Keirstead (2007), for instance, commented that it is not clear how fuel poverty and quality-of-life data can be combined into a single social sustainability metric. Even if data can be normalised and weighted, it proves difficult to aggregate social, environmental, economic and institutional metrics into a composite index that can be compared at both spatial and temporal levels.

At present, a well-established and widely used methodology to aggregate incommensurable data into a composite index is to use a 'common currency', such as money and land, or to use matrices and 'rose diagrams' that pull out data as colours (Therivel, 2004). After a common currency (often monetary) is established, this is predominantly used for cost-benefit assessment or analysis. This technique, however, has been considered ethically inadequate to take into account certain environmental and social issues. Gasparatos *et al.* (2007) noted that aggregation tools, such as cost-benefit analysis, have the great advantage of strong theoretical foundations in economic theory but they can be inadequate in certain situations as progress towards sustainability goes beyond economic efficiency to include equity considerations. Similarly, Cavanagh *et al.* (2007) pointed out that monetisation predominantly relies on assumptions and discount techniques, which focus on absolute figures, disregarding the importance of subjectivity and perceptions.

The development and integration of indicators is hindered further by the shift in the social sustainability discourse from the in-depth analysis of 'hard' themes towards the inclusion of 'soft' themes, as reviewed earlier. As a result, new sustainability indicators are increasingly focused on measuring these emerging themes rather than improving the measurement of more traditional, long-standing concepts such as 'equity' and 'fairness'. For example, a growing number of variables and factors are being proposed to deconstruct and measure happiness and well-being of individuals and communities worldwide (Veenhoven, 2002; Veenhoven & Hagerty, 2006) but the main approach to equity still relies on a fairly crude analysis of income and relative prosperity, as shown for example by the UK *Green Book* (HM Treasury, 2005), the recent guideline document for the appraisal of governmental policies, plans and projects, which was reviewed earlier.

Recent sets of sustainable development indicators also illustrate the tendency of favouring the investigation of softer themes at the expense of developing the measurement of more established social sustainability criteria. For instance the set of sustainable development indicators released by the UK Government in 2007 (ONS & DEFRA, 2007) contained a 'Sustainable Communities' and a 'Fairer World' cluster of indicators, addressing social sustainability concerns. This cluster suggests several indicators to assess different aspects of sustainable communities, including well-being, life satisfaction and so on. However, it does not recommend any index to deal with the interlinked subjects of social justice, equity, fairness, and cohesion (ONS & DEFRA, 2007: 96). Similarly, a recent study commissioned by the EU Parliament (EP, 2007) to look at the implementation of the sustainable communities approach in the EU concluded that fairness cannot be adequately measured through existing indicators and that further research work is needed in this area.

Conclusions

The chapter has illustrated how the progress toward sustainability is increasingly being assessed by extending and integrating 'Impact Assessment' and 'Strategic Impact Assessment' methods into 'Sustainability Assessment'. Early forms of impact assessment, such as Environmental Impact Assessment, Social Impact Assessment and Health Impact Assessment were not designed to address the complexity inherent in the measurement of sustainability. However, they are being amalgamated into a new independent form of assessment rooted in the philosophical and methodological framework provided by sustainability, despite the widespread uncertainty concerning how these different techniques should be integrated together.

Furthermore, this has created methodological and theoretical quandaries regarding sustainability indicators, including: (i) the need to improve the neglected measurement of traditional social sustainability themes before addressing emerging concerns; (ii) the challenge of enhancing actual participation in the selection process; (iii) the pitfalls of using a 'single currency' to produce composite indices; and (iv) the practical difficulties of gathering relevant data for measurements at different spatial and temporal scales. These will be examined in more depth in Part II of the book through the case-study analysis. In the meantime, the next chapter completes the theoretical framework of the research in Part I by illustrating the increasingly important role of Public Private Partnerships (PPP) and other delivery vehicles in current urban regeneration practices and how these are linked to the social sustainability agenda and other related agendas.

4

Urban Regeneration: Delivering Social Sustainability

Introduction

Urban areas are a vital part of the social and economic landscape of Europe. In what is a highly urbanised continent, European cities act as the engines for innovation and economic growth, but are also subject to serious problems of inner-city decline, unemployment, crime and multiple deprivation, including social exclusion (EIB, 2005; ULI, 2009).

A complex set of demographic, social and economic forces have interacted to transform the structures of European cities, often resulting in urban sprawl, but also urban decay, and therefore the need for continuing adaptation, renewal and regeneration (Roberts, 2000; EIB, 2005). Increasing migration and population growth in some cities present challenges of their own, and as the recent *State of European Cities* report pointed out, urban life in Europe is increasingly dominated by one-person households surrounded by a wide diversity of neighbours and with very different capacities to participate in the urban economies that are developing around them (EU, 2007a). Often the better-educated members of society are able to exploit these opportunities more than those on lower incomes. Therefore addressing this 'duality' is key to addressing social cohesion and social sustainability issues in Europe's cities. As the Territorial Agenda of the EU suggested (EU, 2007b:1):

> In the long run, cities cannot fulfil their function as engines of social progress and economic growth ... unless we succeed in maintaining social balance within and among them, ensuring their cultural diversity and establishing high quality in the fields of urban design, architecture and environment.

Urban Regeneration & Social Sustainability: Best Practice from European Cities, by Andrea Colantonio and Tim Dixon © 2011 Andrea Colantonio and Tim Dixon

This raises the issue of how urban-regeneration projects across Europe are tackling such issues and how the financial delivery of such projects can best be managed to address the substantial investment gaps in Europe's cities, particularly in the face of the current recession and economic downturn.

Drawing on experience from the UK, USA and elsewhere, this chapter therefore examines the nature of urban regeneration and how it has evolved in policy terms over the last fifty years. The chapter also examines the growth of corporate responsibility and responsible investment agendas and how, linked to the rise of the sustainability agenda, these have driven by and linked to an increasing trend towards institutional involvement in urban regeneration. The diversity of partnership models, which have been developed to deliver urban regeneration projects, is examined together with the emergence of more recent urban development fund models, such as JESSICA and local asset-backed vehicles. The chapter concludes by summarising how attempts have been made to measure social sustainability in the context of urban regeneration.

A question of definition

The term urban regeneration conjures up different meanings to different people and can range from large-scale activities promoting economic growth through to neighbourhood interventions that improve the quality of life (CLG, 2008; IPF, 2009). In the UK, the government has defined regeneration as a set of activities that reverse economic, social and physical decline in areas where the market will not resolve this without government support (CLG, 2009). From this point of view regeneration should aim to (CLG, 2008: 6–7):

- Secure long-term change, by tackling barriers to growth and reducing worklessness;
- improve places and make them more attractive to residents and the investment community so that new and existing businesses can prosper;
- foster ambition and unlock potential in the most deprived areas by breaking out of the cycles of poverty in an area;
- enable everyone in society to be empowered to participate in decision making and to take advantage of the economic opportunities that regeneration brings;
- supplement and help improve the flexibility and targeting of mainstream government services in those areas which under perform;
- deliver sustainable development, which contributes to people's satisfaction with where they live as well as wider government goals; and
- open up opportunities to create more equal communities.

Table 4.1 Characteristics of the three phases of regeneration.

Regeneration phase	Main activity	Characteristics	Institutional involvement	Funding options
Remediation/infrastructure	Site assembly Site remediation Infrastructure provision	High cost High risk Potential for high return	Certain institutional activity through bond issues	Higher yielding or protected bonds Indirect property investment Private equity Bank finance
Development	Construction of property asset Letting property to tenants	Debt-financed High risk (notably in the early stages) Potentially high return Lack of income stream Uncertain capital values	Bank-lending dominant Limited institutional involvement	Direct property investment Indirect/direct property investment Private equity Bank finance Bonds
Investment	Sale of occupied property asset in the investment market	Secure revenue streams Capital value growth Lower risk Returns above bonds Diversification benefits	Main entry point for many institutions Under-weight in regeneration property	Quoted equity Indirect/direct property investment – including Real Estate Investment Trusts (REITs) Private equity

Source: IPF (2006). Reproduced by permission of IPF.

This also recognises therefore that regeneration is dynamic and is about creating sustainable communities, increasing economic value, promoting entrepreneurialism and attracting inward investment (IPF, 2006, 2009). It should also be emphasised that although regeneration and economic development have always been closely related their focus is different. It cannot be claimed, for example, that all activity that promotes economic development is regeneration and much of the evidence from the UK suggests that the goal of economic inclusion does not necessarily follow from increased economic growth (CLG, 2008; IPF, 2009). In this sense, therefore, regeneration is about delivering increased economic inclusion and ensuring that economic development improves the lives of those living in the most deprived areas. In other words, regeneration is seen as a subset of economic development. In another sense, development is about a focus on profit if it is property led, whilst regeneration, although commercially viable in its focus, must also incorporate elements of social and economic diversity to benefit existing communities (IPF, 2009). Therefore an alternative definition may be more appropriate (Roberts, 2000: 17):

> Regeneration is comprehensive and integrated vision and action which leads to the resolution of urban problems and which seeks to bring about a lasting improvement in the economic, physical, social and environmental condition of an area that has been subject to change.

Regeneration consists of three distinct phases (i.e. remediation, development, investment; Table 4.1) in areas characterised by:

- Location in inner-city areas;
- secondary nature of sites;
- adverse impacts from neighbouring land uses;
- associated social and environmental problems; and
- perceived low return and high risk.

Therefore each phase of the regeneration process has distinct characteristics within the overall risk–return profile: remediation/infrastructure is characterised by high risk/high return (often exacerbated by contamination problems) through to investment, with low risk/low return.

Evolution of urban regeneration policy

The history of urban regeneration in the UK has been characterised by a number of distinctive phases during the 30 years since the seminal White Paper on *Policy for the Inner Cities* (DoE, 1977). Moreover, the period before this was also a time of shifting emphasis (Figure 4.1).

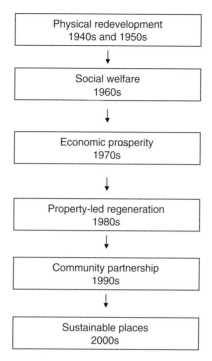

Figure 4.1   Evolution of urban regeneration policy.

As IPF (2009) suggested, following the emphasis on physical redevelopment and social welfare in the 1940s–1950s and 1960s, respectively, by the 1970s there had a been a shift away from a welfare emphasis towards economic prosperity, driven largely by criticisms of existing policy and a desire to move towards a more mixed approach in tackling urban issues through partnerships.

By the 1980s, and with the advent of the Thatcher Conservative Government, the emphasis had shifted again with a bigger role played by the private sector in a world of 'de-regulation' and 'privatism', at the expense of the public sector. Essentially a period of property-led regeneration, this borrowed heavily from US policy with an emphasis on flagship projects (Blackman, 1995).

However by the 1990s, and following the emergence of recession, it was clear that this approach was unbalanced and limited and so policy swung towards placing greater emphasis on partnership-based structures and economic prosperity, through, for example, such initiatives as City Challenge. There was thus a greater role again for local communities. Local residents and businesses were expected to play an increased role in tackling urban deprivation problems within their areas. This was continued through the Blair Labour Government's focus on a New Deal for the Communities.

More recently, sustainability has become a key focus for UK Government policy with an emphasis on social, economic and environmental well-being, or what, in academic literature, is often referred to as the 'Triple Bottom Line' approach to sustainable development (Elkington, 1997). This approach attempts to achieve development that promotes economic growth, but maintains social inclusion and minimises environmental impact (Dixon, 2007; Dixon & Adams, 2008). In turn this has been under-pinned by policy guidance (*Securing the Future*), which seeks to set a new framework goal for sustainable development (SD; HM Government, 2005) and revisions to national planning guidance that aim to strengthen the focus of SD principles within the wider UK planning system – for example, PPS1: Delivering Sustainable Development (CLG, 2005) and PPS 23: Planning and Pollution Control (CLG, 2004). Moreover, as European urban regeneration policies themselves have become more developed (for example the Rotterdam and Leipzig 'Charters', see Chapters 1 and 12), there have been parallel trends in the UK towards a more integrated approach, which has also been closely tied to the concept of 'sustainable communities'. Nonetheless, this period has also included a substantial number of proper-ty-led regeneration projects, the sustainability of which has been ques-tioned (Dixon *et al.*, 2007b).

This period has, however, also coincided with a period when significant investment gaps have been highlighted as a key issue for EU states including the UK. For example in 2007 an EU Member State Expert Working Group reported (EIB, 2007: 1):

> Despite substantial investment needs and substantial funds available through capital markets and financial institutions, there is a widespread perception of an investment gap in cities and towns. This includes a per-ceived failure to translate investment needs into effective demand (bank-able projects and propositions) and a failure to attract effective supply, in the form of readily available financial products and instruments, for sus-tainable urban development. The challenges are especially acutely felt in the new Member States and accession countries, which can however count on support from the EU Structural Funds as well as on the transfer of know how from the EU institutions and other Member States.

This issue has also been starkly highlighted with the collapse of the US sub-prime mortgage market, and the related turbulence in lending markets worldwide, which have exacerbated a downwards trend in land and property asset prices. It is still too early to say what the long-term consequences of the current recession will be, but recent research in the UK suggests that the effects have already fed through into investment, development and occupa-tional demand. The potential slowdown is seen as being deeper and more severe than the 1990s recession posing a significant threat to the long-term viability of some regeneration projects in the UK and elsewhere (GLA Economics, 2008; APUDG, 2009; Dixon, 2009a; Parkinson, 2009).

This had led to an increased emphasis globally on how cities and major urban areas can maintain their global competitiveness. For example a recent study of success and failure in European cities (ULI, 2009) found significant gaps in the following areas:

- Capital gaps;
- knowledge (skills and management) gaps;
- institutional framework gaps; and
- collaboration (communication, leadership, and trust) gaps.

There is, therefore, a perception amongst many commentators that the need for urban investment is greater than ever if cities are to become more 'invest-able' and 'investment-ready' (Clark, 2007). In the EU15 there has been a gradual decline of public investment from about 5% of GDP in the 1970s to 2% today, for example (CLG, 2007). Therefore private finance is critical to city and regional development (Clark, 2007) because it:

- Provides capital in a fast and effective manner;
- can help rebuild local investment markets and avoid disinvestment;
- creates greater commercial and professional discipline within city development policies and initiatives;
- attracts wider interest from other commercial players and can raise confidence in a city;
- can help develop a sustainable finance strategy in city development initiatives and help unlock public finance for alternative use; and
- repositions beneficial city development as 'investment' rather than 'expenditure' in a modern economy.

Essentially this means that cities need to be financially sustainable in both public and commercial terms, which requires a good internal rate of return (IRR) for private investors and a good external rate of return (ERR) for public investors (ULI, 2009). As Figure 4.2 shows, public sector actors may need to invest in those activities where there is limited scope for private sector input (for example, welfare services) (Box B). In the same vein, private actors may wish to invest in projects that have a high IRR and have no potential for public sector involvement (Box A; for example, retail development). However, there is a consensus that some activities (Box C) can offer both an acceptable IRR and ERR. Such projects include major regeneration programmes, infrastructure projects and public service provision. Such partnerships are even more important for risk sharing in times of economic turbulence but making those partnerships work effectively can be even more challenging as a result of the recession (ULI, 2009).

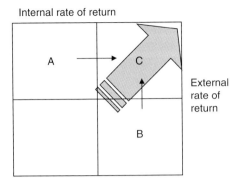

Figure 4.2 Rates of return from city investment. *Source*: ULI (2009). Reproduced by permission of ULI Europe.

Table 4.2 City investment trends: Three levels of approach.

	Level 1	Level 2	Level 3
Methodology	Clear long-term strategy. Public sector investment and energy committed to creating an investment attractive and investment ready urban environment	Articulation and provision of specific investment opportunities to initiate and reinforce development momentum	Innovative mechanisms engineered to overcome the challenge of accessing conventional sources of finance. These mechanisms can also incentivise investment where traditional methods are likely to have already failed
Increasing degree of public sector innovation and risk taking	← ————————————————————————— →		
Increasing degree of private sector leadership/participation	← ————————————————————————— →		
Increasing directness of funding	← ————————————————————————— →		

Source: ULI (2009). Reproduced by permission of ULI Europe.

Recent research from ULI (2009), in a study of 38 cities, has suggested that they have responded to the investment gap with a range of specific strategies ranging from hosting international events and direct state funding to value capture, municipal bond finance and national lottery contributions. These can be further characterised as operating at three distinct levels through an increasing maturity of investment strategy (Table 4.2).

In terms of regeneration, the attractiveness of such projects for the private sector, besides financial return, also lies in the desire of investors to be seen to be 'doing well by doing good', and this has connotations for the growth of corporate responsibility and responsible investment agendas, which are now explored in the next section.

Responsible investment practices

Socially responsible investment (SRI) has become a well-established term in the realm of institutional equities investment portfolios, and increasingly investors have looked to realise the opportunities in alternative assets such as property (Rapson *et al.*, 2007). Alternative definitions of SRI have been offered as the concept has evolved. For example, the Social Investment Forum in the USA define SRI fairly broadly as (SIF, 2006):

> An investment process that considers the social and environmental consequences of investments, both positive and negative, within the context of rigorous financial analysis.

However, Kinder (2005) suggested that SRI has evolved into 'responsible investment' (RI) with the omission of 'social' signalling the emergence of a new perspective.[1] This is founded on the following definition of RI by the World Economic Forum (2005: 7):

> Responsible investing is most commonly understood to mean investing in a manner that takes into account the impact of investments on wider society and the natural environment, both today and in the future.

The recent growth of 'socially responsible investment' (or 'responsible investment') has paralleled a similar elevation in the importance of 'corporate social responsibility' (CSR) or 'corporate responsibility' (CR) in corporate business agendas, including those of the real estate or property sectors (Dixon, 2007; Pivo & McNamara, 2008; Dixon, 2009b). Moreover, it has mirrored a parallel growth in the engagement with the wider sustainability agenda, which, in the real estate and urban regeneration sector, has been impacted, and primarily driven, by legislation and business-related benefits (Dixon, 2009b).

---

[1] The 'S' word appears to have dropped out of the vocabulary of many businesses. Terminology has shifted away from the 'social' towards a more generic descriptor, perhaps reflecting the 'political' connotations of the term (Kinder, 2005); a recognition that responsibility is wider than a 'social' one; or that social sustainability is perhaps the most difficult dimension to measure (Dixon *et al.*, 2007a).

RI's increase in importance for financial institutions and others potentially investing in urban regeneration projects should be seen in the context
of other trends towards the diversification of investment portfolios, including the role of real estate in helping spread risk, and the emergence of the
concept of responsible property investment (or RPI; Rapson *et al.*, 2007).
Historically, prime real estate has tended to dominate as a sub-category of
real estate in the majority of investors' portfolios, but increasingly the performance of urban regeneration real estate markets is being closely examined by investors. Previous research has shown that there is immense
potential in urban regeneration areas, which often coincide with inner-city
locations (Porter, 1995), and in the UK, recent real estate performance measures have also highlighted the sound financial returns that can be made
through engagement in urban regeneration. As a result, combined with the
clear benefits for CR and sustainability (often focusing on brownfield developments) offered by these locations, there has also been a real interest in
understanding how private sector finance can best be attracted into investing in urban-regeneration locations.

The quest for diversification has undoubtedly also led to institutions allocating funding to RI-based investments. This has also led to the development of the concept of 'responsible property investment' (RPI) or 'socially
responsible property investment' (SRPI).[2] Pivo and McNamara (2005) for
example defined RPI as:

> Maximising the positive effects and minimising the negative effects of
> property ownership, management and development on society and the
> natural environment in a way that is consistent with investor goals and
> fiduciary responsibility.

This definition has been made more precise through the work of UNEPFI
(2007) which suggested that RPI:

> … is an approach to property investing that recognizes environmental and
> social considerations along with more conventional financial objectives.
> It goes beyond minimum legal requirements, to improving the environ-
> mental or social performance of property, through strategies such as urban
> revitalization, or the conservation of natural resources.

---

[2]   Kinder (2005) provided a valuable deconstruction of the term SRI. For example the
term 'socially' can imply: (a) that the individual's and society's concerns and aspirations
must be given equal weight in investment decision making; or (b) that society's interests
take precedence over the individual's. For Kinder both of these implications deeply dis-
turb non-SRI adherents, and the semantic connection between 'socially' and 'socialism'
magnifies the upset.

In this sense RPI can be implemented throughout the property lifecycle, as shown by the following examples (UNEPFI, 2007):

- Developing or acquiring properties designed with environmentally and socially positive attributes (e.g., low-income housing or green buildings).
- Refurbishing properties to improve their performance (e.g., energy efficiency or disability upgrades).
- Managing properties in beneficial ways (e.g., fair labour practices for service workers or using environmentally friendly cleaning products).
- Demolishing properties in a conscientious manner (e.g., reusing recovered materials on-site for new development).

This view of 'responsibility' is predicated on the fact that the built environment is a major contributor to carbon emissions and pollutants (RICS, 2007) but also that the social and economic impacts of property investment strategies need to be considered (Pivo & McNamara, 2005). There is, therefore, a strong link between RPI and the concept of sustainable development (Pivo & McNamara, 2005; Rapson *et al.*, 2007)

Although examples of RPI are growing, there is still an apparent reluctance to apply RI approaches directly to commercial property investment portfolios and this is often linked to investment managers' concerns over their fiduciary responsibilities (Rapson *et al.*, 2007). Most investors believe that it will lead to increased costs, which are not immediately translated into higher asset values, thereby diluting investment returns (Pivo & McNamara, 2005).

However, proponents of RPI argue that by considering the potential impacts over a longer term, ignoring sustainability issues begins to contradict fiduciary responsibility (Pivo & McNamara, 2005). Although the wider sustainability benefits to society are well understood and form the basis for the moral case for more sustainable buildings, it is the benefits to occupiers and investors that make the economic case a stronger one. For example, it is thought that as occupiers become aware of these benefits, their attitudes toward 'bad' buildings are likely to change, leading to their avoidance. This could result in increased letting voids and reduced asset values for these properties, while those with better sustainability profiles enjoy higher demand and increased returns (see McNamara, 2005).

Given the emphasis on sustainability within the RPI process, therefore, it comes as little surprise that a strong market in urban regeneration areas in the UK has developed, which seeks to attract institutional investment. Such sites and the property development and investment benefits associated with them can offer characteristics that might appeal to RI funds or institutions seeking to diversify into RPI. For example, IPF (2006) suggested that such projects may offer:

- Investments based on commercial and ethical criteria;
- cross-asset opportunity;
- diversification benefits; and
- regeneration as a clear focus.

Institutional involvement in urban regeneration

Despite the growth of RPI, private capital (or equity) has often been deterred from investing in regeneration because of (CLG, 2007):

- Perception of risk and poor returns;
- high transaction costs; and
- perceived long-term time frames of the public sector.

Other barriers include complexity and cost of clean-up/remediation; fragmented land ownership and a slow planning system (APUDG, 2007a).

However, in recent years financial institutions have become more interested in investing in regeneration areas because of evidence of higher returns, the potential for RI and for other related reasons. This has also led to the development of a range of property investment vehicles.

It is also clear that commercial banks have become important players in the capital market for urban finance (Figure 4.3; IPF, 2006; CLG, 2007). For example, Abbey National, HBOS and Barclays have all lent to urban regeneration projects in the UK. IPF (2006) suggested that the weight of money from banks is for investment (about 70%) with the balance for development (30%). Essentially banks who act as venture capital providers are looking to obtain a capital gain in the short term with the average deal length being three years with an outer limit of ten years. Evidence from IPF (2006) suggests that banks have become involved in a range of regeneration products including:

- Opportunity funds to target infrastructure investments;
- equity-based positions in property development; and
- joint ventures with banks taking an equity stake and partnering with local authorities.

Ultimately banks are more likely to lend where there are returns that are linked with capital growth, perhaps from mixed use developments, for example.

The increase in the role of bank finance in regeneration is also partly as a result of the good credit ratings of local authorities (and related to this increased borrowing powers provided by central government), but also

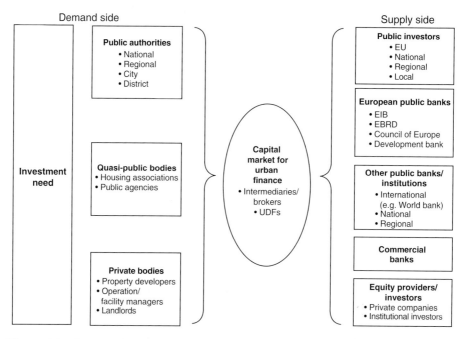

Figure 4.3   A model for urban finance. *Source*: CLG (2007).

because the overall level of urban finance grants is set to decline, because the EU Structural Funds allocation is due to fall in the next few years by 40% (CLG, 2007). As a result, the European Investment Bank (EIB) has become a medium-sized player in the urban-lending market in the UK (CLG, 2007). Since 2001, for example, the EIB has lent €4 bn to 21 projects in the UK and is seen to offer key advantages:

- Competitive interest rates;
- not a profit maximiser lender;
- commitment to supporting projects with a social element;
- provision of technical support with loans; and
- willingness to lend on complex long-term projects.

Financial institutions such as pension funds, insurance companies and banks therefore play a major role in financing the urban regeneration process in the UK. The main drivers for the increased institutional involvement in urban regeneration projects are now discussed. These include:

- The development of a literature that highlights the importance of underserved markets, capital gaps and the role of financial institutions in achieving targeted returns in such markets.

- The growing trends towards RI in the context of CR and sustainability agendas.
- The increased evidence of strong financial returns from urban regeneration.
- Underinvestment in infrastructure and regeneration by the public sector.
- The availability of new investment and partnership vehicles.
- The role of mixed communities as 'social engines'.

Underserved markets, capital gaps and institutions

The intellectual arguments for investment in underserved markets, or inner-city areas, in the UK have their roots in the USA (Dixon, 2005). The decline of the manufacturing sector in the UK and the long-term trend towards a service-sector economy has also led policy makers in the UK to champion the importance of retailing as a potential creator of jobs, and economic vitality, not only nationally, but more locally in local regeneration projects, especially in disadvantaged, inner-city areas. The intellectual roots for this lie with the work of Michael Porter (1995) and his close relationship with the Initiative for the Competitive Inner City (ICIC) in the USA in 1994. Porter's work suggested that, despite the disadvantages of crime, poverty and capital shortages, inner city[3] areas retain four strategic advantages:

- Location;
- untapped local market demand;
- clustering; and
- human resources.

The latent demand, and in particular retail demand, of inner cities was also the subject of a separate, and ongoing, research programme at ICIC. A survey by Boston Consulting Group (BCG) and ICIC (1998) found, for example, that US inner cities have some $85 bn of retail spending power (or 7% of US retail spending), of which some $21 bn is unmet locally by inner-city retailers. Indeed, retail demand per inner-city square mile is often 2–6 times greater than each metro square mile, and inner-city shoppers are surprisingly well connected to the internet, although they are half as likely to have online access as the general US population. Policy themes in the UK have therefore been developed around such initiatives as City Growth Strategies, Inner City 100 and Underserved Markets (Dixon, 2005).

---

[3]   Inner cities are defined by ICIC (www.innercity100.org) as core urban areas that currently have higher unemployment and poverty rates and lower median income levels than the surrounding Metropolitan Statistical Area (MSA).

Trends towards RI in the context of CR and sustainability

As we saw above, there is a strong and increasing emphasis on RI amongst investing institutions, driven by a range of related factors such as legislation and the business case, alongside the growth in the sustainability and CR agendas (Dixon *et al.*, 2007a). These factors also provide implicit drivers for urban regeneration as a focus for RI and RPI, in terms of direct or indirect property investment. Frequently, real estate investors are now targeting brownfield sites in such areas because they provide not only payback in terms of return but also the opportunity to highlight sustainability credentials (Dixon, 2006; Dixon *et al.*, 2007b; Pivo & McNamara, 2008). For example, in the UK, Morley Fund Management created the world's first sustainable property fund. The California Public Employees' Retirement System (CalPERS) in the USA created the California Urban Real Estate (CURE) programme as part of a portfolio of property investment, which focuses on low/middle-income housing, urban-infill projects and community-level investments.

Evidence of strong financial returns from urban regeneration

Until recently it was not possible to determine the investment performance of regeneration property in any detailed shape or form nationally in the UK. However, research by Adair *et al.* (2003) developed a regeneration index based on properties within UK regeneration areas (i.e. subject to some form of intervention) in eight major cities. The research showed that over a 22-year period from 1980, but more specifically from the mid 1990s, investment returns from regeneration property (12.8% annualised return) exceeded the Investment Property Databank (IPD) UK benchmark (10.2%), with similar trends existing on a sector basis. In the same way, the risk per unit of return was lower for regeneration areas (0.69) compared with the UK all property index (0.88), so that regeneration investment provided both a higher return and a higher risk-adjusted return.

This research was paralleled by the development of the IPD Regeneration Index, which is now in its fifth year of operation, and shows that over the five years from 2002 to 2007 the index outperformed the IPD All Property Index in each of those years (IPD, 2007; Table 4.3). The index is based on a sample of 581 standing investment properties in regeneration areas with a total capital value of £7.5 bn, using some 20 Urban Regeneration Company areas, typically fringe central core urban areas in the UK.

As a result, investing in regeneration areas within key sectors (including commercial and residential property) is no longer a 'niche sector', but is now considered 'mainstream' (IPD, 2007). More recently, despite the recession, the index has also shown not only a 'surprisingly resilient' regeneration sector, particularly at an individual sector level, but also that long-term

Table 4.3 UK regeneration property performance.

	2006		10 year (annualised)	
	Regeneration areas	All UK	Regeneration areas	All UK
Total return	16.2	18.1	13.7	13.6
Income return	5.0	4.9	6.5	6.5
Capital growth	10.7	12.6	6.8	6.6
Rental value growth	2.7	4.2	3.5	3.7
Yield shift	−9.5	−8.6	−4.3	−4.0
Yield impact	10.5	9.4	4.5	4.2
Residual	−2.8	−1.4	−1.4	−1.5

Source: IPD (2007).

incentives for investment in regeneration have not been impaired by the market downturn (IPD, 2009). For example, while regeneration returns of −22.6% in 2008 have correlated closely with the downturn in the wider property market with returns of −22.1%, office and industrial properties still outperformed the UK average at that time, although more recently the recession has affected regeneration performance adversely (IPD, 2009).

Underinvestment in infrastructure and regeneration by the public sector

In a more negative sense, the private sector has also been courted because of well-documented deficiencies in governance structures, financial fragmentation in funding streams, weak strategy and lack of capacity and skills (APUDG, 2007b; Dixon, 2007). Partnerships which can cut through these problems, bring the private sector into regeneration and create value over the long term are therefore seen as advantageous.

Availability of new investment and partnership vehicles

Demand and supply side restrictions have frequently led to the lack of appropriate finance for urban regeneration. However, building on such initiatives as the Igloo Fund, developed by Morley, several innovative methods of financing have also been developed to stimulate private sector involvement (CLG, 2007). The involvement of the private sector has also been encouraged by new ways of thinking within government as to how to deal with the public sector's asset base in the UK (Sorrell & Hothi, 2007). Reviews such as the Lyons (2004) report and Gershon (2004) report, for example, have supported the government's view that it needs to devolve £30 bn of assets in public ownership by 2030. There is now, therefore, a complex array of investment vehicles for urban regeneration, which form part of a wider 'Public–Private Partnership' (PPP) concept. Examples include (IPF, 2006; CLG, 2007; Sorrell & Hothi, 2007):

- Limited partnerships and unit trust models (classified through their legal status); and
- outsourcing and joint venture models (classified through their asset-management status).

Examples of these structures are discussed in more detail in the next section of this chapter.

The role of mixed communities as 'social engines'

In a recent review of UK experience in regeneration Anne Power and John Houghton (2007) argued that mixed communities have become the 'holy grail' of urban policy. For Power and Houghton (2007: 194) a mixed community:

> ... houses people from different incomes and varied ages, different tenures, ethnic and cultural backgrounds, providing within walking distance a mix of activities, spaces and services, close to a public transport hub. It always implies at least moderate density; otherwise a mixed community of varied services, tenures and types of people cannot work. It may not mean the top elite living next door to the very poor – such utopias rarely if ever, exist – but it does mean a range of different people.

In this sense a mixed community implies mixed uses and services and mixed tenure (Power, 2007), building on the key UK policy concept of 'sustainable communities', perhaps even in some circumstances carrying connotations of 'social engineering', and has been promoted as a way of increasing institutional involvement in regeneration (Savills, 2005). Despite this, accusations of 'gated communities' are frequently attached to regeneration projects (Minton, 2002) and barriers often mitigate against their success, either through polarisation issues or existing problems of neighbourhood decline (Dixon, 2007; Power, 2007). Previous work, for example, which focused on brownfield regeneration in the Thames Gateway and Greater Manchester (Dixon, 2007), has pointed to the difficulties of creating new communities on derelict sites without appropriate infrastructure and the different issues associated with integrating new communities with existing communities (see also NAO, 2007). These problems and issues are also relevant to consider, for example, in the context of the regeneration of the Lea Valley for the London Olympics in 2012.

Box 4.1   OECD LEED principles of sustainable finance for cities

i.   Smart finance for smart localities and cities: Promoting the fiscal relation-ships with higher tiers of government right.
ii.   Promote active private sector leadership in local investment.
iii.   Metropolitan finance for metropolitan amenities: Sharing costs and ben-efits between cities and their neighbours.
iv.   Capturing and sharing the financial and fiscal benefits of growth locally.
v.   Flexibility in public funding to enable private co-investment in local development.
vi.   A new approach to the management of public assets locally to achieve financial leverage.
vii.   Fostering financial innovation in public and private sectors locally.
viii.   Long-term market building in local economies by the private sector.
ix.   Focus on the quality of the local financial propositions not on the supply of finance.
x.   Build capable specialist local financial intermediaries.

Source: Adapted from Clark (2007).

Partnership models

The development of PPPs in urban regeneration is one facet of the drive towards sustainable financing for cities and city regions (Clark, 2007). Indeed the OECD LEED programme suggested ten principles for sustainable finance for cities (Box 4.1), which are intended to offer a means to promote long-term investment in cities to achieve improved value for all stakeholders. PPPs are just one of a number of alternative financing mechanisms for secur-ing private-sector input into urban renewal and infrastructure development (others include supplementary business rates, tax increment financing and road pricing; Clark, 2007; Webber & Marshall, 2007).

Throughout Europe, therefore, there has been a growing interest of the role of PPPs in urban regeneration (see Trache & Green, 2001; European Commission, 2003, 2004; Ball & Maginn, 2005; Trache & Green, 2006; URBACT, 2006). Trache and Green (2006: 11) have provided a general defi-nition of a PPP as: '... (existing) when the public sector (federal, state, local or agencies) joins with the private sector or service providers, to attain a shared goal'.

For Trache and Green (2006) each partnership is unique but they share common characteristics such as:

• Bringing together public/private sector partners;
• working together toward shared goals or objectives;

Table 4.4   Key elements of urban regeneration PPPs.

✓	Interactive mechanisms that bring together, coordinate and enhance the potential of the public and private sectors in the context of public policies.
✓	Formal (or informal) association of public and private partners who have common objectives and cooperate to achieve them.
✓	Partnership contract stating what the various partners have to do within a given context.
✓	A single legal entity having a stake for both public and private sectors.
✓	Imply the involvement of the private sector in fields of intervention that are usually undertaken by the public sector, by creating tools of conciliation between both sectors.
✓	Result in a mutual added value and a sharing of the tasks. Each partner undertakes to carry out the tasks for which they are most suited.
✓	Renewal programmes based on common public (local government, local people or public interest) and private interest.

Source: Trache and Green (2006). Reproduced by permission of URBACT.

- contributing time, money, expertise, and other resources; and
- sharing decision-making and management responsibilities.

Trache and Green (2006) also highlight key characteristics of PPPs in urban regeneration (Table 4.4).

Van Boxmeer and Van Beckhoven (2005: 3) adopted a more specific definition of a PPP (in relation to their study of Spanish and Dutch housing markets) as:

> An institutionalised form of co-operation between government and one or more private partners in a project with common interests via a distribution of decision rights, costs and risks. A PPP is characterised by common responsibility; the final result for every individual partner strongly depends on the action of the other partners involved in the project.

Previous literature, highlighted in Van Boxmeer and Van Beckhoven (2005), suggested that there were four potential benefits resulting from the concept of a partnership (in generic terms):

1 *Synergy*: where there is additional benefit gained from working together (either through increased profit or new resources (resource synergy), or through innovative solutions (policy synergy).
2 *Transformation*: challenging the aims and operating cultures of the respective parties.
3 *Budget enlargement*: opportunity for further funding from other parties.
4 *Capacity enlargement*: the potential to spread responsibilities between parties.

In relation to urban regeneration, the benefits of PPPs[4] include (URBACT, 2006):

- Finance and access to additional finance through the private sector often in a 'funding pool'.
- Helping organisations learn and innovate in both the public and private sectors.
- Providing the opportunity to minimise the partners' individual limitations through joint working and joint action.
- Bringing 'know-how' to a project through the use of the private sector.

In the UK, an added advantage of PPPs in regeneration is that profitable and unprofitable investment projects can be bundled together to create better scale to development and more certainty, so that investors are more prepared to take a higher risk in the early stages of development (Mills & Atherton, 2005). The variety of models that have been developed is therefore extensive.

The UK continues to be the most highly developed global PPP market (Global Legal Group, 2007). Generally in the UK the structure of a PPP aims to match public-sector funding and surplus/development assets with private-sector funding and expertise (Mills & Atherton, 2005). In order to attract private investment the public sector offers cash or assets, with the private sector investor offering cash in the partnership as an equity stake or through raising debt against the land and other assets.

In the UK the main types of PPP structure in relation to urban regeneration are as follows:

- Limited partnerships and unit trust models (classified through their legal status); and
- Outsourcing and joint venture models (classified through their asset management status).

Proposals for other more sophisticated models have also included Real Estate Investment Trusts (REITs), which benefit from tax transparency (IPF, 2006), and more recently urban development funds such as JESSICA have emerged within the EU. These four PPP models are explored below.

Limited partnership

IPF (2006) suggested that typical co-investment models include both the English limited partnership and unit trust models. The former is typically structured with a single general partner and one or more limited partners.

---

[4] In the UK the term Property Regeneration Partnership (PRP) has also been used to characterise vehicles that operate in an urban regeneration context.

The general partner is responsible for the management of the business of the partnership and its assets (although it is common for certain duties to be delegated or contracted to advisers such as development and asset managers). A general partner has unlimited liability for the debts and obligations of the partnership and so is often a special purpose vehicle to protect against this exposure. The limited partners are prevented from being involved in management of the partnership business but benefit from having limited liability status so that their financial exposure is limited to the amount that they invest in the partnership. In a typical regeneration partnership the limited partners would be institutional and other investors providing the equity finance for the project. One or more companies that are associates of one or more of the limited partners will usually own the general partner. In limited partnerships the institutional investor provides equity funding and so can secure a foothold in large-scale investments. With changes in tax (for example, Stamp Duty Land Tax) the market for such vehicles, however, is in decline.

Unit trusts

This is an arrangement where the assets of the trust are held by the trustee for the benefit of the unit-holders or investors. The funding of a regeneration project through a unit trust is similar to the arrangements in a limited partnership structure. Institutional investors subscribe for units in the trust in exchange for cash. The cash is then combined with bank debt to fund the project. Once income producing, the income passes through to the investors, with capital proceeds being returned on a sale of the asset (IPF, 2006). In the UK both unit trusts and limited partnerships may be combined within a single regeneration structure.

Outsourcing and joint venture models

Sorrell and Hothi (2007) highlighted two alternative models of partnering. In what they referred to as the 'outsourcing' model the public sector contributes assets and the private sector cash, which are both then used to provide medium term funding. The public sector receives deferred consideration for transferring its assets and this is payable by the partnership vehicle on an agreed basis over the lifetime of the project. In this model the arrangement is '50/50 deadlocked', which gives shared control over the assets.

In contrast, the joint venture model may mean the private sector already owns the land and will grant the vehicle rights over the land and provide the required infrastructure and remediation work (i.e. creating 'development platforms'). The public sector may also own land in this model but can also bring compulsory purchase powers to the partnership. In return the private sector brings its expertise to completing the project, in which case the pub-lic sector monitors progress against the agreed business plan.

Recent developments in partnership models: The emergence of UDFs and other financial vehicles

In the UK, alternative funding mechanisms to grant funding (or 'gap' fund-ing) are also being explored, in the wake of the recession and its perceived negative impact on regeneration projects. These alternatives include Accelerated Development Zones (ADZs), which are a UK variant on tax increment financing schemes (TIFs), and are intended to fund infrastructure from future increases in tax revenue created by new development (APUDG, 2009; Deloitte, 2009; Hackett, 2009; IPF, 2009; King Sturge, 2009a, b; ULI, 2009).

Moreover, within the EU and its Member States there has also been much discussion over how to lever private-sector investment into urban-regeneration projects. The concept of an 'urban development fund' or UDF is core to this. Essentially a UDF is a fund that invests in public–private partnerships and other projects included in an integrated plan for sustaina-ble urban development and provides the key implementation tool for JESSICA initiatives within the EU (King Sturge, 2009a, b).

The European Commission (EC) and the European Investment Bank (EIB) announced the development of the JESSICA initiative in the EU in 2005, in cooperation with the Council of Europe Development Bank (CEB). JESSICA[5] is the Joint European Support for Sustainable Investment in City Areas, which aims to promote sustainable investment, growth and jobs in Europe's urban areas. This initiative offers the managing authori-ties of Structural Funds programmes the possibility of taking advantage of outside expertise and of having greater access to loan capital for the purpose of promoting urban development, including loans for social hous-ing where this is appropriate. Managing authorities (such as the Regional Development Agencies in England) wishing to participate under the JESSICA framework, would contribute resources from the Structural Fund programme, while the EIB, other international financial institutions, private banks and investors would contribute additional loan or equity capital as appropriate.

Since projects will not be supported through grants, programme contribu-tions to urban development funds will be 'revolving' and help to enhance the sustainability of the investment effort. The programme contributions will be used to finance loans provided by the urban development funds to the final beneficiaries, backed by guarantee schemes established by the

---

[5] See http://ec.europa.eu/regional_policy/funds/2007/jjj/jessica_en.htm.

funds and the participating banks themselves. No state guarantee for these loans is involved, hence they would not aggravate public finance and debt (European Commission, 2007).

The overall aims behind JESSICA are to make Structural Funds in the EU more efficient and effective by using non-grant financial instruments, which would create stronger incentives for successful project implementation; mobilise additional financial resources for PPPs and other development projects that focus on sustainability; and to utilise financial and managerial expertise from leading financial institutions (King Sturge, 2009a, b). The idea is that these funds will be invested in a particular delivery vehicle, such as an urban regeneration corporation, or within a specific urban renewal programme, and this public funding will at least be matched by private equity from the EIB, CEB and other banks (MacDonald, 2007).

The JESSICA model builds on other similar models in the UK, for example, the North West Development Agency's Space North West PPP, and other local asset-backed vehicles (LABVs). Another example is the Blueprint model based in the East Midlands (see Box 4.2). Essentially LABVs are special-purpose vehicles owned in equal shares by the public and private sector partners with the main aim being a programme that focuses on area-based regeneration or the renewal of operational assets. Effectively the public sector invests property assets and the private sector matches this with cash input so that the partnership can use these assets as collateral to raise debt finance (IPF, 2009; King Sturge, 2009a, b). 'Pure' JESSICA initiatives, however, are yet to be implemented in the UK although recently the London Development Agency announced its intention of using the vehicle to improve London's environmental infrastructure (EIB, 2009).

Box 4.2   Blueprint

Blueprint was launched in 2005 to develop regeneration projects in the East Midlands. Blueprint comprises a partnership of East Midlands Development Agency (EMDA), the Homes and Communities Agency (HCA), both public sector bodies and igloo Regeneration, from the private sector. igloo invested £12.5 m of equity with the two public sector partners investing £6.25 m each. Blueprint's remit is to generate social, economic and environmental benefits within a commercial framework by delivering sustainable and well-designed development. Blueprint is focusing on the East Midlands priority Urban Areas, which includes projects based in Nottingham, Leicester, Derby, Northampton and Corby.

For further information see: http://www.blueprintregeneration.com/

Integrating and measuring social sustainability in urban regeneration

Given the growth of institutional investment in RI, RPI and urban regeneration, the synergy with the sustainability and CR agendas also becomes evident. If institutions investing in urban regeneration projects are to prove their credentials in these arenas they need robust and consistent metrics systems to measure the economic, environmental and social impacts of their investments, and fully engage with communities. For example, Frankental (2001) suggested that issues of RI could only have real substance if they were reinforced by changes in company law relating to governance; they were rewarded by financial markets; related to the goals of social sustainability, with implementation benchmarked and audited; if they were open to public scrutiny; if the compliance mechanisms were in place; and if they were embedded across the organisation horizontally and vertically. It is frequently the 'social dimension', however, that is the most problematic and controversial in terms of measurement (see also Roberts *et al.*, 2007).

Developing metrics systems to assess the impacts of investment in property (and regeneration) based projects has not been straightforward therefore. As Pivo and McNamara (2005) suggest there is no set of broadly accepted metrics for evaluating the 'commitment of real estate investors to principles of RPI', often arising from the different metrics that are required for different countries and different properties. In related research in the USA, Hagerman *et al.* (2007) suggested (in terms of pension fund investment in urban revitalisation) that the investment returns from community-based investing should include financial, social and environmental outcomes. Financial returns, for example, can easily be measured through risk-adjusted internal rates of return and in investment multiples, assessed against bond indices and property indices. Indeed Pivo and McNamara (2005) suggested that social investing does not appear to require concessions in financial performance, and this view is supported in relation to real estate investment in regeneration areas in the UK (IPD, 2007). However, Hagerman *et al.*, also suggested (2007: 62):

> On the social impacts there is no universally accepted industry yardstick to date for testing how well an investment vehicle performs on its targeted social returns.

It is therefore the social dimension to investing (and indeed to sustainability) that still lacks a cutting edge in the institutional investment sector in the context of urban regeneration.

Despite these issues, outside the banking sector, there has been some developmental work in relation to metrics systems that attempt to incorporate

Table 4.5   Assessing social impact: Key methods.

Method	Process	Impact	Monetisation	Non-profit	For-profit
Theories of change	X			X	
Balanced scorecard	X			X	
Acumen scorecard	X			X	X
Social return scorecard	X				X
Atkinson Compass assessment for investors	X	X			X
Ongoing assessment of social impacts	X	X		X	
Social return on investment		X	X	X	
Cost-benefit analysis		X	X	X	
Poverty and social impact analysis		X	X	X	

Source: Clark *et al.* (2004).

a triple bottom line approach in relation to property (Pivo & McNamara, 2005; Dixon *et al.*, 2007a). In a more generic sense there have also been advances in methodology in relation to assessing social impact in community investment projects in the USA through the work of Clark *et al.* (2004) and the Community Development Venture Alliance (CDVCA, 2005). For example, Clark *et al.* (2004) listed a number of techniques to measure social impact (Table 4.5 and see also Chapter 3 and Appendix 4).

Nonetheless, in comparison with the environmental and economic dimensions to sustainability, social sustainability remains a 'poor cousin' (Dixon, 2009b). We have to turn to specially developed financial vehicles for investment to see more radical and robust ways of integrating and measuring the social dimension of urban regeneration, which are examined later on in this book.

Conclusions

It is clear that the growth of 'responsible investment' (RI) has paralleled a similar rise in the importance of 'corporate responsibility' (CR) in the agendas of business, including the real estate or property sector. RI's rise has been partly driven by legislation, but also the importance of an increased institutional interest and appetite for investment in urban regeneration and a growing industry-wide sustainability agenda.

The key themes emerging from this chapter are therefore that:

- RI's increase in importance for financial institutions should be seen in the context of parallel trends towards diversifying their investment portfolios, including the important role of real estate and the potential for urban regeneration investment, and the emergence of the concept of responsible property investment (or RPI).

- There has also been a real interest in understanding how private sector finance can best be attracted into investing in urban-regeneration locations. This has spawned increased attention on how private public partnership (PPP) vehicles can be developed to attract private institutions and bank finance, and a range of delivery mechanisms and models has been developed.
- Institutions have come under closer scrutiny to measure and evaluate the impacts of their investments in such locations. Although a variety of tools has been developed to assess impacts in terms of the environmental, economic and social dimensions of real estate projects (including regeneration) these measures tend to be relatively underdeveloped in relation to the social dimension.

This shows how important it is to understand both the context of urban regeneration and the evolution of PPPs if we are to understand how institutional and development actors are engaging with the social sustainability agenda.

The next part of this book sets out the EU policy context, and then examines how five major cities in Europe have integrated social sustainability within substantial urban regeneration programmes; the partnership models on which the delivery of the projects are based; and the measurement systems that are in place to quantify success or failure in terms of social sustainability outcomes.

Part II

Socially Sustainable Urban Regeneration in Europe

5

Integrated Urban Regeneration and Sustainability: Approaches from the European Union

Juliet Carpenter

Introduction

Throughout Europe, the issue of urban regeneration has risen up the policy agenda in Member States since the mid 1990s (Berg *et al.*, 1998). It is being increasingly recognised throughout the European Union (EU) that cities are the motors of regional economic growth and often the location of significant prosperity. Yet within European towns and cities, there exist considerable disparities between different social groups, in terms of their access to employment opportunities, decent housing and environmental conditions, and socially inclusive networks. It is these disparities that urban regeneration policies aim to address, often taking an integrated approach to tackling the physical, economic and social challenges that they present (Parkinson, 1998).

The Commission of the European Communities (CEC), the executive body of the European Union, has only lately started to embrace these urban challenges, by putting greater emphasis on urban interventions. The principle of subsidiarity framing EU policies envisages that decision making takes place at the level where it is most effective, usually the one closest to citizens affected by the measure. Urban policy was therefore considered to be essentially the responsibility of national, regional and particularly local government. However, as 80% of Europe's population currently live in urban areas (CEC, 2007), it is clear that the majority of EU policies have a strong local impact and it seems therefore logical that some common action at the urban level is undertaken in order to ensure the effectiveness of European policies such as innovation, energy efficiency, the environment and, in particular, social cohesion. In the social arena this need is particularly acute, as disparities are often more dramatic within particular regions and cities themselves, rather than amongst the wealthier regions and the 'convergence' regions supported by traditional EU regional development policy. No real convergence in the quality of life of EU citizens could be achieved globally without attacking urban inequalities.

In parallel with this increased attention given to urban areas, there has been a drive to encourage partnership working within EU programmes. This reflects a more general shift throughout the EU to develop modes of governance (as opposed to government) that are inclusive, responsive and proactive in addressing policy challenges (CEC, 2001a).

The aim of this chapter is to set out the context for, and evolution of, the way in which the EU has addressed urban regeneration issues, particularly in relation to social sustainability. The next section addresses the policy framework that forms a backdrop to urban interventions within the EU. The chapter then explores the role of the mainstream Structural Fund programmes in urban regeneration, followed by a review of specific urban interventions through the URBAN Community Initiative. The chapter then brings the review up to date, setting out the reforms of the Structural Funds covering the period 2007–2013, in particular bringing out the importance of competitiveness and cohesion to current debates about the reform of the Structural Funds post-2013.

The EU policy framework

Since 2000, the EU policy agenda has been dominated by the so-called 'Lisbon Strategy' that was set out by EU Heads of State and Government at a summit in Lisbon in March 2000. The Lisbon Strategy focused on employment, economic reform and social cohesion with the aim of making the European Union (Lisbon European Council, 2000: 2):

> the most dynamic and competitive knowledge-based economy in the world, capable of sustainable economic growth with more and better jobs and greater social cohesion, and respect for the environment by 2010.

The Lisbon Strategy was relaunched in 2005 with a clearer focus on growth and jobs, emphasising the importance of both competitiveness and cohesion for Europe's future. As will be shown, these two concepts are embedded within the EU's regional policy agenda.

In June 2001, the European Council in Gothenburg complemented this strategy by adding a sustainability dimension. The EU's Sustainable Development Strategy (CEC, 2001b) encourages the assessment of environmental, as well as social and economic aspects, in the drafting of all future policy documents, thus confirming the EU's commitment to sustainability. These two strategies, Lisbon and Gothenburg, have set new priorities for the EU's policy agenda since 2000.

A history of the EU urban policy agenda

The urban agenda has only recently been integrated into EU policy making. The principle of subsidiarity within the EU governance agenda calls for intervention at the 'most appropriate level' in the particular policy context. It was therefore argued that, as urban issues are intrinsically local, they should not be addressed at the EU level, but rather by lower levels of governance that are closer to citizens. Indeed, up until the late 1990s, there was no explicit urban policy at the EU level.

However, during the 1990s, there was a growing awareness of the importance of cities and the pivotal role that they play in delivering EU policies, particularly in relation to the environment, economic and social cohesion, as well as employment and innovation. It also became increasingly apparent that while cities are the motors of regional, national and by implication EU economic growth, significant disparities exist both within and between cities, even inside the more developed regions, and that this warranted attention at the EU level. The European Spatial Development Perspective (ESPD), adopted in 1999, reinforced this view, with the aim of achieving a balanced and sustainable spatial development strategy (CEC, 1999).[1] Given the different experiences across Europe, particularly with the imminent accession of new Member States, it was felt that 'cross-fertilisation' and exchange of good practice at the EU level could help to address these disparities.

As a result of the awareness of the key role of cities and the need to share experiences, the European Commission began to develop policy statements setting out the EU's urban policy agenda. In 1997, the Communication 'Towards an Urban Agenda in the European Union' (CEC, 1997) was published, which set out the challenges facing Europe's cities, as well as directions for the future. Following wide consultation with economic, social and political partners, this was followed up with a further Communication

---

[1] The European Spatial Development Perspective (ESPD) is an informal document adopted by Member States in 1999, which sets out guidelines to strengthen the coordination of national regional planning policies (CEC, 1999).

'Urban Sustainable Development in the EU: A Framework for Action' (CEC, 1998), which was subsequently discussed with local, regional and national partners at the Urban Forum conference, held in Vienna in November 1998.

The Framework for Action set out an agenda for policy and action on urban issues at the EU level, with four interdependent goals:

- Strengthening economic prosperity and employment in towns and cities;
- promoting equality, social inclusion and regeneration in urban areas;
- protecting and improving the urban environment, towards local and global sustainability; and
- contributing to good urban governance and local empowerment.

The twin themes of sustainable development and urban governance combined to produce a strong policy manifesto in the Framework for Action. It was rooted in an integrated place-based approach and advocated area-based regeneration initiatives combining economic, social, cultural and environmental dimensions, being managed through partnerships with strong civic involvement.

The concept of partnership was woven into the Framework for Action, with proposals for good practice based on partnerships involving the public, private and voluntary sectors. Thus, the Framework for Action states (CEC, 1998: 5):

> At the local level, it is important to involve citizens and the private and community sectors, thereby ensuring that the aspirations of all the main actors are taken on board, that the needs of targeted local beneficiaries are met, that all possible resources are mobilised and that 'ownership' and commitment are enhanced thus increasing policy legitimacy and effectiveness.

However, the underlying principle was not to prescribe solutions, but to encourage the analysis of local conditions as the starting point, and to take account of the institutional context of each Member State.

Recent developments in EU urban policy

Since the Lisbon strategy was adopted in 2000, there has been increasing recognition of cities' potential contribution to achieving the Lisbon objectives, given their role as the motors of regional and national economies. The European Commission published its Communication 'Cohesion Policy and Cities: The Urban Contribution to Growth and Jobs in the Regions' in July 2006 in which it set out guidelines for achieving sustainable urban development in the context of European regional policy and the Lisbon Agenda.

Box 5.1 Eight key characteristics of 'Sustainable Communities'

1 *Active, inclusive and safe* – fair, tolerant and cohesive with a strong local culture and other shared community activities
2 *Well run* – with effective and inclusive participation, representation and leadership
3 *Environmentally sensitive* – providing places for people to live that are considerate of the environment
4 *Well designed and built* – featuring quality built and natural environment
5 *Well connected* – with good transport services and communication linking people to jobs, schools, health and other services
6 *Thriving* – with a flourishing and diverse local economy
7 *Well served* – with public, private, community and voluntary services that are appropriate to people's needs and accessible to all
8 *Fair for everyone* – including those in other communities, now and in the future

Source: ODPM (2006).

While the Commission has been promoting the urban agenda in recent years, Member State ministers have also been moving closer to a common position on urban policy. Partly inspired by the development of the 'Sustainable Communities' agenda that had recently been developed within the UK (ODPM, 2003), European ministers met in Bristol under the UK Presidency in December 2005, and signed the Bristol Accord. The Accord defined what is meant by a 'sustainable community' and set out eight characteristics of such places (see Box 5.1 and Chapter 2).

Following the Bristol Accord, European ministers signed a further agreement in May 2007, the 'Leipzig Charter on Sustainable European Cities' (EU Ministers, 2007). The charter outlines an ideal model for the 'European city of the 21st century', and sets out common principles and strategies for urban policy. Focusing on urban challenges related to structural change, social exclusion, ageing, climate change and mobility, it lays the foundation for an integrated urban policy at the European level.

The Charter contains two key policy messages:

1 Greater use should be made of integrated urban development policy approaches, by:
   • creating and ensuring high-quality public spaces;
   • modernizing infrastructure networks and improving energy efficiency; and
   • introducing proactive innovation and educational policies.

2 Greater focus should be placed on deprived urban neighbourhoods, by:
- Pursuing strategies for upgrading the physical environment;
- strengthening the local economy and local labour market policy;
- using proactive education and training for children and young people; and
- promoting socially acceptable urban transport.

In the context of the Charter, 'integrated urban development' is defined as (EU Ministers, 2007: 2):

> a process in which the spatial, sectoral and temporal aspects of key areas of urban policy are coordinated. The involvement of economic actors, stakeholders and the general public is essential.

The Charter provides the basis for common principles and strategies related to urban development, and has been welcomed by many commentators as an important step in addressing Europe's urban challenges, making links between the economic, social and environmental aspects of regeneration. However, there has been criticism that it does not provide any follow-up programme or action points for Member States to adopt, and it remains to be seen what action Member States will take to operationalise the Charter in the future.

The Structural Funds and Cohesion Fund to 2006

The Structural Funds are the European Commission's financial instruments for regional policy. They address economic development and socio-economic disparities within and between Member States[2] and regions. The two main Structural Funds relating to urban areas are the European Regional Development Fund (ERDF) and the European Social Fund (ESF):

- The ERDF provides support for building infrastructure, productive and job-creating investments, local development projects and aid for SMEs.
- The ESF supports training actions and employment schemes, and promotes the social and labour market inclusion of unemployed people and excluded groups.

The Structural Funds support national, regional and local priorities, within an overall strategic framework, oriented towards regional economic

---

[2]   However, the instrument specifically devoted to support the poorer Member States is the Cohesion Fund, originally created to assist them to compensate themselves for the burden of monetary union. See the end of the section for further details.

development, that must be approved by the European Commission. The funds are organised around programming periods, with the most recent periods running from 1989–1993, 1994–1999 and 2000–2006.

Up until 2006, the Structural Funds were organised around so-called 'Objectives', with Objectives 1 and 2 being focused geographically, and Objective 3 taking a thematic approach:

- *Objective 1* was targeted on regions whose development lagged behind the rest of the EU, with a gross domestic product (GDP) below 75% of the EU average, (including the whole of Greece, southern Italy, parts of Spain and the former East German Länder). These regions were typically characterised by problems of economic adjustment or competitiveness, including low levels of investment, high unemployment rates and a lack of infrastructure for businesses. Structural Fund support provided basic infrastructure and investment for businesses. Although largely regional programmes, some Objective 1 regions, such as Merseyside in the UK (the Liverpool city-region), were essentially conurbations, with the whole strategy focused on urban development.
- *Objective 2* supported economic and social conversion in industrial, urban, rural or fisheries-dependent areas facing structural difficulties. With the defining indicators including measures such as long-term unemployment and poverty, high crime rates, poor environment and low educational achievements, many urban areas qualified for support.
- *Objective 3* was a thematic objective, not focused on geographic areas, but implemented at the national level. It focused on human resources, aiming to modernise training systems and promote employment among socially and economically excluded groups. Objective 3 therefore addressed many issues of relevance to urban areas, such as the skills agenda and social inclusion, although it was not targeted on urban areas as such.

Box 5.2 provides examples of Objective 1, 2 and 3 interventions in urban areas.

It is worth noting here that, in addition to the Structural Funds, a Cohesion Fund was created in 1993 to help the least prosperous countries of the Union to prepare for economic and monetary union. At that time, Greece, Ireland, Portugal, and Spain, whose GNP per capita was less that 90% of the EU average, qualified for the fund. Today, all new Member States qualify as well, although Ireland is now excluded as its economy has considerably improved. The aim of the fund is to reduce economic and social disparities by investing in major projects, rather than programmes, in two key areas: environmental infrastructure and trans-European transport networks. Typical examples of Cohesion Fund projects include the Dublin ring road in Ireland, treating urban waste water in Greece, and improving railway links in Portugal and Spain.

Box 5.2   Examples of Structural Fund support in urban areas

Objective 1 – The Athens Metro

Athens is home to 1.4 million people and was one of the most polluted cities in Europe. Prior to the construction of the metro, the city relied on one over-ground electrified line, and a complex network of bus services. The public transport system was so poor that the level of usage had collapsed. Following investment from the Structural Funds Objective 1 programme, as well as loans from the European Investment Bank, the Athens metro opened in 2000, with two new underground lines. A total of 15.5 km of track serve 19 new stations in the city, with a rush-hour service frequency of every 3 minutes. It is esti-mated that there are now 250 000 less private car journeys per day as a result of the construction of the metro, with subsequent savings in time and energy, as well as improvements in the environment and quality of life for residents.

Source: CEC (2003b: 21).

Objective 2 – An industrial area put to new uses in Trollhättan, Sweden

The city of Trollhättan in western Sweden received Objective 2 funds to help set up a semi-public foundation, 'Innovatum'. The foundation was established by the municipality of Trollhättan, together with the Västra Götaland region and five private companies, to transform an industrial district of the city. The area began to grow from the 1850s, and prospered in the twentieth century in the areas of engine production and printing presses, but since fell into decline. The Innovatum foundation has transformed the area, which now focuses on high technology production and services. There are around 35 companies located in a business park on the site, a 'House of Knowledge', which includes an exhibition and education and training centre on the theme of technology, media and design, and a centre for film production, 'Film i Väst'.

Source: ECOTEC *et al.* (2004: 35, Annex 8).

Objective 3 – Hamburg

In Hamburg, around 30% of the city's school children are of ethnic minority origin, who often leave education at the first opportunity. It is particularly diffi-cult for those school leavers to access employment. Objective 3 funding has helped to set up an Information Centre – BQM – to build up contacts between teachers, social workers and businesses, in order to widen the job network for young immigrant school leavers. Some 1500 businesses currently receive BQM's newsletter on the local labour market, with the aim of matching school leavers with employment opportunities. The centre is also developing training courses on the benefits of vocational training, and preparatory courses aimed at helping young people to integrate into the workforce.

Source: Information sheet: ec.europa.eu/employment_social/esf/members/de_en.htm

The Structural Funds in urban areas

The Structural Funds are primarily regional policy instruments, and are therefore not specifically focused on urban areas. Nevertheless, a significant proportion of spending does take place in cities. The European Spatial Development Perspective noted that during the 1994–1999 period, approximately 30–40% of subsidies from the regional fund (the European Regional Development Fund – ERDF) in Objective 1 regions were spent in urban areas (CEC, 1999). In many Member States, many projects funded in Objective 2 areas are urban in nature.

The most comprehensive assessment of the urban dimension of Structural Fund programmes has been undertaken by the European Policies Research Centre (EPRC) in collaboration with Nordregio. They were commissioned by the European Commission (DG Regio) to assess how far the Objective 1 and 2 programmes, drawn up for each Member State for the period 2000–2006, integrated the principles of two key policy documents: the Urban Framework for Action, and the European Spatial Development Perspective (EPRC and Nordregio, 2001a, b).

They found that programmes rarely included an explicit urban dimension, and also that the inclusion of urban elements within the programming documents varied considerably from country to country, as summarised in Table 5.1. While some countries such as Ireland, Italy and Spain had strongly embedded the principles of the Urban Framework for Action within their programmes, other countries such Austria, Finland, Denmark and Sweden had not included an urban focus. In some cases, this was due to the fact that the programmes covered non-urban areas, but amongst the other Member States there were also differences in approach. The types of action found by the research to have been supported in urban areas are set out in Table 5.2.

The last significant meeting on urban issues in the EU took place in Bristol in 2005, with an Informal meeting of the 29 EU ministers responsible for urban and spatial development. Following this meeting, the most recent

Table 5.1   Degree to which the Urban Framework for Action is included in Objective 1 and 2 programmes, 2000–2006, by country (EU15).

	Objective 1	Objective 2
Strong	Ireland, Italy	Spain
Mixed	Belgium, France, Germany, Greece, Portugal, Spain, UK	France, Germany, Luxembourg, Netherlands, UK
Weak		Austria, Belgium, Finland, Italy
None	Austria, Finland, Sweden	Denmark, Sweden

Source: EPRC & Nordregio (2001a, b).

Table 5.2   Actions supported in urban areas by Objective
1 and 2 programmes.

Theme	Actions in urban areas
Business support	Developing innovative infrastructure
	Supporting SME entrepreneurship
Education and training	Tertiary sector support
Regeneration and exclusion	Support for socially excluded groups
	Development of city centres
Infrastructure	Improving city public transport
	Developing business parks
Environment issues	Tackling urban pollution
	Waste management

Source: EPRC & Nordregio (2001a, b).

communication from the Commission to the Council and Parliament was published, reinforcing the importance placed on urban interventions within the Structural Funds, to achieve the Lisbon Strategy (CEC, 2006).

Governance and the Structural Funds in urban areas

In terms of governance issues, it has already been noted that the Structural Funds place considerable emphasis on the importance of partnership working, through encouraging the inclusion of relevant actors in the design, management, implementation and evaluation of programmes. This particular issue was examined by ECOTEC *et al.* (2004) in their report into the territorial effects of the Structural Funds in urban areas. Taking a case-study approach, one of the aspects that the project aimed to explore was governance structures and levels of engagement of different local actors in Structural Fund programmes with an urban impact.

Within the 27 case studies, the project identified five broad groups of actors involved in Structural Fund partnerships in urban areas: (i) regional authorities; (ii) city authorities (local or sub-regional); (iii) NGOs; (iv) local community or voluntary groups and businesses; and (v) other agencies. The regional authorities often took the role of managing authority with financial responsibility for the programme. In some cases, city authorities were also involved, to a greater or lesser degree, depending on the national Structural Fund management system. The categories of community or voluntary groups, NGOs, and businesses included both economic and social partners relevant to the programme. For example, trade and business organisations were often involved in management and implementation, municipal enterprises such as those related to waste disposal or culture were partners, as well as social actors such as voluntary organisations and citizens' groups.

A range of other actors were also identified as partners, such as employment agencies, universities and vocational colleges, and trade unions.

The study also found that the Structural Funds have had considerable influence on governance arrangements within the programme areas. Applying the partnership principle and encouraging economic and social partners to be engaged in the programme have had a significant impact on modes of governance at the local level. In particular, there have been positive effects in two areas: in terms of networking and organisational innovation, with partnerships leading to new cooperation networks and more inclusive management structures; and in terms of citizen participation and identity-building for local residents.

However, the study showed that in many cases, the extent of partnerships was not as inclusive as it could have been, and that more could be done to involve a wider range of economic and social actors in the partnership. This finding is also reflected by the EPRC/Nordregio study (2001a, b), which showed that, of the four principles from the Framework for Action being examined, the one related to 'good urban governance and increased participation of local actors and citizens' was the least developed.

The ECOTEC *et al.* (2004) study also found that partnership working created extra administrative burdens and potential delays in the programming. These findings are also backed up by Atkinson (2000), who highlighted the challenges of partnership working in urban Structural Fund programmes.

The Structural Funds and sustainable development

The Structural Funds support regional economic convergence within the EU. But written into the Council Regulations relating to the Structural Funds is also a commitment to support the balanced and sustainable development of regions (Council of European Communities, 1999: 1–2):

> [in the] efforts to strengthen economic and social cohesion, the Community also seeks to promote the harmonious, balanced and sustainable development of economic activities, a high level of employment, equality between men and women and a high level of protection and improvement of the environment ....

An evaluation carried out for the European Commission has sought to assess the contribution of the Structural Funds to sustainable development (GHK *et al.*, 2002). At the level of the overall programme, the evaluation identified an increased level of integration between the Structural Fund programmes and broader regional development strategies, suggesting an overall approach that is more supportive of sustainable development in the long term.

At the level of individual measures, the evaluation applied the four-capitals model to assess the contribution of the Structural Funds to sustainable development (for further details of the methodology see GHK *et al.*, 2002; Ekins & Medhurst, 2006). The study found that the Structural Funds have made a positive contribution to manufactured and human capital, that is, physical infrastructure and human resources, but had in some cases made negative contributions to natural capital (i.e. the environment) and social capital.

In the case of natural capital, the negative effects were largely due to the impacts of new infrastructure investment, especially roads. However, it was found that these negative impacts were generally agreed by policy makers as an acceptable trade-off in the wider context, given the increase in economic opportunities and social welfare that such investment brings. In terms of social capital, the contribution of the Structural Funds is less clear, due to the difficulties of untangling the cause and effects in relation to the stock of social capital, social policy outcomes and economic development measures. The indicators used in the study included the evolution of poverty rates, disparity between average income of highest and lowest deciles, the number of social welfare recipients, and crime and youth criminality rates. The evaluation showed that there are signs of a decline in social outcomes despite increased employment and incomes more generally, raising questions about the contribution of Structural Fund programmes to social sustainability.

In terms of governance and management structures to ensure sustainability, the evaluation found that there had been a strong positive impact on the development of institutional capacity at the regional and local levels, including 'the ability to take strategic views, adopt coordinated policy approaches, apply methods for policy evaluation and to adopt consultative and partnership approaches' (GHK *et al.*, 2002: viii). The evaluation concluded that this impact will have lasting benefits in the regions receiving Structural Fund support.

Thus, while the ECOTEC and EPRC/Nordregio studies found that partnership working could be better developed and red tape reduced, the GHK *et al.*, evaluation highlighted the positive institutional impacts and long-term benefits of the Structural Funds, and more generally the importance of governance for sustainable development.

Evolution of the partnership ideal within the Structural Funds

Within the EU, the principle of partnership has been particularly influential in the operation of the Structural Funds. The concept of partnership within the Structural Funds was initially defined as: 'close consultations between the Commission, the Member State concerned and the competent authorities … at national, regional, local or other level, with each party acting as a partner in pursuit of a common goal' (Council of European Communities, 1988: 5). However, since then, the notion has strengthened to include 'the economic and social partners designated by the Member State' within the competent bodies and authorities (Council of European Communities, 1993). As a concept, partnership now includes social, sectoral and territorial partners involved in the programme, including community and voluntary sector partners, local and regional authorities, and the private sector.

The key drivers that lie behind this push for greater partnership working are varied. At a broad level, there has been a cultural shift across the EU that has encouraged organisations to work together, cutting across traditional divides and well-established boundaries. There are two main reasons for this shift. The first relates to the complexity of the socio-economic problems facing cities and regions, which are often beyond the remit of just one organisation working on their own (Carley *et al.*, 2000). The second relates to the underlying belief that partnership working generates a number of positive benefits and produces better outcomes in terms of, for example, greater effectiveness, greater legitimacy and transparency, greater commitment and ownership, and opportunities for capacity building and learning across traditional divides (Tavistock Institute, 1999).

Within the EU, it is also widely held that good governance and effective institutional structures are crucial for regional competitiveness and these are facilitated by cooperation and exchange of information between actors, including those in the public and private sectors (CEC, 2004: 58). This cooperation in turn stimulates collective learning and the creation, transfer and diffusion of knowledge, which are all critical for innovation (Simmie, 2001). A further spin-off from partnership working is the networks that are created, which can contribute to social capital (Putnam, 1993) in a city or region, thus supporting sustainable development (Ekins & Medhurst, 2006).

It is in response to these considerations that, over the successive programming periods, partnership working has become more deeply embedded in the operation of the Structural Funds, from being defined as close cooperation between different tiers of government (vertical partnerships) to the inclusion of different social and economic partners (horizontal partnerships). With the requirement to implement Structural Fund programmes in partnership, the EU has played a significant role in introducing the partnership principle to many Member States, where it had not previously been normal practice.

The URBAN Community Initiative

Up until 1994, the European Union's involvement in specific urban interventions was relatively limited. The Structural Fund programming period 1989–1993 had seen major investment in infrastructure and human resource development, some of which was focused on urban areas, but explicit urban interventions had not been a feature of regional policy during that period.

The URBAN Community Initiative was launched in 1994 (CEC, 1994) in response to the growing awareness at the EU policy level of the challenges facing Europe's towns and cities. URBAN I was implemented during 1994–1999 and the specific focus for these programmes was deprived neighbourhoods in need of regeneration. In comparison with the first URBAN Community Initiative, URBAN II, which ran from 2000–2006, placed greater emphasis on the importance of integrated programmes, including transport interventions, and also provided for more structured transnational learning between programme areas, through the network-focused URBACT programme.

However, the actual scale of the URBAN programmes is very small within the Structural Fund programmes as well as within national budgets for regeneration. For the period 2000–2006, €700m were committed to the URBAN II Community Initiative in EU15, representing just 0.3% of the total EU15 Structural Funds budget of €213 bn. The actual funding per programme is also relatively small. The 70 URBAN II programmes received on average an EU investment of around €10m over seven years. This contrasts with national programmes such as the New Deal for Communities (NDC) in the UK, where individual programmes receive an average of £50m per programme (around €55m) over ten years (Lawless, 2004).

Most programmes were situated in areas that were already eligible for support under Objectives 1 or 2, but the URBAN programme opened up the possibility for cities outside these priority areas to apply for funding. This was in recognition of the fact that even in more prosperous cities of the EU, there were still pockets of poverty and deprivation that warranted further public investment. Having previously been seen as an environmental issue, urban regeneration was now presented as an issue of social cohesion that needed to be addressed independently of geographically-based regional disparities. The focus of the URBAN programmes was narrower than the mainstream interventions, and particularly aimed at targeting urban deprivation, and therefore social sustainability. In addition, the active involvement of citizens through partnership arrangements was specifically encouraged throughout the programme.

An evaluation of URBAN I (1994–1999) showed that it was largely successful in terms of its impact at the local level, although due to the small scale of each programme, these impacts were necessarily limited (GHK, 2003). Nevertheless, it has been argued that the wider impacts of the programme have been significant, particularly in terms of partnership working (Carpenter, 2006). Partnership working has been one of the most important legacies of the URBAN programme, and has paved the way for lasting relationships and the creation of networks of public- and private-sector organisations. City authorities were directly responsible for the management of the programme, and in many Member States, different services of the local authority and other agencies were involved in the implementation of the project, depending on the issues involved. While some URBAN programmes, such as those in Portugal and Greece showed less evidence of additional value from local delivery (Chorianopoulous & Iosifides, 2006), many of the URBAN programmes showed that there was real 'community added value' in managing regeneration using a partnership approach, despite the challenges and delays that were often incurred.

The national mid-term evaluations of the URBAN II programmes in 2003 showed that in general, URBAN II has improved on URBAN I, particularly in the integrated nature of the programmes and the simplification of processes and management arrangements. For example, in the UK it was found that URBAN II programmes were now better integrated with other regeneration initiatives and existing partnerships and local authority departments than before (DTZ Pieda Consulting, 2005). Emerging findings from the final evaluation of URBAN II suggest that some 4000 gross jobs have been created with 65 000 people trained (ECOTEC-ECORYS, 2009). However, from initial results, there appears to be limited evidence of real community involvement in URBAN II, which could call into question the strength of social sustainability within the programme.

Some research has also argued that the neoliberal rationale to EU urban policy, emphasising competitiveness as a means of promoting social cohesion is not an effective approach to tackling neighbourhood deprivation (Chorianopoulous & Iosifides, 2006). Nevertheless, the URBAN programme, in its limited capacity, appears to have had an impact in particular spheres, as Box 5.3 illustrates.

Structural Funds 2007–2013

The current programming period for the Structural Funds covers the period 2007–2013, and also includes the theme of partnership working as an important principle within the programmes. Indeed, the Leipzig Charter places emphasis on partnership working within the context of building sustainable urban communities (EU Ministers, 2007: 3):

> Integrated urban development programmes … should be coordinated at local and city-regional level and involve citizens and other partners who can contribute substantially to shaping the future economic, social, cultural and environmental quality of each area.

The partnership principle is therefore embedded in the EU's most recent urban policy charter, and is likely to play an increasingly significant role in the management and operation of Structural Fund programmes in the future.

Box 5.3　Example of an URBAN case study

URBAN II: Renovation of an abandoned historic building as a community facility, Pamplona, Spain

The Pamplona URBAN II programme is focused on the historic centre of the city. A number of buildings in the centre were derelict and had been abandoned, including the sixteenth-century Palacio del Condestable. The URBAN programme aimed to renovate the palace for use as a community facility, for training, social, and cultural activities. One of the key features of the project has been the extensive consultation that has taken place, including with residents and associations of local businesses. At each stage, local people have been actively involved in putting forward proposals and defining the project, and residents' and businesses associations are well represented on the monitoring committee. The project has taken an integrated approach, through environmental improvements and historic restoration, social inclusion through training and social activities, as well as economic regeneration including pacts for employment with local businesses.

Source: CEC (2003a: 17).

The 2007–2013 Structural Fund programming period follows enlargement of the EU to include 12 new Member States. Given that some of these States face considerable challenges, the Structural Funds have been reorganised to take account of the shifting map of the EU.

Driven by the Lisbon Strategy, with its focus on competitiveness, and a wider neoliberal agenda that has permeated policy making in many EU countries (Boddy & Parkinson, 2004; Buck *et al.*, 2005), the new architecture of the Structural Funds is based around three objectives (the 'three Cs'): convergence, competitiveness and cooperation:

Convergence　The 'convergence' objective is allocated, like the previous Objective 1, on the basis of GDP per capita using the criteria of 'GDP per capita less than 75% of the EU-25 average'.

A number of regions are also eligible for transitional support (called 'phasing-out'), if they would have been eligible for the convergence objective if the 75% threshold had been based on the average GDP of EU-15 and not EU-25. This includes regions such as the Algarve in southern Portugal and the Highlands and Islands in Scotland.

Included in the 'convergence' heading is the Cohesion Fund, which benefits those countries whose Gross National Product (GNP) is less than 90% of the EU average and Spain ('phasing out' of the Fund).

Together, the Structural Funds and Cohesion Fund, which make up the convergence objective, account for 82% of the total cohesion budget.

Regional competitiveness and employment The 'competitiveness' objective applies to all other regions not covered by the convergence fund, supporting activities to achieve the Lisbon agenda's competitiveness targets set for 2010 (to create the most advanced knowledge-based economy in the world, with at least 70% of the adult workforce in employment by 2010). The absence of zoning (characteristic of the previous Objective 2) is recognition that there are pockets of deprivation even in the most prosperous regions. For a successful region to remain competitive, it needs to be adaptable to change, with possible implications for public-sector investment in supporting opportunities for change.

Within the competitiveness priority, there are two elements, one channelled through regional programmes to promote economic change in industrial, urban and rural areas (not dissimilar to the previous Objective 2 initiatives), and the other channelled through national programmes aimed at promoting employment, structured around the European Employment Strategy (modelled on the previous Objective 3 arrangements).

As with the convergence objective, there is transitional support available for regions that were covered under the previous Objective 1, but whose GDP now exceeds 75% of the EU-15 GDP average (called 'phasing in'). This includes regions such as Sardinia in Italy, and the Canary Islands in Spain.

The competitiveness objective accounts for 15% of the total cohesion budget.

Cooperation Building on the success of the INTERREG Community Initiative programme, which promotes cross-border cooperation, the 'cooperation' objective is aimed at communities in border regions, supporting joint territorial cooperation programmes and projects that forge links between communities in different Member States. This accounts for the remaining 3% of the total budget.

As these programmes are currently being implemented, their impact specifically on urban areas has not yet been assessed. On the surface, it would appear that the urban dimension is less evident, as the URBAN Community Initiative has not been maintained. However, there is a requirement for Member States to incorporate an 'urban dimension' into their National Strategic Reference Framework (NSRF), which sets out the broad priorities for future Structural Funds Programmes in each country. All countries have 'mainstreamed' urban considerations in their development strategies and there are therefore increased opportunities to incorporate urban issues into cohesion policy, with the potential to delegate power to urban authorities to manage aspects of the programme. Local authorities can be key partners, and the commitment and participation of the private sector is also required. The extent to which the urban dimension has been incorporated into the NSRF varies between Member States, and the mid-term evaluations in 2010 will provide the first opportunity to assess how far urban issues are being addressed within the new programmes. Nevertheless, there has been concern expressed about the loss of the distinct and explicit 'urban' focus within the Structural Funds (Atkinson, 2007), which some see as a disadvantage for urban areas in the future.

There is currently an on-going debate at the time of writing over the future of the Structural Funds for the post-2013 period. The Barca Report published in 2009 provided an independent review of the effectiveness of cohesion policy to date, including an assessment of core priorities that could be the focus of any future cohesion policy. The report argued strongly for a place-based strategy to continue, with core priorities that involve both 'economic' and 'social inclusion' objectives, including a so-called 'territorialised social agenda' (Barca, 2009). Although the details are still to be clarified, it appears that social sustainability and competitiveness in urban areas will continue to be priorities for EU cohesion policy.

Conclusions

There has been a significant sea-change in the attitude towards EU-led interventions in urban areas since the 1980s and the first programming period of 1989–1993. At that stage, it was felt that urban areas were a priority for national governments rather than the EU, in line with the principle of subsidiarity. However, during the intervening 20 years, there has been increasing recognition of the importance of addressing urban challenges at the EU level, primarily for two reasons: first, because cities are the engines of regional, national and thus EU economic growth; and second, because of the marked disparities that exist within and between cities, which call for a wider response from a social-inclusion perspective.

In parallel with this increased interest in urban issues has been a growing emphasis on the importance of partnerships in planning, managing and delivering EU interventions. This has evolved from being essentially a passive consultation role, to economic and social partners being expected to take a full and active role in all stages of Structural Fund programming and delivery.

The most recent development on the EU urban policy scene, the Leipzig Charter, looks set to take these two developments further. Ministers for the first time have recognised collectively the importance of integrated urban development and the role of partnerships, which in theory lay the foundations for greater emphasis on urban policy in the future. Given these policy priorities, it is likely that the social sustainability agenda will come to dominate urban policy at the EU level in the years to come.

Having set out the EU urban policy context, the next five chapters of this book explore different local city responses to the challenges of urban regeneration, in five national contexts: the UK (Cardiff), Spain (San Adria de Besos), Italy (Turin), the Netherlands (Rotterdam) and Germany (Leipzig). Each case study examines the different approaches to integrating dimensions of social sustainability, the issues that arise in delivery partnerships, and the challenges of measuring the outputs and outcomes of the regeneration programme in terms of social sustainability.

6

The Future Regeneration
of Roath Basin, Cardiff Bay

Tim Dixon and Austine Ng'ombe

Introduction

Cardiff's wealth and prosperity was historically based on iron and coal, but when trade began to decline the city faced a battle to 'reinvent' itself. Initially the focus for regeneration in the city, following the demise of the docks, was the city centre, but this shifted in emphasis during the 1980s to south Cardiff and the area known as Butetown or Tiger Bay, in what is the wider Cardiff Bay area. Today the overall strategic emphasis in the city is very much based on developing its competitiveness, locally/regionally, nationally and internationally. The planned regeneration of Roath Basin in Cardiff Bay is linked to this agenda, with the potential for further employment space to underpin Cardiff's recent, and relatively strong, economic growth.

This chapter therefore begins by examining the evolution of Cardiff as the capital of Wales and places the Cardiff Bay regeneration project in historic perspective. The chapter then goes on to examine recent developments in policy and context before examining the Roath Basin development in terms of its planned social sustainability outcomes and the framework for its measurement. It should be noted that the chapter draws on existing literature as well as interviews with key stakeholders, and also highlights and describes igloo's social responsibility investment (SRI) framework: *footprint*™ (igloo, 2010).

Urban Regeneration & Social Sustainability: Best Practice from European Cities, by Andrea Colantonio and Tim Dixon   © 2011 Andrea Colantonio and Tim Dixon

Historic perspective

Cardiff's origins as a major settlement stretches back to Roman times, and following the Norman invasion in the eleventh century it developed into an important administrative centre for the surrounding agricultural area, although for many centuries it followed, rather than led, Bristol and Swansea as a port (Rakodi, 2009).

However, it was only during the late eighteenth and early nineteenth century that Cardiff really started to expand, first as an export centre for iron, and then subsequently for coal. The completion in 1794 of the 50 km-long Glamorganshire Canal, which was specifically constructed for the purpose of exporting iron and coal overseas, and which also linked Cardiff to Merthyr Tydfil to the north of Cardiff, was the beginning of what was to become the busiest port in the world, with a range of docks serving the port (Thomas, 2003; Rakodi, 2009).

In 1798, a basin was built to link the canal to the North Atlantic Ocean to facilitate iron/coal exports, and further calls for more modern dock facilities in the area prompted the Marquess of Bute, Cardiff's foremost landowner, to promote the construction of West Bute Dock, which was completed in the 1830s. This marked the birth of the modern dock business in Cardiff, as more docklands were subsequently constructed, thereby making coal export the most lucrative business of the time in the area. Indeed, by 1835 Cardiff itself was declared a borough with an elected council, and in 1839 the first modern deepwater dock was constructed (Rakodi, 2009). Moreover Cardiff's growth was further fuelled by the development of north–south rail connections between the docks and the coalfields to the north (from 1840 onwards) and east–west along the coast, from 1850 (Hooper, 2006; Rakodi, 2009).

Following these transportation improvements, the industry was exporting two million tons of coal as early as 1862, and this rose to over 10 million tons per annum within the space of just two years, and increasing trade in the area led to the construction of Roath Dock in 1897 and Alexander Dock ten years later (Thomas, 2003). By 1850 Cardiff's export trade in coal had enabled it to overtake Bristol as the major commercial centre for the south west (Rakodi, 2009), and by 1880 its dominance was such that it was known as the 'coal metropolis of the world' (Davies, 2002; Rakodi, 2009). Although coal exporting began to decline in relative terms during the 1890s Cardiff's dominance as a coal-exchange port continued and by the end of the century it had become the acknowledged regional capital of South Wales (Hooper, 2006).

As a result of these developments, Cardiff was granted city status in 1905, and by 1909, Cardiff Bay was already the biggest coal-exporting port in the world (Thomas, 1999a; 1999b; 2003; Hooper, 2006). Coal production rose from 16.9 million tons in 1874 to 53.9 million tons in 1914, and during the same period, Cardiff's population grew from 65 000 to 185 000 (Thomas, 2003).

Cardiff's growth and physical configuration was also heavily influenced by the development of its infrastructure: within the old town alongside the east–west highway, the central business district developed whilst the docks also gave rise to a burgeoning centre of commerce and business, some 2 km from the centre, which was to have significant implications for future regeneration in the area (Rakodi, 2009). The city's growth during the nineteenth century was also based on a large number of migrants from the coalfield areas to the north and from overseas, and although social tolerance was often a hallmark, there were tensions throughout this period and up to the present day (Hooper, 2006; Rakodi, 2009).

The booming coal-export business was also evidenced by the presence of shipping companies in the area. By 1920, for example, a total of over 120 shipping companies were operating in Cardiff. Therefore Cardiff grew to be one of the major economic hinterlands in Europe and became the capital city of Wales in 1955 (Thomas, 1999b, 2003; Hooper, 2006).

By 1914, however, coal exports were already declining, with a further decline during the 1920s (as a result of the general strikes) and during the end of World War II (as a result of falling demand), so that by 1964 they had dried up, leading to underutilisation of the docks and subsequent abandonment (Rakodi, 2009).

As a result, Butetown (commonly known as 'Tiger Bay'), with its high levels of migrant workers, and the area closest to the docks, became one of the most impoverished wards in Cardiff. For example, Thomas (1999a) reported that by the 1980s 47% of Butetown residents were Anglo-Negroid; 19% were Arab/Somali born from an Egyptian father and white mother; 19% were white, and 14% from other nationalities. In 1981, the area scored lowest in a range of social development indicators, including employment levels; households with cars; and housing standards.

The decline of the city in the south was paralleled with expansions in the north, west and east of the centre during the twentieth century, and this physical decentralisation was paralleled by boundary extensions from 1875, which increased the administrative area to 14 000 ha by 2000 (Davies, 2002; Rakodi, 2009). Moreover its population also grew from 305 000 in 2001 to 315 000 in 2004.

Part of this expansion was founded on the provision of new housing to accommodate those relocated from poor-quality inner-city housing that had to be demolished. For example, the council built 20 000 housing units (as compared to 17 000 units built by the private sector) between 1945 and 1974 (Thomas, 2004). These house-building policies enjoyed massive support from both Labour and Conservative parties during their respective reign within the reference period. At the same time, the quality of council houses in Cardiff was categorised as 'better than average' (Thomas, 1999b).

However, in the 1970s the growth of business and commerce in the centre of Cardiff and improved motorway links led to the city shifting its emphasis on growth and renewal away from the dockland area (Hooper, 2006). During this period, and subsequently, the 'Hook Road' improvement scheme and a new retail centre, St David's Centre, were completed. Other developments included a 2000-seater concert hall, leisure facilities, multi-storey car parks and further pedstrianisation of streets. As a result, Cardiff shopping centre was ranked by Hillier Parker, as one of the top 20 British shopping centres (Thomas, 1999b).

Regeneration policy: Cardiff Bay

On the basis of the council-house building immediately after World War II, and city redevelopment between the 1950s and 1980s, it could be argued that Cardiff had delivered in terms of urban development. But for some, these developments were not executed under the banner of 'Cardiff regeneration'; rather they were 'business as usual' developments, carried out on a piecemeal, ad hoc basis (Punter, 2006a). Moreover, these developments were only executed in the north, west and eastern parts of the city, while the southern part remained relatively marginalised.

However, with growing worries about the declining industry in the docklands, coupled with the realisation of the dockland area's potential for upmarket housing and a variety of commercial uses, the planning policy of the city shifted again, as the docklands in the south became the target for redevelopment during the 1980s.

There were certainly sound economic reasons for trying to arrest the decline of South Cardiff, not least the continued job losses as many companies went bust. For example, as a result of the economic decline, the population (which had been rising since the 1900s) began to fall for the first time in 1980, as residents were moving out of the city, and de-industrialisation also saw the departure of Land Rover's car-manufacturing plant, and the closure of the giant East Moors Steelworks (formerly Dowlais Works). As a result manufacturing employment in the city fell from just over 20% to only 6.7% in 2003 (Radoki, 2009).

Nonetheless, it was not until the early 1980s that the County Council actively suggested that economic regeneration should shift from the promotion of manufacturing to service sector development in South Cardiff (Rakodi, 2009). Despite concerns over competition for the city centre, the early 1980s therefore saw the development of Atlantic Wharf, a small, speculative site of some 40 ha, which combined residential, offices, hotel and leisure uses with the refurbishment of a disused dock (Rakodi, 2009). The real impetus for a shift to the south, however, came with the establishment of Urban Development Companies during the 1980s. In Wales a UDC was established (alongside the 12 in England) to provide a new vision for what became known as Cardiff Bay, but which would also overcome the rivalry and disagreement between the city and county levels of government.

A key, initial role for the Cardiff Bay Development Corporation (CBDC) was to build the Cardiff Bay Barrage, which dams the Ely and Taff Rivers (and which ultimately created a 200 ha freshwater lake), and to redevelop the 1100 hectares of derelict and contaminated land (Thomas, 2003). Essentially the aim of the Development Corporation was to (CBDC, 2000: 8, quoted in Thomas, 2003: 24):

> Put Cardiff on the international map as a superlative maritime city, which will stand comparison with any such city in the world, thereby enhancing the image and economic well-being of Cardiff and of Wales as a whole.

The CBDC aimed to achieve the above aim by (Punter, 2007):

- Reuniting the city centre with its waterfront;
- promoting development that could provide a superb environment in which people would want to live, work and play;
- achieving the highest standards of design and quality in all types of investment;
- bringing forward a mix of development, which would create a wide range of opportunities and would also reflect the hopes and aspirations of the communities;
- stimulating residential development, which provides homes for a cross-section of the population; and
- establishing the area as a recognised centre of excellence and innovation in the field of urban regeneration.

This vision of a vibrant 'Cardiff Bay' was in fact inspired by a visit to the USA by one of the county councillors, and was also heavily influenced not only by the emerging idea of 'urban entrepreneurialism' or city marketing as a away of attracting inward investment, but also the successful London Docklands model of public-sector intervention in decision making, land assembly, infrastructure modernisation, and levering private-sector funding (Punter, 2007; Rakodi, 2009).

CBDC therefore adopted the American Baltimore Harbour model of regeneration (Locum Destinations Review, 2000; Punter, 2007), which was essentially 'property-led', but also 'design-led', regeneration (Thomas, 2004; Francis & Thomas, 2006). For Punter (2006a) a key driver and distinguishing feature in property-led regeneration is the concept of 'boosterism', focusing on the creation of an enabling environment to attract private investment. Nonetheless, private investment cannot be attracted unless an area provides a physically acceptable image, and, in this sense, private investment could also be attracted by increased positive publicity of the area through effective marketing programmes.

These, therefore, were seen as being the key characteristics of the Cardiff Bay Regeneration project that could transform Cardiff into a 'recognised centre of excellence and innovation in the field of urban regeneration' (CBDC, 1987, cited in Punter, 2007: 2). Accordingly, a total investment of about £1.2 bn was set aside by CBDC to achieve this, and the city underwent a vigorous land reclamation, and a re-imaging and remarketing exercise, so that by 2001 the initial budget of £1.2 bn was exceeded by 51% to reach £1.815 bn, making the project 'one of the biggest and most impressive regeneration programmes of modern times' (Punter, 2007: 1).

Figure 6.1 shows the CBDC expenditure in 2000 towards the regeneration project. As the chart shows, the largest portion of the budget went towards infrastructure/property development, with the construction and running costs of the barrage alone costing £210 m. Key to attracting business was the location. In a survey in 2004, some 24% of businesses in the area suggested this was a key reason for locating in Cardiff Bay (Figure 6.2).

Ultimately the aim of the regeneration project was to 'resurrect' Cardiff Bay in order to make it one of the major cities in Europe. By adopting the Baltimore property-led regeneration model, CBDC aimed to regenerate

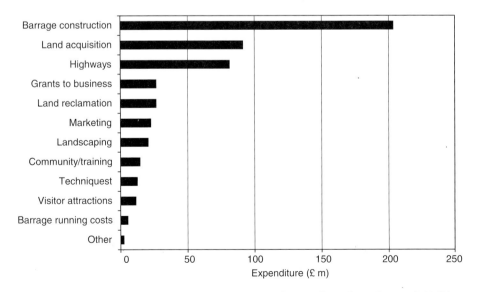

Figure 6.1 Cardiff Bay regeneration expenditure. *Source*: Data from Punter (2006b).

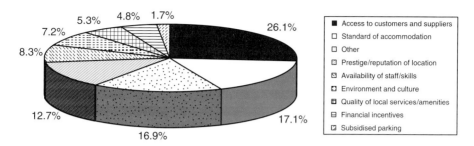

Figure 6.2   Reasons for locating in Cardiff Bay. *Source*: Data from Cardiff Council (2005).

and commercialise the waterfront, replete with iconic buildings and designer spaces to serve as an urban playground for high-class, affluent residents, tourists and conventioneers whose expenditure would drive economic development. This has created Europe's largest city centre waterfront with more than 13 km of frontage for hotels, leisure, business and new residential areas. Key characteristics of the property-led model included among others, a focus on attracting private investment, and a top-down approach in defining the goals of the regeneration project. As a result a network of high-quality infrastructure (roads, electricity, drainage, telecommunications) and a range of state-of-the-art buildings have been constructed in Cardiff Bay, including the 5 star St David's Hotel, the Millennium Stadium, the Oval Basin (public space), Techniquest (science museum), the Mermaid Quay (restaurants/festival shopping), Pierhead Building, Senedd building (the Wales debating chamber), International Pool and about 6000 housing units like the gated ones at the Century Wharf (Punter, 2006b; Rakodi, 2009).

Despite the achievements of the property-led Cardiff Bay regeneration, the project has not been without its critics and a key criticism has been that the property-led regeneration falls short in terms of social sustainability (Thomas, 2003; Punter, 2007; Rakodi, 2009). The regeneration has also been accused of neglecting the needs of the majority of residents in the area, especially in Butetown. For instance, it has been suggested that the project's emphasis, in the case of housing, was to build more expensive, socially exclusive, gated units that could only be accessed by the rich, while those in Butetown – where, according to Thomas (2004), very few, low-class units have been built – are perceived as being more isolated from the rest of the area and the city. Overdevelopment of expensive housing units has therefore bred new fears of high vacancy rates as many of the units are never occupied. This has prompted others to warn that Cardiff Bay risks being a slum of the future because of high housing vacancy rates (Punter, 2008).

Furthermore, by the time the CBDC was wound up in 2000, it was suggested that its activities had created less employment than intended, with some of the planned infrastructure and other projects remaining uncompleted (Rakodi, 2009). It was also suggested that the private investment gearing ratio of 1: 2.38 was below the average of other UDCs (Punter, 2006a).

Environmentally, the barrage is said to have permanently covered mudflats, which were for a long time feeding grounds for wading birds. These criticisms notwithstanding, after the CBDC wound up (Locum Destination Review, 2000), the successor organisations (e.g. South Glamorgan Council, Cardiff Council) have continued with the same regeneration model (Thomas, 2004).

To sum up, the property-led regeneration of Cardiff, driven by boosterism, has been only a partial success story. Its focus on physical transformation in meeting two of the CBDC's objectives – *reuniting the city centre with the waterfront*, and *achieving the highest standards of design and quality* has been successful. Arguably, however, the project has failed in promoting social sustainability with social inclusion objectives being voiced but not prioritised (Thomas & Imrie, 1999).

As the brief historical review above suggests, Cardiff Bay has played a part in the trajectory of Cardiff as a city which has undergone massive transformation from, to borrow Hooper's (2006: 1) words, 'Coal Metropolis to Capital Cardiff'. However, to date, Cardiff Bay, especially Butetown, remains the most socially deprived area of Cardiff city (Thomas, 2004). The communities in these areas have been bypassed by this physical transformation of the city. In Thomas' (2004: 275) words, the regeneration project has left these people 'as islands in a sea of rising land values and upmarket developments'. However, Thomas (2004: 278) also suggests that:

> ... an alternative to [property-led] regeneration must address any injustices associated with these social relations of inequality. If the Cardiff Bay story provides a lesson about the limitations of one approach to regeneration, then it also provides an example of a promising alternative, an alternative that provides a basis for critical engagement within and outside the community. It is an approach that tries to provide an improved environment and marketable skills, but not at any cost; and does so while remembering that it is important to improve the quality of life of those without any possibility of inclusion in the labour market (such as the elderly).

Key to explaining the successes within Cardiff Bay, therefore, is the formation of a common vision, through the 1980s and 1990s, which not only overcame political uncertainties, and effectively coalesced political interests and private-sector commercial development interests, but also brought together a strong public–private partnership (Hooper, 2006; Rakodi, 2009). As an example, Punter (2006a) suggested that in only 5 of the 3000 planning decisions made during the life of the CBDC were differences between the agencies referred to the Welsh Office because they were unable to be resolved by negotiation.

Policy and context: Recent developments

But what of Cardiff and the wider vision of Cardiff Bay today? Today Cardiff Council is primarily responsible for the social, economic and environmental regeneration of Cardiff Bay, and the Council's responsibilities include Cardiff Harbour Authority, which is tasked with managing the barrage and the 200 ha inland bay.

Indeed, the continued vision for Cardiff Bay should also be seen in the context of the wider Cardiff Economic Strategy, which promotes Cardiff as a 'city region', and emerged from the Council's Community Strategy, 'Proud Cardiff', and the Council's Corporate Plan (Cardiff Council, 2007). This recognises the importance of cities in their regional context, but also as engines of economic growth nationally, and also parallels the competitiveness of the cities agenda, which sees cities as providing opportunities to narrow the economic gap between regions and to tackle deprivation at local and neighbourhood levels (ODPM, 2006). In this sense competitiveness is the ability of an economy to attract and maintain firms with stable or rising market shares while maintaining stable or increasing living standards for those who are participating in the economic activities (Storper 1997; European Institute for Urban Affairs, 2007). Work for the UK Government and others (Parkinson & Karecha, 2006) has identified six critical drivers of urban competitiveness, which are:

1 Innovation in firms and organisations.
2 Economic diversity.
3 A skilled workforce.
4 Connectivity – internal and external.
5 Quality of life – social, cultural and environmental.
6 Strategic capacity to mobilise and implement long-term development strategies.

These drivers also form the basis for the narrative of the Cardiff Economic Strategy, which is built around the following themes (Cardiff Council, 2007):

- An International Capital City – which aims to increase the competitiveness of Cardiff as a leading International Capital City, and to project the vibrancy, culture and verve of the City and the Welsh nation to a national and international audience.
- A Business City – which aims to establish Cardiff as a widely recognised international business location that encourages growth and innovation in thriving sectors.
- An Innovative City – which aims to accelerate the diversification of the City's economic base by encouraging and facilitating growth, enterprise and innovation in thriving high-value-added knowledge sectors.
- A Skilled City – which aims to create a highly skilled qualified workforce to drive forward the knowledge economy and provide an excellent quality of service.
- An Enterprising and Inclusive City – which aims to tackle deprivation and promote economic and social inclusion by regenerating local communities and providing a sustainable future for local businesses.
- An Accessible City – which aims to ensure that Cardiff has a modern, world-class transport infrastructure that meets the ambitions and needs of residents, businesses and visitors alike and assists in achieving sustainable economic growth.
- A Sustainable City – which aims to build on Cardiff's reputation as a quality-of-life City by progressing improvements in the quality and performances of businesses in the context of sustainable development and a high-quality built and natural environment.

Research has recently suggested that between 1998 and 2004 Cardiff experienced the largest percentage increase in total employment of any of the UK core cities, with private sector jobs growth in Cardiff outnumbering public sector growth (Cardiff Council, 2007). A recent research report (Robert Huggins Associates, 2005) also placed Cardiff as third in the UK (behind Edinburgh and Bristol respectively) on the basis of competitiveness, as measured by economic activity rates, business start-up rates, number of businesses, proportion of working age population with NVQ Level 4 or higher, proportion of knowledge-based businesses, GVA per head, productivity, employment and unemployment rates and gross weekly pay). Nonetheless, in comparison with other European cities, its performance is respectable but not outstanding (Parkinson & Karecha, 2006).

Cardiff's continued shortcomings, therefore, are partially based on its failure to tackle deprivation in the south of the city, as the council acknowledges (Cardiff Council, 2007). The challenges of physical renewal, jobs creation, community integration and transport links are therefore key to the future development of the bay and, not least, the planned Roath Basin redevelopment, where sustainability is a key outcome.[1]

Regeneration of Roath Basin

Background and approach

The land to the south side of Roath Basin (Figure 6.3) has been planned to be an integral part of the Cardiff Bay development since the original plans for regenerating the wider Cardiff Docks were drawn up in the 1980s (igloo/DEGW, 2008).

Roath Basin was built between 1868 and 1874, and the planned regeneration scheme for the area will be targeted at the southern part of the basin, the last major derelict site in the inner harbour. The area represents a sizeable eastern extension to the existing urban area and its waterfront comprises approximately a third of the total inner bay water frontage.

The Welsh Assembly Government (WAG) is promoting the regeneration as a major new commercial, residential and leisure centre following the master plan prepared by Sir Terry Farrell (a leading British architect) in 2004 on behalf of the former Wales Development Agency (WDA). The project is intended to create a liveable neighbourhood with a range of housing and workspace opportunities tailored to a range of incomes and needs. It is estimated that the project will create about 100 000 square metres of new commercial space, which will accommodate, among others, media, creative and life science sectors and 20 000 square metres of leisure and retail space (Figure 6.4). The scheme will also create some 1010 new homes (including affordable units), and some 4000 job opportunities. Two dry docks will be flooded in order to provide this spectacular site with over 1.6 miles of waterfront.

---

[1] The Welsh Assembly Government is responsible for the overall framework of the planning system in Wales, and operates with the aim of meeting its objectives for sustainable development. The delivery of everyday planning services is normally carried out by the 25 LPAs in Wales. Section 121 of the Government of Wales Act 1998 places a legal obligation on the Assembly to prepare a scheme showing how it would promote sustainable development in the exercise of all its functions. More specifically, the Act requires the Assembly to consult with all the relevant stakeholders both internally and externally on the development of its sustainable development scheme, to undertake regular reviews in the form of annual reports, and to gauge the effectiveness of its actions and activities every four years by formal evaluation exercises. Only two other governments in the world – Estonia and Tasmania – have a comparable duty, although environmental protection in various forms features in other regional and national constitutions, notably those of Hawaii, France and India (Williams, 2006).

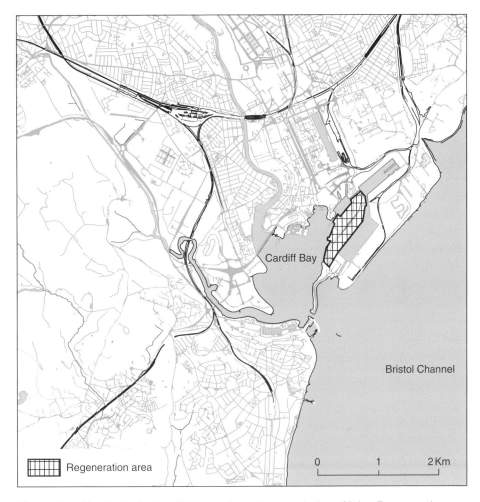

Figure 6.3   Roath Basin, Cardiff. Reproduced by permission of igloo Regeneration.

Figure 6.4   Roath Basin: BBC Drama Centre. *Source*: igloo (2008). Reproduced by permission of igloo Regeneration.

According to the master plan, the site is designed in such a way that a network of public spaces (e.g. waterside walkways and gardens) framed by office, laboratory and research buildings will overlook the waterfront, whilst the northern and southern parts of the site will accommodate a mixture of houses, shops, leisure and hotels. The plan will also provide significant infrastructure improvements for the area, including (igloo/DEGW, 2008):

- A new road link to the barrage;
- extensions to the bus network serving the bay area;
- pedestrian bridges allowing for access around all sides of Roath Basin; and
- the completion of the missing link, allowing for pedestrian and cycle access around the Bay.

The driving framework of regeneration, as originally developed by the WDA, and taken forward by the WAG, will be a *Public Realm Strategy*, aimed at creating sustainable places (LDA DESIGN, 2006; igloo/DEGW, 2008). This will include new open spaces, waterside walks, and, for the first time, the opening of former working docks as 'new and vibrant' additions to the public realm of the Bay. The key objectives of the regeneration project are to:

- Increase the economic competitiveness of Cardiff and retain local graduates;
- provide work and regenerate an urban village where people can live, work and play;
- promote a creative industries cluster;
- provide a high percentage (25%) of affordable housing; and
- employ and train as many local people as possible.

igloo was selected to undertake the regeneration scheme because of the company's socially responsible investment policies and urban regeneration experience and, in particular, the recognition by the United Nations of the company's SRI contributed to its selection by WAG (Colantonio & Dixon, 2009). Mixed-use development was preferred to single use because it is a prerequisite for the provision of vibrancy and life to a place. Furthermore, the mix of use acts as a hedge against a possible decrease of the investment/project value prompted by a market sector slow down (e.g. the decline of the office market may be cushioned by the better and stable housing market).

The regeneration scheme will be implemented under the igloo Regeneration Partnership, the fund developed by igloo Regeneration Limited and Morley (an Aviva Company), the latter currently having more than £12 bn of property investment funds under management. igloo currently has a range of investment models covering a diverse asset portfolio, and the fund is committed to a policy of Socially Responsible Investment (SRI), which, according to the UK Social Investment Forum (EUROSIF, 2008: 6), is:

> a generic term covering ethical investments, responsible investments, sustainable investments, and any other investment process that combines investors' financial objectives with their concerns about environmental, social and governance (ESG) issues.

igloo's SRI policy

As Roath Basin has still to be developed it is not possible to determine the success or otherwise of the project. What is important to note, however, is that the SRI framework, which will be used in the project by igloo, is intended to remedy some of the key issues (particularly social and to some extent environmental) that have until now been relatively neglected in what has been an essentially property-led regeneration of Cardiff Bay. The information presented in the remainder of this section is therefore based on interviews conducted for the project.

Essentially, 'Social Sustainability' is seen as being at the heart of igloo's SRI strategy. According to Stren and Polese (2000: 15), social sustainability is:

> Development that is compatible with the harmonious evolution of civil society, fostering an environment conducive to the compatible cohabitation of culturally and socially diverse groups while at the same time encouraging social integration, with improvements in the quality of life for all segments of the population.

A regeneration project is thus said to be social sustainability compliant if it endeavours to address the thematic issues of, among others, employment, inclusive designs, capacity building, participation and empowerment, happiness, health, gender equity, justice and equality (of opportunities), personal security, cultural promotion, access to resources, well-being, social diversity, multiculturalism.

The SRI policy at Roath Basin will be executed under four key themes[2]: health, happiness and well-being; regeneration; environmental sustainability; and urban design (igloo, 2010).

The *health, happiness and well-being theme* is designed to focus on investing in people and communities in order to change lives and realise potential. Its primary emphasis is on supporting healthy living; creating opportunities for the community and changing lives and realising potential.

---

[2] The theme of 'health, happiness and well-being' was recently added into the framework by igloo.

The *regeneration theme* will not only ensure economic sustainability of the regeneration but also 'social sustainability' that seeks to achieve:

- A high density urban living accessible to all;
- strong social contracts to ensure the vitality and quality of the public realm;
- street, community and family life, which creates the social glue of neighbourhoods; and
- provision of valued community facilities and resources.

The above will be achieved through a diversity of tools, including stakeholder engagement; creating attractive and liveable neighbourhoods by ensuring a range of basic amenities and services, a choice of (affordable) housing, and quality public realm; and creating neighbourhoods that contribute to rebuilding the social fabric of the city through combining careful integration with measures to actively foster community cohesion and long-term stewardship.

In terms of the *environmental sustainability theme*, igloo will endeavour to observe strategies that aim to minimise waste, carbon energy and transport (by, for example, reducing car dependence), combined with an efficient water-resource management. For example, igloo has signed up to WRAP Cymru's (Waste and Resources Action Programme in Wales) initiative to halve construction waste sent to landfill from the project.

Finally, within the theme of *urban design*, the project will seek to ensure not only a permeable street network but also a well-designed and maintained public realm; acceptable density levels and mix of uses; and high-quality urban designs with a distinctive and diverse range of buildings. This theme also incorporates the promotion of greater respect and value for nature by ensuring that the regeneration scheme protects and creates biodiversity 'by design', thereby improving the quality of the urban environment.

Guided by these *footprint*™ themes of health, happiness and well-being, regeneration, environmental sustainability and urban design, the SRI policy will be assessed (against each of the above four themes) at four stages.

The first will be a screening stage (inventory stage) aimed at taking stock of all the necessary aspects of the scheme before 'take-off'. The second stage will involve a detailed assessment of the scheme prior to an outline of planning application. It is during this stage that the SRI characteristics will be determined. The third stage will involve the actual construction, and will be concerned with the monitoring and evaluation of the scheme against the SRI characteristics determined in stage 2. The final stage will be about post-occupancy, and will deal with how the scheme is going to be managed/run after completion. In other words, the four stages could be restated as initiation, planning, implementation and maintenance. Performance in each of the above stages for each of the themes will be measured against the UK and EU best practice benchmarks. Therefore criteria will be ranked as:

- Bad practice – demonstrating fundamental weaknesses and inadequacies in terms of response to key requirements of policy.
- Market practice – demonstrating average practice with minimum compliance to laid-down requirements.
- Good practice – performance that is better than market practice and addresses key requirements.
- Best practice – this is a performance that meets many aspects of the SRI policy and is comparable to most leading UK examples.
- Exemplar practice – performance that exceeds the key policy requirements and compares with leading EU examples.

With the aim of achieving exemplar practice scores, igloo will endeavour to 'import' and learn lessons from case studies within and outside the UK. Potential case-study projects include the Southall Gas Works in London (on stakeholder engagement), Nottingham Science Park, Nottingham (on energy systems), Vauban in Freiburg, Germany (on car dependence reduction) and urban renewal in Berlin, Germany (on urban design and regeneration). This is intended to be inspirational to the project teams in their quest to fulfil the aspirations of igloo in terms of the regeneration, environmental sustainability and urban design. Appendix 5 is a summary of the igloo's SRI policy, showing how achievement of policy objectives will be assessed. The next section highlights how igloo will achieve the social sustainability in the regeneration of the Roath Basin.

Social impacts at Roath Basin

The underlying principle upon which the Roath Basin regeneration project will be executed will be the 'urban village' concept. This entails designing a 24/7 neighbourhood within which residents are able to work, live and play, thereby avoiding a situation where a neighbourhood becomes a 'ghost neighbourhood' during the day as many people leave to work elsewhere, and is only vibrant in the evening when they return.

   Therefore, employment generation is one of the key social impacts that is expected from the scheme. In fact, one of the key underlying reasons for the regeneration was to curb the 'brain drain' where university graduates from Welsh universities migrated to some other parts of the country because Cardiff and Cardiff Bay did not have employment opportunities. It is for this reason that about half of the land at Roath is allocated for employment use. Igloo's social sustainability approach also endeavours to facilitate long-term employment through skills training of the residents, who will be trained in a variety of skills during the building phase of the project. Furthermore, it is intended that the provision of public spaces/facilities in the form of streets/ paths, for example, will boost residents' well-being and happiness with the creation of a high-quality public realm environment. It also hoped that the 'stigma' attached to Butetown will also diminish following completion of the regeneration as new, state-of-the-art infrastructure and services are introduced into the area.

The mix of tenures of house types is also seen as having a positive social impact as this will encourage the exchange of cultures and ideas/knowledge as people of different professional/ethnic backgrounds, age, and so on, interact within one neighbourhood. Indeed, it is only as a result of the regeneration project that the public will, for the first time, be allowed access to Roath Basin, as it was, effectively, a protected, 'no go zone' for many years. Access to public spaces/facilities, coupled with social housing, will also be factors that should bring positive social impacts not only to the residents of Roath Basin but also to all other visitors.

However, the regeneration of Roath Basin also risks displacement to both residents and industry. According to one interviewee for the research, for example, the regeneration scheme will bring about demographic changes as residents of Butetown move out because they are likely to sell their investment/property following the likely increase in values as a result of the regeneration. This will also apply to industry as some will be replaced while others will be abandoned completely as employment and jobs are re-constituted. There are also doubts about whether the 'pepper-potting' of social housing alongside high-quality apartments will be successful.

Innovative tools and initiatives

In order to achieve its ambitious SRI policy, igloo has developed a unique, bespoke assessment tool (*footprint*™) to be applied at Roath Basin. The strength of the tool lies in its ability to:

- Meet the need for an assessment tool specially tailored for mixed use, neighbourhood scale urban renaissance schemes;
- bring together in a holistic manner the four themes of 'health, happiness and well-being', 'regeneration', 'environmental sustainability' and 'urban design' as discussed earlier;
- place a strong emphasis on the need to respond to the opportunities created by the site and its context, including engagement with all stakeholders – by so doing the tool will enable igloo to meet one of the key requirements for every regeneration project: that is every sustainability initiative should be context/place specific (Bell & Morse, 2008);

- encourage developers and project teams to think more strategically, enabling the added value of SRI implementation to be realised; and
- consider the development and innovation process, thereby seeking to benchmark the performance of the project against European Union and global industry practices as well as identifying potential risks to implementation.

igloo is very much aware of the potential risks that could arise as a result of adapting *footprint*™ as the main assessment tool during the implementation stage of the project. In order to cushion this risk, igloo will adopt a hybrid approach whereby it will seek other existing support tools and techniques that will act as back-ups to *footprint*™. These will include the Building Research Establishment Environmental Assessment Methods (BREEAM/EcoHomes), the new Code for Sustainable Homes, sustainable development checklists and design quality indicators. Additionally, project managers and their professional teams will undergo a thorough induction in the SRI policy in order to ensure that they are familiar with its aims and objectives. Furthermore, igloo will ensure that the project teams set performance benchmarks at the outset in response to the opportunities created by the regeneration scheme, and, finally, in addition to adopting other existing tools as back-ups as stated above, igloo will continue to develop its own bespoke toolkits such as the *comfort-zone*™, *evolve*™ and *engage*™. This will uniquely help support policy implementation.

Management of the Roath Basin Regeneration Scheme

As stated earlier, the regeneration of Roath Basin is a joint venture between the public and the private sectors, or in other words a Public Private Partnership (PPP) in which there are different actors, each performing different roles.

The key stakeholders in the scheme are the Welsh Assembly Government (WAG), which represents the public sector, and igloo, who represent the private sector. Being the owners and initiator of the scheme, the WAG (formerly WDA) plays the role of a project overseer, and played a key role in not only compulsorily purchasing the (derelict) land for the project, but also appointing Terry Farrell for the initial master plan.

igloo are the private developer, funder and long-term investor. In order to ensure a smooth and efficient running of the scheme, both igloo and WAG engage their own consultants – engineers, architects, planners, landscapers, etc. For instance, igloo's consultants include DEGW (master plan custodians), Sjoerd Soeters (block master planners), Davis Langdon (project managers), Gehl (key stage review architects), Bay Associates (structural engineers), Martin Stockley Associates (civil engineers), RW Gregory (monitoring and evaluation engineers), and Gardner and Theobold (quantity surveyors). The other key player in the scheme is Cardiff Council, which is the main planning authority. Other actors include Scarman Trust and the Youth Construction Trust, who are community representatives. They act as an interface between the community and the scheme in terms of looking at ways in which the project will benefit the community in the long term.

The first key advantage of the joint venture lies in the potential speed and efficiency for project completion, which is potentially brought to bear from the close working of the public and private sectors. Often the public sector has fallen short in terms of efficiency when it comes to executing projects of this magnitude. The reasons for this may vary but could include ongoing political commitments of the public sector agencies. Thus, the inclusion of the private sector in the scheme brings in some degree of efficiency. Also, since igloo is a private investor, their overall aim is to speed up the project so that they start recouping their investment.

Furthermore, the PPP approach brings in an exchange of expertise/skills that would not be available in either the public or private sectors alone. From the point of view of the public sector, the most important advantage is perhaps the transfer of the financial risks to the private sector. The public sector gains by minimising what it spends while maximising what the private sector spends and yet realising the same outcome. Clearly, the public sector alone would not have managed to finance such a huge project: in the case of the Roath Basin regeneration, the financial contribution of the public sector is only about £10 to £12 m while the private sector contributed about £350 m. Also, in its capacity as owner of the land, the public sector exercises some degree of control in that land can only be released if the private developer meets the required aspects of the project, and this would not necessarily be the case if land simply belonged to the developer.

From the point of view of the private sector, it is also easier for the developer to obtain clean title to the compulsorily purchased land if the private sector is in partnership with the public sector.

Despite the above advantages, however, joint ventures may also face issues over execution and quality of outcome. Certain tasks in such projects depend on the sanction of the public sector but bureaucracy may delay progress and may be in conflict with the interest of the private sector whose objective is to speed up the project in order to start recouping their investment. The other disadvantage is related to the investment orientation of the private investor. Since their interest is on maximising returns to investment, private companies may tend to compromise quality in order to make savings.

Post-project maintenance and long-term monitoring

Many regeneration projects lack an effective post-project sustainability strategy, but in the case of Roath Basin igloo have set up a legacy fund, which will manage the scheme during the building phase and after completion of the project. igloo will retain what it calls the 'golden share' in the company and, after the site is fully developed, igloo will hand over their golden share to a community trust, thereby creating a sense of ownership within the community.

Conclusions

The Roath Basin project is still to be fully completed, and so is 'work in progress'. However, experience so far suggests that the SRI framework *footprint*™ appears to provide a valuable framework for assessing critical dimensions of sustainability in a robust and effective way.

Previous experience with Cardiff Bay suggested that community engagement was not a strong feature of the regeneration programme and the focus has historically been on 'property-led' regeneration. There is a strong sense that Roath Basin will attempt to achieve more 'people-based' regeneration outcomes with the intention of bringing benefits to the wider Butetown community.

Nevertheless, a number of issues remain to be resolved. For example:

- *Transport*: One of the objectives of igloo is to reduce car dependence within the Roath Basin. This means encouraging public transport and walking/cycling but without major investment in transport infrastructure this may be problematic.
- *Displacement and social mixing*: On the negative side the regeneration of Roath Basin risks having the impact of displacement of both residents and industry. For example, the regeneration scheme could bring about demographic and cultural changes as residents of Butetown move out either as a result of rising property values or redevelopment pressures. Despite its many advantages, it is possible that mixing social housing with top-class apartments may discourage potential buyers of the apartments.

Despite the economic recession, at the time of writing the Roath Basin project is still planned to proceed.[3] Time will tell whether the final piece of the jigsaw in the Cardiff Bay regeneration has a socially sustainable and inclusive outcome for the wider community in the area.

---

[3]   The first phase of the infrastructure is now complete with the next phase of construction set to start in March 2010. However, plans to relocate the BBC's production HQ from Llandaff to the site remain on hold currently.

7

The Regeneration of La Mina – Sant Adriá de Besós

Venere Stefania Sanna and Andrea Colantonio

Introduction

Sant Adriá de Besós is a municipality with 33 223 inhabitants and an area of 3.87 square kilometres in Catalonia, Spain (Ine, 2008). Situated at the mouth of the Besós river, from which the city takes its name, and bordering Barcelona's eastern urban perimeter, Sant Adriá forms a continuous urban area that is part of Barcelona Metropolitan Region (BMR), together with Badalona and Santa Coloma de Gramenet and several other municipalities. The city extends to both sides of its estuary, and is made up of six districts: Sant Adriá Nord, Sant Joan Baptista, Montsolís – Trajana, La Catalana, El Besós and La Mina.

As has been the case with other Catalan cities, Sant Adriá de Besós experienced a sustained urban and population growth between the 1950s and the 1970s, prompted by a steady national immigration influx from less developed Spanish regions, such as Andalucia, Extremadura, Castilla, Murcia and Aragon, as well as Catalan rural areas. Over the years, the close proximity to Barcelona provided development opportunities for the city, especially when in the 1960s an industrial development cluster was located at the mouth of the river Besós. At the same time, some areas of the municipality of Sant Adriá exhibit the characteristics of peripheral neighbourhoods, including the existence of mono-use 'sleeping communities', a high concentration of

Urban Regeneration & Social Sustainability: Best Practice from European Cities, by Andrea Colantonio and Tim Dixon © 2011 Andrea Colantonio and Tim Dixon

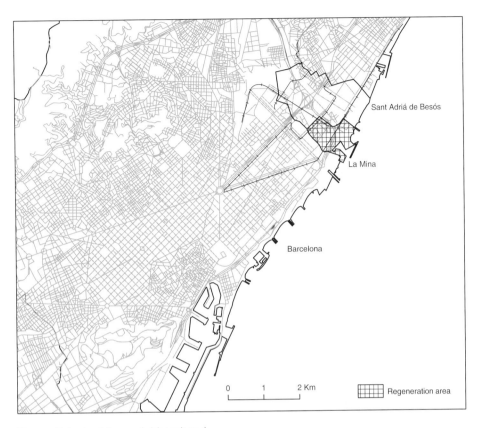

Sant Adriá de Besós

La Mina

Barcelona

0   1   2 Km

Regeneration area

Figure 7.1   La Mina neighbourhood.

housing with insufficient social and commercial services, and a low-quality urban, social and green infrastructure.

However, due to the eastern expansion of Barcelona, over the years the territories belonging to the Sant Adriá de Besós municipality have earned a new 'centrality', and therefore a (new) functional value, within the urban hierarchy of Barcelona Metropolitan Region. As a result, since the 1980s Sant Adriá has been cooperating with Barcelona's municipal authorities, the Catalan (*Generalitat*) and National Government, to promote the regeneration of La Mina neighbourhood (see Figure 7.1), one of the poorest and most marginalised areas of Sant Adriá de Besós.

This chapter therefore begins with an overview of the urbanisation process of Sant Adriá de Besós and the progressive marginalisation of La Mina neighbourhood since its establishment in the 1960s. The chapter then examines the policy context in which several regeneration plans for the neighbourhood were formulated in the 1980s, until their replacement by the promotion of an integrated approach to the regeneration of La Mina in the 1990s. The chapter then goes on to investigate the social dimension of the regeneration process of La Mina, with a special emphasis on the institutional arrangements that led to the formation of a consortium of public institutions in Catalonia. It concludes with a review of the indicators used to monitor the evolution of social sustainability in this neighbourhood.

Urban development and decline

Significant settlement in Sant Adriá de Besós dates back to the early eighteenth century, when the progressive reclamation of marshes along the river Besós allowed agricultural and urban development in the area. During the nineteenth century, the urban expansion of Barcelona led to the demolition of the city walls that historically protected the city, providing urban development opportunities for nearby villages and towns, including Sant Adriá de Besós. Indeed, it can be argued that since the 1860s when the *Cerdá Plan* was designed to control the expansion of Barcelona outside its walls, the municipality of Sant Adriá has been included in several urban development plans of Barcelona, becoming *de facto* part of the planning system of the Catalan capital.

However, the first real urbanisation process in Sant Adriá was originally a product of the industrial revolution. Indeed, at the turn of the nineteenth and twentieth centuries Sant Adriá experienced a modest industrial development, which led to the embryonic establishment of the urban grid of the city. The industrial focus of the municipality was subsequently consolidated in the early twentieth century when two power plants, Power of Catalonia (later FECSA) and the Fluid and Electrical Company (known as La Catalana), were located next to the mouth the river Besós.

As Gutiérrez Palomero (2005) noted, for many years the excellent location of Sant Adriá has been the main asset of the municipality, offering the prime conditions necessary for industrial agglomeration, which included, for example, proximity to the city of Barcelona, good communications network, availability of agricultural land, and sources of water supply. This provided good urban economic development opportunities for the city of Sant Adriá but also led to the peripheralisation of some of its areas, such as La Mina. Indeed, in the late 1960s, at the peak of Francoism's economic development, the Housing Department of Barcelona Municipality bought the land on which La Mina is currently located from the municipal council of Sant Adriá de Besós (Consorcio del Barrio de la Mina, 2008) with the objective of: (i) rehousing a Roma community living in a nearby slum and the inhabitants of Barcelona's shanty towns, such as El Camp de la Bota, La Perona, Can Tunis, Carmel, and Pequín; and (ii) providing housing for migrants coming from 262 towns and villages around Spain (Ajuntament de Sant Adriá de Besós, 1996).

The neighbourhood was built mainly in the late 1960s and early 1970s in two distinct stages. In 1970 the first five-storey buildings in La Mina Vella (Old La Mina) were completed. However, when it became clear that these apartments were not sufficient to meet the increasing demand for new housing in Barcelona, an additional area (New La Mina), based around a complex of much higher density apartment blocks, was built by the mid-1970s to house the regular flow of newcomers arriving from Spain's poorer regions, with few resources and no access to traditional housing.

However, the speed of construction and the lack of planning left the neighbourhood completely disconnected from Barcelona. The mono-use residential area lacked basic urban and social infrastructures, such as schools, medical centres, markets, or public transport. In addition, most of the people who settled in the district were young migrants and travellers arriving from Spain's poorer regions, with serious shortcomings in their education. As a result of widespread illiteracy and general low levels of education, unemployment grew dramatically over the years, becoming a serious problem for the area (Consorcio del Barrio de la Mina, 2008).

Indeed, it can be argued that, since its establishment, the area has been characterised by a lack of social cohesion due to the cultural diversity of its inhabitants. Insufficient government intervention over a number of years produced significant levels of exclusion and marginalisation, as well as social conflict and a deterioration of community life. In addition, La Mina began to be characterised by crime, social degradation, drug trafficking, and other illegal activities, which projected a negative external image of the neighbourhood and prompted safety issues for local residents, in turn. The stigmatised image of the neighbourhood has also been romanticised and fictionalised in several gangster movies, in which La Mina has often been depicted as a place of crime and violence (CCCB, 2008). All these elements influenced the development and implementation of urban regeneration policies and projects, which are now reviewed in more detail in the remainder of this chapter.

The policy context

Traditionally, the national and local governments are the main actors in urban regeneration projects (or interventions/processes) and urban development policies in Spain. The central government merely sets up the general framework policy that is to be implemented at a regional and local level, but remains silent in terms of the division of powers and responsibilities between the different levels of government. Broadly speaking, it is often difficult to identify an 'overall' national or local urban regeneration policy because projects and schemes are often decided and initiated on an *ad hoc* basis with the participation and coordination of several governmental agencies and departments. On the one hand, this helps secure political backing and speedier planning permissions for regeneration projects, but, on the other hand, it has often left the decision-making process too reliant on political power relationships and the availability of state funding, as confirmed by several interviews of key stakeholders.

Since the approval of the 1978 Constitution, Spain has been divided into 17 Autonomous Communities, or regions, which play an important role in land and urban planning. Some of these Communities have also been granted an even greater autonomy in terms of planning, land-use and housing policies, including, for example, Catalonia through the 1979 Statute of Autonomy and the 2006 Statute. At municipal level, local authorities are entitled to design their own Spatial Planning Plans, which have to be subsequently approved by regional governments, which also check for consistency amongst different spatial and sectoral municipal plans (CIVITAS, 2007).

Within the Catalan context, at present, three main urban and territorial planning tools have been established from the 1983 'Territorial Policy Act', and modified by the 'Urban Planning Act' in 2002 (CIVITAS, 2007). These include:

- 'General Territorial Plan' for Catalonia as a whole;
- 'Partial Territorial Plans' for a *comarca* (district);
- 'Territorial Master Plans' for lower spatial areas of interventions; and
- 'Urban Master Plans' (*Plans Directors Urbanístics*), at city level.

These area-based tools are integrated and complemented by specific development policies and plans for urban infrastructure, ranging from public transport and roads to green infrastructures.

The Catalan Government has also promoted additional local development programmes, including, for example, the *Programa de Barris* (Programme for Districts), and the *Plan de Desenvolupament Comunitari* (Community Development Plans – CDPs). The former established a fund by the Catalan Government for financing regeneration projects that fulfilled specific criteria. This fund is allocated by the government, which sets up an annual call for tenders for co-financing (almost half of the total costs) regeneration projects proposed by local neighbourhood councils, with a special emphasis on projects fostering bottom-up grassroots participation. CDPs are set up once a regeneration project is planned and then started. Indeed, at the beginning of regeneration projects, local authorities identify a broader development plan for the local community to accompany the physical regeneration of the area with residents' participation. CDPs are subsequently incorporated in what is known as a 'neighbourhood contract' or 'city contract', which is a document outlining key issues and actions to be included in the regeneration process. These include diagnoses, objectives, programmes to be developed, stakeholder mapping, sources of funding, a monitoring system and evaluation criteria.

Among more recent relevant initiatives, in 2002 the Catalan Government enacted a 'New Urbanism' law, which was subsequently amended in 2004. The main objectives of the new law were to: (i) make land available for affordable housing; (ii) emphasise criteria for environmental sustainability; and (iii) promote a more balanced distribution of powers and local competences within the Catalan urban planning arena (Generalitat de Catalunya, 2004). In 2008, under this law a total of 94 'Strategic Residential Areas', scattered across 80 Catalan municipalities, were identified with the main objective of building 91 000 new dwellings (of which 48 000 were to be affordable housing) in areas, colloquially referred to as the 'new towns' of Catalonia (Nelo, 2008). According to Oriol Nelo (2008), these plans have benefited suburban neighbourhoods, such as La Mina, because they have acquired a new centrality in Barcelona's urban system, and its eastward expansion. This point is now explored in more detail in the next section of this chapter.

Urban regeneration and partnership arrangements

Since the 1980s, Sant Adriá has been cooperating with Barcelona's municipal authorities, the Catalan (*Generalitat*) and national governments to promote the regeneration of some of its most deprived areas, including La Mina neighbourhood.

For example, in 1983 the 'Urgency Plan' was approved in order to encourage interdepartmental cooperation aimed at improving local social and housing conditions in La Mina. There is, however, general agreement that the interventions envisaged within this plan were not grounded in a first-hand knowledge of the main social problems of the neighbourhood and there was minimal integration of, and coordination between, programmes and projects implemented, leading to ineffective results (Ajuntament de Sant Adriá de Besós, 1996). As a result, in 1990, the 'Besós Plan' was agreed and embarked upon by Sant Adriá de Besós City, Barcelona City, the *Generalitat* and the Ministry for Public Works, with the aim of integrating fragmented policies, programmes and projects, which had hitherto been individually implemented by a disjointed variety of public stakeholders involved in the regeneration process. The Besós Plan provided the platform for drawing up several drafts of 'La Mina Transformation Plan' (CIREM-GES-TRS, 1997), on which the current urban regeneration process of La Mina is based, and which is discussed later in this chapter.

The regeneration of La Mina

In recent years, regeneration efforts in La Mina (see Figure 7.1) were prompted and influenced by three main factors. First, after more than 20 years of investment in social services and infrastructure, the low social benefits stemming from the investment programmes were deemed insufficient to justify expenditure thus far. As a result, a new approach to regeneration was required. Second, the eastwards expansion of Barcelona, which began with the 1992 Olympics, and led to the implementation of the 2004 Barcelona Project and the building of the Universal Forum of Culture just next to La Mina, provided a development opportunity for the regeneration of the neighbourhood; and third, a new political cycle began in 2000 with the arrival of the Sant Adriá de Besós administration, which expressed a willingness and resolution to avoid the political exploitation of La Mina (i.e. previous administrations promised the implementation of new programmes prior to political elections in order to acquire votes), and to promote an integrated approach to regeneration.

Although not forming part of our analysis in the rest of this chapter, it is also important to understand that the broad eastwards expansion of Barcelona incorporates developments that have been controversial in terms of their relationship with La Mina. The district of Poblenou, which adjoins La Mina, and is located on the coast to the North East of Barcelona, includes two interlinked developments: Diagonal Mar and the 'Forum'. Diagonal Mar is a residential and commercial district, which is based around private sector investment – €490 m between 2001 and 2004 (Majoor & Salet, 2008) – and contains the largest foreign real estate operation developed by the private sector in Barcelona (the US developer, Hines). This therefore departs from the strong combination of public and private funding found in the traditional 'Barcelona model' of regeneration (Miranda, 2006). Critics have also suggested that Diagonal Mar's 'gated' community and high-end shopping are at odds with the contrasting income profile and immigrant, working class culture in La Mina (Project for Public Spaces, 2010).

The larger Forum project, which combines housing, hotels, offices and other uses including public space, a marina, conference centre and a new university campus, was funded through public investment of some €1749 m, beginning with an event based around '2004 Universal Forum of Cultures' (Majoor, 2009; Majoor & Salet, 2008). At present, the Forum of Culture is already operating whilst other projects of this development scheme, such as the university campus, are still in their planning stages. The Forum project also suffered criticism in some quarters as it was claimed it was simply an outward expression of a 'revanchist' city, which squeezed the poor and other local residents out of the way – at least prior to the formal launch of the La Mina regeneration programme (Miranda, 2006).

The Poblenou area also includes what is essentially a new media, knowledge-based centre called '22@, Barcelona's City of Knowledge' (colloquially known as the 'Catalan Manchester'), which is designed to attract invest-ment and high-tech workers, but at the same time maintain the identity of a neighbourhood with a strong working-class legacy (Walisser, 2004; Pareja Eastaway, 2009). Although still in the process of attracting businesses this area brings together a strong Barcelona-based brand and strategic planning to create an 'innovative district' (Evans, 2009; Pareja Eastaway, 2009). This development is also closely linked with the further development of Sagrera/St Andreu, which is a based on a mixed-use project, and the Forum itself (Majoor & Salet, 2008).

Three main tools played a pivotal role in the urban and social regeneration of La Mina. These include: La Mina Masterplan, The Special Plan for the Redesign and Improvement of La Mina District (Plan Especial de Reordinacion y Mejora, PERM), and The Integrated Development Plan for La Mina (IDPM, 1998). La Mina Masterplan, is one of the urban and territorial planning instruments available to local planners. The Masterplan for the local area was developed in 2005 with the objective of shaping the urban transforma-tion of La Mina and building better public spaces, streets and squares capa-ble of facilitating interactions between residents and promoting community life in turn. In this context, one of the most significant new urban-design elements of the area is the construction a new *Rambla* (a wide street with large pedestrian areas depicted in Figure 7.2) running across La Mina, which

Figure 7.2 The newly built *Rambla* in La Mina with a new tram route crossing the neighbourhood. *Source*: Photograph by Andrea Colantonio (2008).

provides a meeting point for residents and allows the physical opening up of the place through a tram line that connects the neighbourhood to Sant Adriá and Barcelona.

The Special Plan for the Redesign and Improvement of La Mina district (Plan Especial de Reordinacion y Mejora, PERM), has been developed since 2000 through public consultations in order to establish a legal framework for the urban transformation of the neighbourhood around three main guiding principles (Consorcio del Barrio de La Mina, 2008):

- *Centrality*, which envisaged the development of an identifiable physical and social centre for the area.
- *Diversity*, in terms of the type of housing and mixed use.
- *Exchange*, required to improve the connections between La Mina, Sant Adriá de Besós and new developments along East Barcelona's coast line.

The inclusion of these propositions in PERM confirms the importance of overarching principles from a sustainability perspective, which has been highlighted in Chapter 2 of this book.

The Integrated Development Plan for La Mina (IDPLM) perhaps provided the most important framework for the regeneration process and established the overarching roadmap for the integrated redevelopment of the neighbourhood, as illustrated in Box 7.1. According to Gutiérrez Palomero (2005), in essence, the main objectives of the IDPLM can be grouped into three main policy areas including urban regeneration, housing and social development. The latter two aspects will be discussed in more depth in the remainder of this chapter. Here it suffices to point out how, within the context of urban regeneration, IDPLM set out to redevelop the urban and physical infrastructure of

---

Box 7.1   Integrated development plan for La Mina

Priority axes for the redevelopment of La Mina:

1 Social development plan.
2 Development of social, educational, cultural and sport facilities.
3 Housing rehabilitation and improved accessibility.
4 Improvement of the public realm.
5 New affordable housing.
6 Urban management.
7 Improved security for the area.
8 Communication plan to help publicise the implementation of the regeneration process and improve external perceptions concerning La Mina.

Source: Consorcio del Barrio de La Mina (2008).

the area: for example, by opening a new *Rambla* and building a new school, a municipal library, a sports centre, a civic centre and a local police station. Physical renewal efforts also included the restoration of common areas, the construction of green areas and the improvement of access to buildings.

Partnership arrangements

Despite the declared importance of public and private collaboration in the original 1990s Barcelona model of regeneration (Miranda, 2006), 'pure' Public–Private Partnerships in urban regeneration are still at a very embryonic stage in both Catalonia and Spain as a whole for several reasons. For example, as pointed out earlier, historically, local governments are still the main actors in regeneration and so the role of the private sector is still less important than in many other parts of Europe. In addition, Spain is a relatively young democracy and so the idea of involving private sector actors in public policy making, sharing responsibilities and power is itself relatively new (Van Boxmeer & Van Beckhoven, 2005). However, it has also been argued that current state regulations and building requirements limit *de facto* economic profitability in urban regeneration (Pareja Eastaway, 1999). For instance, 'private developers', banks and insurance companies are often not involved in regeneration projects that include social housing (*Vivienda de Proteccion Oficial*) because current requirements (for example, floor space and maximum selling price) render this sector unprofitable for them at present (Pareja Eastaway, 1999). As a result, 'public developers', or organisations and companies linked to local governments, despite the recent increase in private investment inflows, frequently are the main actors participating in Spanish regeneration projects, especially when social housing is involved.

In the context of La Mina, in 2000, an *ad hoc* consortium of local authorities (*Consorci del Barri de La Mina*) with a ten-year life span was set up to carry out the regeneration of this neighbourhood. The main stakeholders of the Consortium included the Municipality of Sant Adriá de Besós, the Municipality of Barcelona and the Government of Catalonia, as shown in Figure 7.3. The Consortium functions as a single task agency responsible for the design and implementation of the vast majority of area-based projects to regenerate La Mina neighbourhood.

The government of the Consortium has been assigned to four main organisations: the Governing Council, the Executive Committee and their two respective presidents. The Governing Council is therefore at the top of the Consortium hierarchy, setting out the political guidelines and priorities for the approval of the 'Plan de Transformación del Barrio de La Mina'. The Executive Committee, on the other hand, manages the actions linked to annual programming cycles and also coordinates the actions of other public

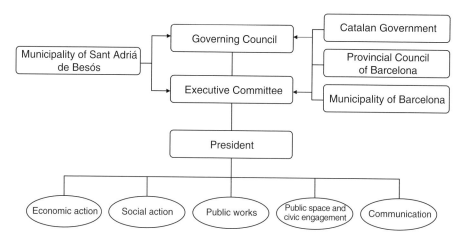

Figure 7.3 La Mina District Consortium. *Source*: Elaborated from the La Mina District Statute (Consorci del Barri de La Mina, 2009).

agencies or entities located in the territorial remit of the Consortium. The presidents of these two organisations have the institutional representation of the Consortium. The President of the Governing Council is elected by the members of the Municipality of Sant Adriá de Besós but the President of Executive Committee is elected by its own members, and can be considered a 'city manager' responsible for the smooth delivery of the regeneration project. Both the president and the Executive Committee are permanently based in La Mina neighbourhood and can be approached by local residents upon request.

According to Gutiérrez Palomero (2005), the current framework of the Consortium partnership has involved a comprehensive long-term agreement between different levels of government. Regardless of the political views of the different representatives, this multi-level governance system ensures continuity to the activities undertaken by the Consortium. As a result this partnership arrangement shows to the citizens of La Mina that the urban regeneration process of their district is actually taken 'seriously', although it presupposes that all the involved authorities must negotiate to reach substantial agreements.

However, during the implementation of the La Mina regeneration project, the overall system of governance faced problems. Initially, for example, the 'La Mina Transformation Plan' did not find the necessary support from a wide range of administrations. Indeed, when the district was included in the European Urban II project areas of interest, only the Catalan Government was willing to provide financial support to the regeneration project, whilst the national government, despite supporting the candidacy project for the neighbourhood, did not contribute financially to the plan. The reasons

Table 7.1   Funding sources and financial budgeting for la Mina regeneration from 2000 to 2010.

Source	Amount in Euros	Percentage
Partner public administrations	57 700 000	32.0
Debt	46 000 000	26.6
Value of land contribution from private owners	24 610 000	14.2
Value of land provided by administrations	23 000 000	13.3
European Union (ERDF and ESF, Urban Projects)	14 780 000	8.6
Other contributions from partner administrations	3 790 000	3.6
Forecasted financial returns	1 860 000	1.1
Contribution from residents (e.g. introduction of elevators)	950 000	0.6
	172 690 000	100%

Source: Consorcio del Barrio de La Mina (2008).

behind this choice are unclear, but may be linked to Spain's internal politics and the tensions between attribution of power and financial competencies between the autonomous Catalan Government and the central government. However, it is also worth pointing out that the City and Provincial Councils joined the plan only after the Urban II inclusion of Barcelona, probably 'persuaded' more by the economic opportunities of the 2004 Forum of Culture than by a sense of responsibility for La Mina neighbourhood (Borja & Fiori, 2004).

The partnership between public authorities and vertical level of government also meant that the regeneration project has been *de facto* funded through public funding, as indicated in Table 7.1. However, it is important to highlight how the construction of 'free-market housing' (as opposed to 'social' and 'affordable' housing) in the area has been envisaged as an important tool in generating revenues to be partially reinvested locally. As a result, several housing projects have been built by private developers. However, during the conduction of the fieldwork in La Mina, it become apparent that the latter were beginning to be unable to sell many newly built units due to the economic downturn, which has been briefly reviewed in Part I of this book. In addition, new construction has been halted, with financial implications for the economic budget of the regeneration project, the impact of which is difficult to fully forecast at present.

Table 7.1 also shows how the EU URBAN programme has played a key role (not only financial) in helping finance the regeneration of La Mina, as pointed out earlier. Sant Adriá de Besós received financial assistance from the European Union, which came through two channels. First, €1.81 m was provided by the European Social Fund in aid of Objective 3 for Catalonia, a part of which was intended for La Mina district. Second, an amount of €12.3 m was provided by the URBAN II Community Initiative Programme, financed by the European Regional Development Fund (ERDF). In addition,

Table 7.2 URBAN II Sant Adriá de Besós.

Priorities	Measures	Contribution (million euros)
1. Mixed usage and reurbanisation	1.1. Recuperation of abandoned and polluted plots. Rehabilitation of public spaces, including green spaces 1.2. Building, renovating and endowment of buildings in order to develop social, cultural, leisure and sport activities	9.6
2. Employers and pacts for employment	2.1. Support to business activities, to the trade and the crafts, to social economy, to cooperatives, mutual benefit societies and services for small and medium enterprises (SMEs) 2.2. Creation and improvement of health services and other social services, particularly those for the elderly and children (nursery schools) and other disfavoured collectives 2.3. Training actions for the unemployed and the employed in order to update their training and their adaptation to the new working organisation and information technologies and communications, giving priority to integrated itineraries for professional insertion and to the development of new sources of occupation	0.5
3. Integration of marginalised persons and access to basic services	3.1. Creation of workshop schools and training centres. Conditioning and improvement of those already existing	1.6
4. Waste treatment and reduction; water management and reduction of noise; reduction of hydrocarbon consumption	4.1. Promotion of waste reduction, total recycling, gathering and selective treatment	0.1
5. Development of the potential of the technologies in the information society	5.1. Promotion of the use and access to information technologies and communication among citizens, particularly for purposes of training, employability, education and culture 5.2. Development of public interest services, particularly in the fields of education and training, health, information about the environment and support to SMEs, especially when it comes to e-commerce and proximity services	0.1
6. Assessment, management and follow-up. Improvement in the urban government	6.1. Information and publicity campaigns, key actions to improve access to information (especially in terms of environment) and citizen participation in the decision-making processes 6.2. Promotion of networks for the exchange of experiences and good practices, as well as the development of a community database about good practices in management and sustainability of cities 6.3. Expenses deriving from management, monitoring and control tasks	0.4

Source: Elaborated from Consorci del Barri de La Mina (2009) and Inforegio (2009).

in the case of La Mina, to be within the Objective 2 areas of the Structural Funds, actions which were part of URBAN II (Table 7.1) were co-financed (50%) by ERDF.

The URBAN II programme mainly covers La Mina district, which Gutiérrez Palomero (2005) describes as a 'natural' candidate for actions co-financed by the European Commission in the light of its on-going deterioration, economically and socially disadvantaged population, and lack of basic services. Furthermore, the Transformation Plan included potential actions eligible for URBAN II funding, providing a policy framework that made the district's proposal more competitive than others at national level. Once approved by the EU, the strategic objectives set for the local URBAN II programme were structured according to the detailed priorities and measures scheme listed in Table 7.2. More specifically, these included the promotion of new technologies, improvement of the business environment, inclusion of disadvantaged groups into the labour market, and improvement of the urban environment, all of which highlights the newly promoted multidisciplinary and integrated approach of the EU to urban regeneration.

According to Gutiérrez Palomero (2005), the Sant Adriá de Besós URBAN II project encouraged the full participation of local actors in urban planning of La Mina; effective monitoring processes of the project; and further participation opportunities in knowledge sharing networks. In addition, the Transformation Plan complied with the principle of 'additionality and complementarity' (EC, 2004), which is one essential principle of action applied by the EU Commission to funding in urban areas. In this sense, there can be little doubt that the participation of La Mina in several urban-regeneration programmes and knowledge-exchange networks promoted by the EU, including URBAN, URBACT and the REGENERA network, provided momentum to the regeneration efforts of local authorities. They were instrumental in raising the profile of regeneration projects nationally and internationally, allowing the attraction of more funding and the exchange of expertise and best practices in regeneration projects in turn.

Social sustainability

The objectives of the regeneration of La Mina have evolved throughout a thirty-year period, since the regeneration started in the early 1980s. For the purposes of this book, the most important socially-oriented objectives can be summarised as follows:

1 To 'normalise' the area by reducing local social, economic and environmental problems and to foster the development of the local housing market. In this context, even what can be described as gentrification is seen

as a positive element because it indicates that there is a renewed housing market in the area, and the negative perception of the area is changing.

2 Physical opening up of the area to increase its permeability, for example by allowing a tram route to pass through the neighbourhood, connecting it to the rest of Barcelona and the surrounding municipalities of Santa Coloma and Badalona.

3 Opening up of La Mina by promoting social mixing and reducing a high concentration of low-income residents.

4 The improvement of social and cultural infrastructure, including educational, health and sports facilities and services.

5 The provision of a high percentage of newly built affordable housing in order to minimise the involuntary displacement of local residents, which may be prompted by the regeneration process.

6 To attract people back to the neighbourhood who had improved their socioeconomic situation and moved out of the area as a result. This can provide role models and good examples for local people to follow.

From a social sustainability perspective, a critical action at the beginning of the project was the establishment of a police station in the area to re-establish legality and improve safety. For many in the community this paved the way for the concurrent physical redesign and redevelopment of the public realm and the strengthening of local social networks, participation and opportunities for local residents. This latter aspect of the regeneration process is reflected in the significant number of actions envisaged within the 'participation and community development' and 'social and educational support' themes of the social development plan that are linked to environmental objectives, as illustrated in Table 7.3 and Figure 7.4.

Housing has been another key objective of several regeneration plans for La Mina. Indeed, the current housing stock of the neighbourhood consists of 2721 units, which were built in the 1970s as social housing. The regeneration process originally forecast the demolition of 412 housing units that were deemed unsafe, and the building of 1145 new units, 36% of which will be improved social housing, whilst the remaining 64% will consist of free-market housing. It is envisaged that 338 households will be offered relocation packages outside the neighbourhood whilst 74 families will be provided with new local social housing (Consorcio del Barrio de La Mina, 2008: 55). At present, however, it is still unclear how the relocation of residents will be carried out. For example, the La Mina Consortium is discussing voluntary relocations of local residents outside the neighbourhood and considering the option of using a 'random selection' process for the allocation of newly built social housing in the area. However, there can be little doubt that a major challenge for local authorities will be the adoption of policies,

Table 7.3 La Mina social development plan.

Theme	Objectives	Number of actions
Training and employment	To generate employment opportunities in an integrated fashion To improve local access to the job market	7
Professional and private life	To generate equal job opportunities (e.g. gender, age) To allow teenagers to attend school by relieving them of family-imposed jobs and tasks	4
Local economic development	To revitalise local economic fabric To legalise informal local economy To support new local enterprises	3
Participation and community development	To facilitate local development at community, technical and institutional levels To strengthen local community and civic society	12
Improved co-existence and civic engagement	To reduce antisocial behaviour To strengthen local social fabric To facilitate insertion of newcomers (e.g. with higher income) into the area	6
Social and educational support	To foster education and training To reward local bottom-up community projects	14
Public realm	To improve urban milieu To encourage local residents to use public spaces	9

Source: Translated and elaborated by Colantonio from Consorci del Barri de La Mina (2007).

Figure 7.4 Association of local residents promoting recycling and environmental education. *Source*: Photograph by Andrea Colantonio (2008).

rules and instruments, which are able to deliver a smooth and fair relocation of residents whose houses will be demolished.

Creating a sense of community and social mixing have also been key social sustainability objectives of the regeneration efforts. For example, in recent years a Museum of the History of Immigration, which is the first in Catalonia, has been opened to foster a positive sense of belonging and identity amongst local residents. In addition, the Consortium is planning to promote social mixing in order to break the circle of social deprivation in the area and to open up the community socially. To achieve this, the *Consorcio* is preparing workshops for newcomers to the area in order to explain the social characteristics of the area to them. Another important aspect to foster a sense of attachment of residents to their place and encourage mutual knowledge was to ask households to contribute to improving access to their building. Indeed, residents made a contribution of €950 000 or 20% of the costs of the installation of lifts, which amounted to between €2284 and €3449 (2004–2009) per family (Consorcio del Barrio de La Mina, 2008). As a result, 30 lifts were installed, giving service to 300 families. In one building, lifts were installed on floors where formerly there was no access to lifts, giving service to an additional 192 families.

Similarly, one of the main objectives of the regeneration of La Mina has also been the strengthening of both civil and religious society and local residents' associations in order to promote public participation in decision making. The setting up of associations has been promoted through a wide range of activities, including festivals, commemorations (i.e. International Women's' Day and the Migrants' Day), exhibitions, concerts and a variety of social events, which have gathered local residents together. A new 'Cultural Space of La Mina', which was opened in June 2009, exceeded 1200 user cards after just a few months (Viure, 2009). However, there have been instances, especially in the finalisation of the La Mina Master Plan, in which there have been disagreements between local spiritual leaders and planners concerning the localisation of religious and educational infrastructures. These disagreements revealed the apparent tensions between the technical solutions being proposed by planners and the requests of local religious leaders concerning, for example, the relocation of a local church and a school.

The *Consorcio* has also promoted several initiatives to equip youngsters with the knowledge and skills to help improve development opportunities for future generations. For example, the social development plan for the area has been embedded in the construction of schools and educational centres in order to provide the best educational opportunities for young people. This approach clearly emphasises the intergenerational aspect of social sustainability, reviewed earlier in Chapter 2. In addition, in 2009 an ambitious development project for the establishment of a university campus in the area was approved. The project will affect a total area of 170 000 square metres adjacent to the 2004 Forum space designated to be a development park, within which 100 000 square metres will be allocated to the university, 17 000 to research centres and 60 000 to infrastructure (see earlier in this Chapter). Broadly speaking, the development of the university is clearly linked to the promotion of a competitiveness agenda built on growth and knowledge, which has been briefly introduced in Chapter 1. The aim of the project, managed under a synergic model between universities, institutions and innovative companies, is to combine university usage and economic activities. In fact, the park will integrate educational centres and innovation-related research spaces, but will also include spaces intended for exhibitions, business and services.

The approach to regeneration implemented in La Mina has been highlighted as an example of best practices for urban regeneration. For example, Box 7.2 shows how UN-Habitat identified La Mina as an exemplary best practice model in 2006. However, La Mina's approach to regeneration has not been exempt from criticism. For example, Gutiérrez Palomero (2005) argued that one of the most complicated issues for the area to address was improving the co-existence and citizenship of local residents. Despite some

---

Box 7.2   Best practices in the regeneration of La Mina according to UN-Habitat

Transformation plan for the La Mina district

Establishment of priorities: The basic lines of action were established by agreement between political heads and the whole community.

Formulation of objectives and strategies: Based on the initial diagnosis, in which all the agents in the area took part, the means of putting in place the Transformation Plan were laid down.

Process: A group of neighbourhood entities and residents set up a civic platform to manage the projects and resources that were obtained through these plans.... In tandem thematic commissions were set up with the participation of the different agents in the area (politicians, technicians and residents).... These commissions went beyond their diagnostic role and became places for discussion and continuous evaluation of new strategies....

Results achieved: The achievements have been made at both the urban and social levels.... The evaluation of these achievements has been continuous.... Participation of the community and its various agents in the setting of priorities and in the design, development, management and, of course, the evaluation of the results of each product has been ongoing.

Sustainability: ... A fundamental factor has been the inclusion of all residents in the processes of the transformation plan, as a basic component for the sustainability of the changes that the plan has entailed until now and will entail

Box 7.2   *(cont'd)*

in the future.... The impact and degree of sustainability of the social interventions, to a great extent hard to evaluate over a short period of time.... Finally, the day-to-day proximity of the authorities to the general public and to the various social agents has consolidated the bases of a fluent socio-political dialogue that establishes a development framework for the community that will not be easily shattered in the future, especially as it is proving to be satisfactorily effective at all levels.

Lessons learned: We assess the most important lessons in terms of what community agents have been interiorising. On the one hand, there is the desirability of coordinating all of them: entities, residents, services, technicians, politicians, etc. The cross-cutting nature of all the interventions has proved to be fundamental in rationalising and getting the most out of them. Setting up sector and interdisciplinary thematic meeting places has been essential in defining common objectives from the viewpoint of comprehensive service for people. Also vitally important has been the establishment, right from the word go, of an information and communication system at all levels with the involvement of all agents, thus creating a cascading and two-way communication system....

Related policies or legislation: This practice has taken place in the legal framework established at all levels: local, regional, state and European. What is new with respect to policy practice has been the establishment of the Consortium of the La Mina District as a practical experience in the management of a plan for urban and social transformation.... the good prospects for the immediate future, are serving as a catalyst for the replication of the model, as we noted above in the case of the neighbouring town of Badalona.

Source: UN-Habitat *Best Practices Database* (2006).

evident progress, the district needs further and more effective interventions, especially in terms of increased security and reduction in the number of young offenders.

In addition, big question marks remain over what will happen to local residents associations after the Consortium is dismantled at the end of 2010. Indeed, by the end of 2009, many members of staff of the Consortium had already begun to leave the *Consorcio*, moving back to their original institutions. The extent to which local associations will be able to continue their operations without the support and encouragement of the Consortium staff is therefore unclear. Indeed, from a social perspective, it can be argued that most of the local associations in La Mina were set up through forceful intervention by the Consortium and active representatives of local political community rather than through grassroots movements, and, as a result, their long-term viability remains to be seen.

Nonetheless, at present it would seem difficult to assess categorically the social sustainability impact of the regeneration process due to a lack of publicly available data and comprehensive studies. This is despite the monitoring of regeneration projects introduced by the Catalan Government through, for example, the establishment of Committees for Project Assessment and Follow-up within the 'Programme for Districts', which was reviewed earlier in the chapter. These committees include the presence of two members from the *Departament de Política Territorial i Obres Públiques* (Department of Land Affairs and Public Works) of the *Generalitat de Catalunya* (Catalan Government), five members from other departments in the Catalan Government, five representatives from the municipality where the project is carried out, and six members guaranteeing citizen participation (Generalitat de Catalunya, 2006; CIVITAS, 2007). During the project implementation period, the committee meets at least three times a year, and drafts a report on the project's development twice a year as well as an assessment report for the Fund Management Committee of each project funded through the *Programa de Barris*. Nonetheless, there have been paradoxical instances (such as the Integrated Regeneration project for the '*Erm*' neighbourhood in Manlleu, financed in 2004 through the Programme for Districts) where the monitoring committee was set up but no monitoring system agreed (CIVITAS, 2007).

Despite these problems, several sets of metrics deployed for the assessment and the monitoring of projects implemented in La Mina are reported in Appendix 6. The approach adopted by the La Mina Consortium was to compare the social performance of La Mina with the rest of the municipality, Barcelona and Catalonia as a whole, which provided benchmarks and reference values for setting targets and objectives of the local regeneration process. This approach also confirms the findings of the literature explored in Chapter 3, according to which the selection of social targets and objectives is a political exercise, which cannot be easily carried out through a scientific approach, and this point will be explored in greater depth in Chapter 11, within the context of an overview of best practice in the sector.

Conclusions

This chapter has shown how the establishment of the La Mina Consortium has been crucial to promoting an integrated, cross-departmental and interdisciplinary approach to urban regeneration and in avoiding piecemeal interventions, which had characterised the regeneration of this neighbourhood for many years. In addition, this allowed the promotion of an infrastructure-led approach to regeneration, for example by building a new *Rambla* and improving public transport and other elements of the public realm, which have diminished the cumulative deficits in local social and urban infrastructure and provided an institutional and legal framework for the attraction of private investment in the area.

Furthermore, the institutional backing for regeneration has provided financial guarantees for almost one fifth of leverage debt of the project's financial costs. In addition, it has also been essential in formulating long-term development plans for the area, such as a new university campus and research park, which are likely to have both positive and negative social and economic impacts on the lives of local residents. At present, the development of this project is still in its planning stages. However, if approved, the new investment plan could attract young researchers and higher income groups. This process would certainly promote social mixing in the area but is also likely to engender an increase in local property prices, prompting an indirect displacement effect on local residents.

Another key element of the regeneration process has been the location of the offices of the Consortium in La Mina itself. This allowed local residents to identify officers responsible for the implementation of specific programmes and to promote accountability and transparency in the decision-making process and operations of the Consortium. Mistrust and unfamiliarity with city services and agencies are often common in neighbourhoods that are experiencing social and environmental decline, and it can be argued, therefore, that the physical presence of regeneration agencies and actors in these areas, through for example local offices and 'drop-in' centres, are a crucial component of the regeneration process.

8

The Regeneration of Turin and Porta Palazzo

Introduction

Turin is located in the Piedmont Region in the north-eastern part of Italy, and with its 908 825 inhabitants (ISTAT, 2009) is Italy's fourth largest city. The urban area covers an area of 130 square kilometres, has a population density of less than 7000 people per square kilometre, and constitutes an administrative municipality on its own. Its metropolitan area comprises 53 municipalities, whose territorial development has taken on the form and character of a widespread urban suburb (Rosso, 2004). In total the city's metropolitan area has about 1 700 000 inhabitants in 1350 square kilometres (ISTAT, 1997), and it is one of the largest cities in the region.

Turin was the first capital of Italy and played a crucial role in the process of national unification. Due to a post-World War II national economic development strategy, Turin became Italy's main industrial city by the mid-1970s, known also as the 'Italian Detroit' (Salone, 2006) or 'one company city' (Rosso, 2004). This is because until recently, urban growth, economic development and the social transformations of the city have been linked to the development of the automotive industry and the fortunes of Fiat (the car manufacturer).

As did many other manufacturing industrial cities worldwide, in the 1980s Turin underwent a period of major economic and urban transformations, which were prompted by the oil crisis of the mid-1970s. Indeed, the city slowly abandoned its monocentric structure for a more polycentric model of urban development, in which secondary poles gained importance, partly favoured by the delocalisation of several industries in neighbouring municipalities and a suburbanisation process driven by the middle classes moving out of the city

Urban Regeneration & Social Sustainability: Best Practice from European Cities, by Andrea Colantonio and Tim Dixon © 2011 Andrea Colantonio and Tim Dixon

centre. As a result inner-city areas, such as Porta Palazzo and San Salvario, for example, remained populated predominantly by the poorest sectors of society who could not afford to move out to the suburbs. This triggered a process of urban decline of Turin's central areas until local authorities promoted a comprehensive set of urban regeneration projects in the mid-1990s.

This chapter therefore examines the policy context and the set of coordinated actions and mechanisms underpinning the urban regeneration of Turin. It then goes on to investigate the case study of the regeneration of Porta Palazzo, an inner-city neighbourhood, which has been regenerated through the establishment of a local development agency and funding provided by EU URBAN.

Urban development and decline

During the post-World War II period, the population of Turin grew from 700000 inhabitants at the end of the 1940s to 1 202 846 in 1974 (Turin City Council, 2001) predominantly as a result of the rapid expansion of Fiat, which contributed to the generation of a monocentric urban structure, and highly specialised industrial cluster centred around the company's three main factories. The success of Fiat and its spin-off industries prompted a vast migratory influx from impoverished Southern Italian regions, which overwhelmed the local authorities and the city's inadequate infrastructure. According to Winkler (2007), Turin's municipal authorities took little action to remedy the chronic housing, health, transport and education problems in the overdense peripheral areas where most immigrants settled. Instead they adopted a 'laissez-faire' attitude towards urban development projects, allowing free rein to property developers, who neglected the city's severe need for affordable housing, which at the time accounted for just 15% of all new building.

Turin's economic growth and population expansion continued until the first oil crisis hit Fiat and the manufacturing sector during the mid-1970s. During this period, due to increasing prices of raw materials, national financial incentives to invest in southern Italian regions and a growing unionised workforce, Fiat began to shift production out of Turin, prompting a period of economic and social decline for the city. For example, it is estimated that during the 1980s, Turin lost roughly 100000 jobs (Maggi & Piperno, 1999). Between 1986 and 1996, the jobs created by the Fiat group fell from 92 000 to 47 000 (Maggi & Piperno, 1999). Similarly, the industrial group halved the production taking place in its Turin plants from 60% in 1990 to 30% in 2002.

The harsh consequences of the economic decline of Fiat in Turin were exacerbated by the political and social crisis, which stemmed from it. For many years, Fiat played a crucial social role in the city, providing both housing and a range of social benefits to its workers. Therefore the company's decline left a vacuum in many key areas of welfare and service provision, which the municipal authorities were not equipped to deal with (Winkler, 2007). Moreover, the several left-wing coalitions, which governed Turin during the 1970s and 1980s, were unable to develop an integrated and effective strategy for tackling the city's social and political problems. As a result, Turin experienced a volatile cycle of four mayors in seven years (1985–1992), which led to the dissolution of the elected city council in 1992 and the nomination of a government-appointed commissioner responsible for running the city until the 1993 elections.

In 1993 the Italian Government introduced major political reforms to mayoral elections and this played a pivotal role in the economic and political transformation of Turin, as well as several other Italian cities. Until 1993, local authorities operated in a strongly centralised system, in which mayors were indirectly elected by a council of elected politicians. Law 81 was passed in 1993, allowing mayors to be directly elected in their own constituencies in all towns with more than 15 000 inhabitants. The first directly and locally elected mayor of Turin was Valentino Castellani in 1993. He began to formulate a concerted and clear strategy for the renaissance of Turin, which would boost its competitiveness by changing the city's identity from an industrial urban area to an outward-oriented and international services centre. The main milestones of Turin's urban renaissance and its policy context are discussed in the remainder of this chapter.

The policy context

In Italy there is no tradition of nationwide urban development or regeneration policies comparable to those of northern European countries, where urban planning has been well integrated into spatial and economic development policies for many years. Broadly speaking, in Italy the Ministry of Public Works (until 2001), and then the Ministry for Infrastructure, have indirectly shaped national urban development policies through major infrastructure projects and investment programmes. However, after the mid 1990s, the Ministry of Public Works began to promote *ad hoc* urban regeneration programmes, adapting the models of the URBAN schemes launched by the EU in 1994 and the UK City Challenge programme (Bricocoli & Savoldi, 2005) to the Italian context. The new model set out 'competitions' based on regeneration project proposals amongst cities and neighbourhoods in order to target limited national financial resources for urban renewal.

There is general agreement that URBAN had a powerful influence in shaping urban regeneration programmes and plans in Italy (Tedesco, 2006). The centralised top-down approach to urban regeneration and development policies, which envisaged the promotion of physical infrastructure as the main objective of urban regeneration, began to be abandoned in favour of a more integrated and participatory bottom-up approach to urban renewal. Adopting the URBAN methodology and the City Challenge concept, the Ministry of Public Works began to fund local urban regeneration plans through a tendering procedure and a methodology that deployed sets of indicators to rank project proposals to be funded. Although scores were linked to indicators representing the central government's strategic vision, programmes were also proposed or put forward by municipalities according to their own needs and potential. This therefore allowed for national and local urban development plans to meet in a centre ground provided by these programmes.

Before the adoption of URBAN in Italy, other embryonic urban regeneration schemes were piloted at the national level. These provided the platform for the development of several urban regeneration policies and programmes throughout the 1990s and 2000s. The most important initiatives included (Janin Rivolin, 2004):

- Urban Pilot Project (*PPU – Progetto pilota urbano*, ERDF/EU 1989–93, 1997–99).
- Integrated Action Programme (*PRIN – Programma integrato di intervento*, L. 179/92).
- URBAN (ERDF/EU, 1994–99).
- Territorial Pacts (*Patto territoriale*, L. 662/1996).
- Area Contract (*Contratto d'area*, L. 662/1996).
- Territorial Pact for Employment (*Patto Territoriale per l'Occupazione*, 96/C).
- Urban Renewal Programmes (*PRU, Programmi di Recupero Urbano*, DM 1.12.1994).
- Urban Regeneration Programmes (*PRIU – Programma di riqualificazione urbana*, DM 21.12.1994).
- Neighbourhood Contracts (*CDQ – Contratto di quartiere*, DM 22.10.1997).
- Urban Regeneration and Territorial Sustainable Development Programmes (*PRUSST – Programma di riqualificazione urbana e di sviluppo sostenibile del territorio*, DM 8.10.1998).
- Agricultural Pact (*Patto agricolo*, DM 29.06.2000).
- URBAN II (ERDF/EU 2000–2006).
- Integrated territorial programme (*PIT – Programma integrato territoriale*, QCS 2000–2006).
- Neighbourhood Contracts II (DM 23.04.2003).

Although an in-depth analysis of these policies and programmes is outside the scope of this chapter, some of the most important of these initiatives arc briefly reviewed in Table 8.1, which illustrates how they have slowly moved

Table 8.1 Main national urban regeneration programmes in Italy since the 1990s.

Programme	Description and objective	Date
Integrated Action Programme (*PRIN – Programma integrato di intervento*)	The programmes mainly focus on urban infrastructure, public housing and 'aesthetic' renovation of the existing built environment, mobilising public and private resources. There were also instruments to amend Urban Master Plans	1992
PRIUs (*Programmi di Riqualificazione Urbana*)	Programmes proposed by municipalities to the Ministry of Public Works, which entail the participation of private companies as a prerequisite. Unlike PRIUs, Urban Regeneration Programmes are not limited to the refurbishment or improvement of social housing estates and services, and can be located in any city district	1992
PRUs (*Programmi di Recupero Urbano*)	Programmes to improve public services and infrastructure in degraded urban neighbourhoods. These programmes are limited to areas of social housing. PRUs required the participation of the private sector, for example through setting up public–private joint ventures. To this aim, municipal authorities could approve speedier changes to urban development plans to attract the participation of private actors if necessary	Since 1993
Neighbourhood Contracts I and II (*Contratti di Quartiere*)	Experimental programmes funded by the Ministry for Public Works, which do not require participation of the private sector as a pre-requirement. They mainly include the restructuring of social housing rather than projects of new urbanisation	Introduced in 1997
PRUSSTs (*Programma di Riqualificazione Urbana e Sviluppo Sostenibile del Territorio*)	Programmes set up to move away from sectoral interventions in urban areas in favour of a more integrated approach to urban regeneration and sustainable development, which transcended administrative urban boundaries to include metropolitan regions. These programmes epitomise the efforts of central government to embrace sustainability principles and integrate the urban regeneration of single neighbourhoods within the wider urban and city–region contexts. They also encourage public–private partnerships aimed at promoting urban competitiveness and employment	1998

Source: Elaborated by Colantonio from several sources.

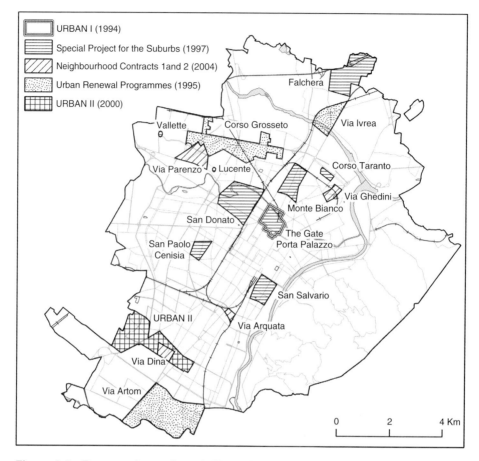

Figure 8.1 Regeneration projects in Turin. *Source*: Drawn by Venere Stefania Sanna (2008) from Officina Torino.

away from the monodimensional and sectoral approach to urban regeneration in the early 1990s (which was mainly limited to housing renewal schemes and environmental improvements) towards the promotion of integrated and multidimensional neighbourhood regeneration programmes in the 2000s. In addition, Table 8.1 demonstrates how the involvement of the public and NGO sector (through the formation of PPP for urban regeneration projects) has been a key feature of urban policies in Italy over the last two decades.

Turin has therefore been able to attract funding for (and implement) several of these policies and programmes, as illustrated in Figure 8.1, because, since the mid-1980s, the municipality has also been involved in several international networks of cities in urban decline, such as the *Quartiers en Crise* network. Through the early participation in these networks, the municipality's policymakers, architects, planners and practitioners were able to develop knowledge and skills in the field of regeneration, which gave the city a competitive advantage when several national and EU programmes of urban regeneration were launched in the 1990s. It is therefore no surprise that Turin has been at the forefront of urban regeneration in Italy for several years, experimenting with new programmes and approaches to regeneration.

Urban regeneration and partnership arrangements

As well as the active participation in international city networks, since the early 1990s, the urban redevelopment strategy of Turin has been based on several important milestones. These include:

- The development of a 'vision' for the city in partnership with key local economic and social stakeholders. This process resulted in the elaboration of Turin's Strategic Plan in 2000 (Torino Internazionale, 2000).
- The ratification of a new Masterplan (*Piano Regolatore Centrale*) in 1995, which the city had not had for almost 50 years. The new plan guided major urban transformations and large-scale infrastructure projects, especially in terms of mobility and transport within the city.
- The promotion of a new image for the city, and the organisation of the Winter Olympics in 2006.
- Urban regeneration of socially and environmentally deprived neighbourhoods through the setting up of the *Special Project for Marginal Suburbs* in 1997.
- The promotion of a new institutional and financial governance model for urban management. The new model restructured and simplified governing local agencies, introduced participatory and partnership-based planning processes and combined several programmes (local, national, European) and funding sources (public, private and NGOs) to support an integrated urban development policy.

These milestones are now discussed throughout the remainder of this chapter and within the context of the Porta Palazzo regeneration process.

The strategic plan

In 2000, Turin became the first Italian city to develop a *Strategic Development Plan*, with a methodology that has been emulated by other Italian cities such as Florence, Venice and Trento since then. The plan was born out of an initiative of Mayor Castellani, who looked at European examples of successful urban and economic regeneration, with special emphasis on the Barcelona model. Indeed, in 1998, Mayor Castellani began a consultation process with the city's most important public and private social, economic, political and cultural actors aimed at identifying an integrated economic development strategy for Turin and a new international identity for the city. The consultation lasted two years, during which time two drafts of the plan were produced, until the Strategic Plan was presented and signed by 57 public and private leaders at the beginning of 2000.

The plan is particularly important because it established a long-term 'road map' for the city's development, and identified some 84 specific actions to be implemented by 2011 (see also Box 8.1). From an operational perspective, the plan created new independent task-oriented bodies and agencies, such as 'Invest in Turin' and 'Piedmont' and 'Turismo Torino', to implement specific elements of the programme, whilst Torino Internazionale Association was set up to coordinate individual activities and promote the plan as a whole. According to Winkler (2007), the plan is possibly the city's most important recovery tool because: (i) it was highly participative, involving leaders from several public and private bodies and hundreds of residents; (ii) it was strongly rooted in the city and its particular characteristics; and (iii) it was informal in style, encouraging the involvement of a wide range of bodies with different operating methods that would have resisted formalised engagement.

Master plan

Another important instrument that played a key role in structuring Turin's urban regeneration was the 1995 Master Plan (*Piano Regolatore Generale*; PRG). Turin had not had a new Urban Master Plan for over 45 years because of a lack of political consensus. The development of the plan entailed extensive public relations exercises and consultations in order to reach consensus and cooperation between private- and public-sector bodies, which was needed to deliver the urban transformation of the city. Thus, the new PRG provided clear guidelines for the city's physical renewal and offered a legal framework for the concerted actions of municipal authorities, private developers and other urban regeneration agencies. There can be little doubt that the new Master Plan stemmed from the political vision of the newly elected Castellani's administration, which envisaged it as a key policy tool to achieve the physical regeneration of the city through the designation of new land uses (such as the proportion of offices, housing, services and so on) and infrastructure planning for a period of ten years.

Broadly speaking, the 1995 Master Plan laid the foundations to enable the reconfiguration of Turin from a monocentric city centred around the Fiat factories to a denser, better connected, post-Fordist polycentric

Box 8.1   The first Turin Strategic Plan (2000)

Turin was the first city in Italy to adopt a Strategic Plan. This plan was promoted by the municipality to give a new international identity to the city and to suggest a strategic vision for its future development.

The content of the Strategic Plan

The Plan reflected the intention of giving to the city the international role it deserved through three strategic visions: (i) Turin as a European metropolis; (ii) Turin as an ingenious city, which gets things done and does them correctly; and (iii) Turin which knows how to choose its development path: the intelligence of the future and the quality of life.

Strategic lines

- To integrate the metropolitan area in the international system;
- to construct the metropolitan government;
- to develop training and research as strategic resources;
- to promote enterprises and employment;
- to promote culture, tourism, commerce and sports; and
- to improve the urban environment.

The governance context

The vision of the plan has been shaped by several actors and stakeholders. The Municipality of Turin was mainly supported by:

- The Development Forum, funded by representatives of the economic, social and cultural elites;
- the Scientific Committee, made of Italian and foreign experts; and
- the Coordination Committee, funded by the Regional Development Agency, the IPT (*Invest in Turin and Piedmont*) and Turismo Torino (the official tourist office for the metropolitan area).

'Torino Internazionale' process

The two bodies responsible for the implementation of the Turin's Strategic Plan were:

- 'Torino Internazionale' Association, a political body constituted in May 2000 and formed by 122 private and public partners: institutions, political representatives, economic organisations and almost 1000 people who were organised into various workgroups and associations; and
- 'Torino Internazionale' Agency, a technical body responsible for following up projects and cooperation support.

Box 8.1   *(cont'd)*

Bringing together public and private sectors

- Specific analytical studies were delegated to external advisors and external teams (i.e. the plan for the integration of the metropolitan area within the international transport system, studies on the international competitiveness of the city in the European context, etc.).
- The private sector provided resources, mainly financial, technical and management. Nevertheless, the contributions of individual firms were limited.
- Numerous and different collective organizations and business representatives were involved in the Development Forum.

Source: Salone (2006) and Balducci *et al.* (2003).

metropolis (Winkler, 2007). Through the new Urban Master Plan the municipality set out a vision for re-zoning industrial land and encouraging private developers to revitalise these areas within the clear guidelines set by the city for land use. Figure 8.2 shows how the Master Plan identified *Spina Centrale* (Central Backbone) as a central axis for the physical transformation of Turin. This route once represented the city's industrial artery, connecting the north and south industrial districts with a railway line. The Spina Centrale was to be created by interring the railway line and replacing it with a 12-kilometre six-lane arterial road into the city centre, flanked by four major industrial brownfield zones to be redeveloped along its length. Redevelopment works have been carried out over a ten-year period, from 2000 with a planned finish in 2010, with the use of both public and private resources, increasing Turin's available land for redevelopment by 2 million square metres.

New plans also proposed the redevelopment of four derelict industrial areas (i.e. Spina 1, Spina 2, Spina 3 and Spina 4 in Figure 8.2) totalling 1.4 million square metres of land, in order to create new mixed-use neighbourhoods with almost half the land (53%) designated for residential use, and the remainder for parks, commercial activities (43%) and public infrastructure (4%). These derelict areas will be linked back to the urban fabric through major transport infrastructure, including Turin's first metro line, and other projects that represent €2.45 bn of public and private investment, with the aim of turning the rail corridor into a new strategic growth corridor (Winkler, 2007). The improvement of transport offers a major incentive to developers to contribute to the strategic transformation of brownfield areas of the city, together with a certain degree of flexibility, which has been left in terms of the designation of specific uses for the four 'spina' redevelopment zones.

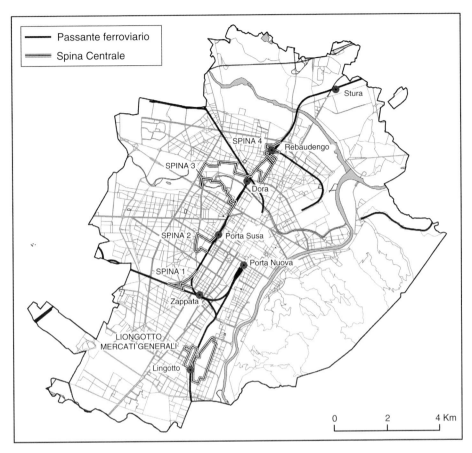

Figure 8.2 The 1995 Turin Master Plan. *Source*: Drawn by Venere Stefania Sanna (2006) from Officina Torino.

Winter Olympics

In 2006, Turin hosted the twentieth Winter Olympic Games, which played a pivotal role in spurring on a wave of physical renewal projects and promoting a new 'post-industrial' service-oriented image for Turin. The pre-Olympics preparations were also instrumental in setting up public–private partnerships in the city, which were deemed an essential ingredient in mobilising local entrepreneurship and in attracting financial resources and private-sector expertise for the timely delivery of key infrastructure projects. Within this context, Essex and Chalkley (2007) have pointed out how mega-events, such as the Olympic Games, have emerged as a significant feature of de-industrialised, post-modern societies and represent a major catalyst for urban change through economic regeneration, infrastructure investment and environmental improvement

Table 8.2 New public–private agencies.

Agency	Nature and objective
Turismo Torino	A tourist agency to promote and welcome tourism in the Torino area
Invest in Turin and Piedmont (ITP)	An agency to draw investments to Torino and Piemonte
Associazione Torino Internazionale	An association to coordinate and monitor the delivery of the Strategic Plan comprising 120 representatives of economic, cultural and social institutions throughout the area
Convention Bureau	An organisation to promote convention activity
Organising Committee of the twentieth Winter Olympic Games	A non-profit private foundation; to organise the Torino 2006 Olympic and Paralympic Games
Film Commissione	A commission to promote the film industry
Six Territorial Agreements	Agreement among neighbouring municipalities
Technological Parks (e.g. Environmental Park and Virtual Reality Multimedia Park)	Parks to attract investments in high added value new economy industries
Fondazione Torino Wireless	A foundation to promote investments in the information and communications technology sectors

Source: Adapted from Rosso (2004).

as well as an opportunity to achieve international prominence and national prestige through 'place marketing'.

The smooth delivery of the Olympics and a new branding for Turin was helped by a range of other activities carried out by several agencies born out of public–private agreements, which are listed in Table 8.2. The in-depth analysis of the impact of the Olympics and the newly created public–private agencies is outside the scope of this chapter. Briefly, however, the 2006 Winter Olympic Games can be considered as a catalyst for urban change, providing a tool to steer and channel public and private resources into an integrated set of concerted urban interventions. However, the games have been criticised for hurrying construction and infrastructure development plans with inadequate planning for the post-Olympic period and the management of the games' legacy. Furthermore, interviews conducted as part of the research process for this book highlighted how this new infrastructure has not been fully integrated into the urban system in Turin.

Special project for marginal neighbourhoods

In 1997, the municipality of Turin developed an innovative programme called the Special Project for Marginal Neighbourhoods (*Progetto Speciale Periferie*; PSP), setting up a dedicated department within the council, called the 'Neighbourhood Unit', the exclusive aim of which was to address the social problems of degraded neighbourhoods across the city as part of the overall recovery effort. This process was part of a broader institutional restructuring process initiated by the first Castellani administration, which streamlined roughly 17 000 municipal employees in 1993 to 12 800 municipal workers in 2004 (Rosso, 2004) and consolidated the 87 departments into fewer administrative units.

Overall, the Special Project for Marginal Neighbourhoods (SPMNs) envisioned a bottom-up and participatory model of urban regeneration, which placed residents' participation at the heart of urban-renewal policies and development projects. According to Magnano (2007) the defining features of SPMNs' approach to urban regeneration included:

- The integration of policies to address social, economic and physical problems in a holistic fashion;
- the fostering of residents' participation in every stage of the regeneration process;
- the promotion of innovatory and experimental ways (e.g. social mixing, etc.) of addressing local problems; and
- a novel interdisciplinary cross-departmental approach to policy making.

One of the main objectives of the Neighbourhoods Unit was to implement interdisciplinary cross-departmental policy making at both neighbourhood and institutional levels. Thus, for each area-based project, a group of city council employees (e.g. housing specialists, social services personnel, teachers, etc.) was set up within the unit to work together with local residents to identify and address the main issues concerning municipal services. At a departmental level, another working group of professionals from several municipal departments was also set up as part of the unit to ensure the integrated delivery of services through the inter-departmental exchange of information amongst municipal actors.

The Neighbourhoods Unit remained operational for over 10 years until 2008, when the working groups were dismantled due to a reduction of funding, and their members returned to their respective departments. It is difficult to quantify the unit's impact on the urban regeneration of Turin, as no comprehensive study has yet been carried out. Nonetheless, the Neighbourhoods Unit managed investments of €450 000 000 (Turin City Council, 2007) in areas of the city covering a total of 200 000 residents.

The regeneration of Porta Palazzo

Porta Palazzo is often held as good example of the success of Turin's urban-regeneration efforts. This district is located close to Turin's city centre (see Figure 8.1). With a (census) population of around 11 000 inhabitants in 2001, the area has historically acted as a first-recipient neighbourhood for the major waves of national and international immigration that character-ised Turin in the 1960s (national) and the 1980s–1990s (international). The area hosts an outdoor flea market, which is amongst the biggest in Europe, covering an area of 52 000 square meters, and which is the main social and physical feature of the neighbourhood. The market comprises roughly 1000 vendors, attracting 40 000 people daily and 100 000 shoppers on Saturdays.

Before the urban regeneration process started the area was a decaying inner-city neighbourhood, characterised by an informal economy and illegal activities, inadequate social services, low cultural integration of interna-tional immigrants, a highly mobile and transient population, a myriad of short-lived micro-enterprises, and a bad reputation linked to local crime and illegal immigrants. At both a household and a building level, Porta Palazzo also exhibited social problems ranging from domestic violence (especially towards women) to a lack of social cohesion, due to limited shared values and common aspirations amongst the many nationalities of immigrants liv-ing in the community.

As a result, the main objectives of the regeneration project included:

- The promotion of an integrated and trans-disciplinary approach to the social, economic, cultural and physical regeneration of the Porta Palazzo neighbourhood, covering an area of 500 000 square meters;
- the achievement of a flexible 'bottom up' redevelopment of the area in order to value and build upon local resources; and
- the mobilisation of internal and external available resources (ranging from financial resources to know how) to be invested in community develop-ment projects.

The identification of these objectives and the call for new delivery vehi-cles and governance models for urban regeneration were also linked to Italy's changing institutional and economic landscape. Indeed, until 1990, Italian local authorities had operated in a strongly centralised system, in which local authorities had limited decision-making power and con-strained financial autonomy. However, by the mid-1990s, the newly intro-duced legislation concerning the direct local election of mayors, and a series of judicial trials against widespread corruption, granted local author-ities greater decision-making capacity and more flexibility to operate at the local level. As a result, relations between citizens, entrepreneurs and the municipality became stronger, and this not only encouraged the set-ting up of public–private partnerships between state agencies, the private sector and non-governmental organisations, but also promoted a more participatory model of urban regeneration, which is now examined in more detail.

Partnership arrangements

In Italy there are several models of public–private partnership as reported by Roland Berger Strategy Consultants (2005) and Poggesi (2007). These include:

- Project finance, where the private sector acts as 'promoter' of public works by submitting an infrastructure project proposal to the public administration body, within its three-year investment plan.
- Concessions on building use and management for the provision of a public service.
- Other management concessions, used for the provision of public services through the management of already existing infrastructure (for example, hydraulic networks and systems, gas, public lighting and so on).
- Mixed public–private companies introduced in the national system by Article 22 of Law 142/1990, as part of the different management types of managing local public services.
- The urban transformation companies, which differ from mixed public–private companies mainly because of their mission to focus exclusively on urban regeneration.

Broadly speaking, public private partnerships in Porta Palazzo were established mostly between civil society associations and micro-enterprise organisations on the one side and municipal authorities on the other. The main objectives of these partnerships were to legalise and regulate services that were often provided informally or illegally, and to organise cultural and educational activities. Therefore examples of PPP in this local context include agreements to run outdoor market activities or run theatre courses. In this sense, PPPs in Porta Palazzo were not set up to implement or run large infrastructure projects or services, but rather to implement economic and social development micro-projects involving local actors.

The promotion of the partnership concept in the regeneration of Porta Palazzo began in 1997 when the City of Turin submitted an Urban Pilot Project proposal, entitled *The Gate: Living Not Leaving* (Curti, 2007), to the European Union to be funded through the European Regional Development Fund (ERDF). The project aimed at improving the quality of life and job opportunities in the Porta Palazzo area through the participation of a wide range of local actors. The proposal was approved and the 'The Porta Palazzo Project Committee', a non-profit body with mixed participation of both public institutions and third-sector companies, was established in 1998 to manage and implement 'The Gate' project.

Figure 8.3 shows how the Porta Palazzo Project Committee was composed of 11 members from public-, private- and NGO-sector organizations.

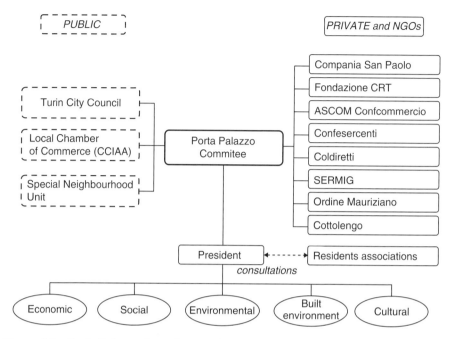

Figure 8.3   Porta Palazzo Committee and its operations.

According to Balducci *et al.* (2003), the creation of the committee stems from Mayor Castellani's political will and his efforts to modernise and re-launch the city of Turin internationally. At the beginning of the Gate Project, the main role of the committee was to build consensus concerning sets of actions and strategies amongst various actors with a stake in the regeneration project. However, the committee soon began to undertake a more proactive leadership and management role in terms of the project and to develop a 'vision' for the neighbourhood and the implementation of its renewal. This continued between 1998 and 2001 when the first phase of the regeneration process was concluded.

Indeed, two main phases can be identified in the regeneration of Porta Palazzo. The first phase lasted approximately five years, until 2001 when the Gate Project was formally concluded. In 2002, at the end of Urban Pilot Project, the committee was transformed into a Local Development Agency in order to continue the work of the Gate Project and build on its initial achievements. The total budget of the project between 1997 and 2001 is summarised in Table 8.3. Under the Innovative Actions Initiative of ERDF, studies or pilot schemes concerning regional development at the community level could receive co-financing grants from the ERDF of between 30 and 75% of the total project budget, depending on the geographic area. For example, Turin was eligible to receive 50% co-financing, and had to match at least EU funding. Within this context, it is worth pointing out that EU/

Table 8.3   Main funding sources for the regeneration of Porta Palazzo.

Source	Amount in euros
European Union (ERDF)	2 582 000
City of Turin	3 582 000
Ministry for Public Works	1 032 913
Total	7 196 913

Source: Winkler (2007) and Curti (2007).

ERDF funding was initially granted because The Gate Project proposal was framed within the city's overall regeneration plan envisaged within the Master Plan, and drawn up in 1995. Indeed, as pointed out earlier, this document provided an overall framework for all the city's redevelopment projects, linking a specific project to the city-wide development plan, and this was a key requirement of major national and EU funding bodies and also helped attract financial resources (Winkler, 2007).

Since 2002, the new Local Development Agency has received continued funding from the municipality and Turin-based foundations, bringing the total amount of investment for the regeneration of Porta Palazzo to €85 000 000 (Curti, 2007).

Social sustainability

For several years, Porta Palazzo exhibited cumulative social problems, which Avedano (2007) and Curti (2007) summarise as follows:

- High concentration of residents with cumulative social problems, especially within immigrant communities;
- difficult cohabitation of several religious and cultural groups;
- commercial decline;
- high levels of unemployment;
- poor and unsafe housing conditions;
- drug trafficking and consumption in the market area;
- crime (e.g. pick pocketing and assaults during outdoor market hours); and
- bad image and reputation of the area at city, regional and national levels.

During the first phase of the regeneration process (The Gate Project, 1997–2002), the Porta Palazzo Committee identified five main themes and a set of 19 actions, ranging from community participation to economic incentives and education to promote the integrated revitalisation of the area, as shown in Figure 8.4.

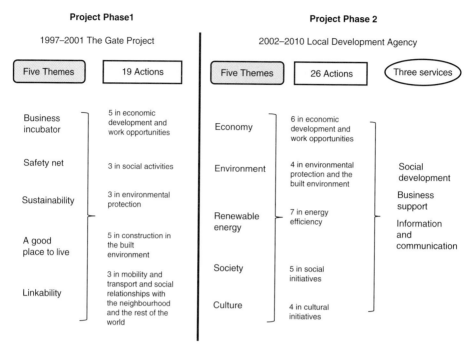

Figure 8.4   Phases, themes and actions of the regeneration process of Porta Palazzo. *Source*: Elaborated from Curti (2007) and Avedano (2007).

During the second phase of regeneration (2002–2006) the newly formed Local Development Agency identified five themes and embarked upon the integrated implementation of 26 actions and three services. The latter included: (i) social support for local community development; (ii) support for micro-enterprises to capitalise on the entrepreneurial and commercial skills of many local residents and the 2300 local micro-enterprises, which employ roughly 7000 workers; and (iii) the promotion and communication services to try to promote a better external image of Porta Palazzo and attract investments.

From a social sustainability perspective, three clusters of objectives and related activities can be identified within the project. The first cluster revolves around fostering participation and empowerment of local residents through the formation of neighbourhood forums (*tavolo sociale*) and the improvement of the skills and education of local residents. Within this context, the location of the local development agency office in Porta Palazzo is at the heart of the municipal authority's efforts to deliver public participation in the decision-making process in the area. Indeed, from the start of the project, the offices of the Gate Committee were located next to the flea market, and this provided the physical and virtual space for the formation of a local neighbourhood forum, which brought together representatives of local residents associations and interest groups, specialists of the Neighbourhood Unit, working groups, and bank foundations. The *tavolo sociale* allowed local residents and their associations to be consulted and deliver aspects of development projects in partnership with municipal authorities and institutional bodies. In addition, they promoted transparency and accountability within the decision-making process as residents could clearly identify the designated representatives of municipal authorities or working group experts responsible for the implementation of specific schemes or projects.

In addition, other initiatives were promoted to ensure maximum participation in the planning process of the regeneration of the neighbourhood, and one of the most important was 'The Planning Weekend', organised in 1999. According to Balducci *et al.* (2003), approximately 200 local residents took part in the event, gathering over 100 ideas for the future development of the area, which were eventually translated into 37 potential proposals. The proposals were distilled into a single proposal for alternative uses for local residents of the market area outside its opening hours.

The second cluster of activities focused on the enhancement of community identity, and a sense of 'belonging' to the place, by strengthening social ties amongst neighbours and building up trust towards public authorities despite the high turnover of residents in the area. A major action in this direction included a programme of small grants to homeowners to improve their own flats, which were complemented by grants targeted towards improving the common areas of buildings, including stairways, roofs, courtyards, gas and water pipes. The main objective of these grants was to provide incentives to improve local housing conditions and not to abandon the area. According to members of the Gate Committee, homeowners who received these grants also acted as ambassadors or liaison representatives for the project and contributed to trust building between neighbours, which helped to reduce mistrust and unfamiliarity with city services and agencies. Indeed, the recipients of home improvement were able to spread information about the project's aims and to refer neighbours to the right member of staff of the Gate. Furthermore, home-improvement grants acted as catalysts to develop a stronger sense of attachment to the place for local residents, providing an incentive not to leave their homes and the area as a whole.

The third cluster of activities endeavoured to reduce crime and to reintroduce legal practices, especially within the context of the outdoor market and local commercial activities, which had attracted around 300 illegal and unlicensed traders during Saturday flea markets. As a result, several activities were implemented, including the Community Warden project (see Box 8.2), aimed at reducing crime and illegal activities with the support of the police and local residents themselves. Their overall purpose was to generate maximum investment opportunities and promote the market as a primary shopping destination for tourists and visitors from other parts of the city,

---

Box 8.2   The 'Neighbourhood Municipal Warden' Project

The 'Neighbourhood Municipal Warden' Project (*Vigili di quartiere*) was launched with the 'Special Project for Neighbourhood' (*Progetto Speciale Periferie*) in 1997.

Objectives

- To identify critical and urgent issues to be dealt with by the service in order to improve safety conditions and reduce risk perception for the neighbourhoods' inhabitants;
- to guarantee a first level of 'proximity' service granted by the local police;
- to activate a constant 'observation point' and establish collaborative relationships among a plurality of actors; and
- to change the image and stereotypes concerning the district.

Working methods

- To establish a direct contact with the district's citizens who comment, warn and/ or notify dangers, risks or illegal situations (i.e. through 'walks for dialogs');
- to draw the district's 'risk maps' and plan actions to solve specific problems (reduce overall crime and antisocial behaviour, build respect across communities, etc.);
- to set up action teams composed by local police officers and social support staff;
- to build networks and coordinate meetings with the aim of exchanging experiences and information; and
- to give direct response (or at least a 'referent') to citizens' needs and requests.

Results

- The introduction of local police officers consolidated reciprocity and cooperation networks between districts and citizens and people-participation in the neighbourhood problems;
- problematic issues have been identified; and priority issues and actions that deal with these have been selected in each district involved in the programme;
- debates over urban safety and risk perception have been stimulated (citizen mobilisation);
- shared security district plans have been drawn up;
- best practices have been identified and evaluated and the relative knowledge has been shared between neighbourhood actors; and
- partnerships between local police and other institutional actors (Polizia di Stato, Guardia di Finanza, Pretura, Tribunale dei Minori, Direzione Investigativa Antimafia) have been reinforced.

Source: Canestri and Leonarduzzi (2006).

generating business for merchants, shaping a positive identity for the market, and reconnecting the neighbourhood with the urban fabric of Turin (GMF, 2008).

Although there is a dearth of evaluation studies to assess the social sustainability of these initiatives a 'mid-term' evaluation study was commissioned by the Porta Palazzo Committee from Cicsene at the end of the Gate Project. The Cicsene study (Cicsene, 2002) provides a comprehensive overview of the main social, economic and physical transformations of the neighbourhood between 1997 and 2001, together with the analysis of the media coverage concerning the changing perceptions of the area. The study uses a variety of data sources and indicators, ranging from official statistics to questionnaires and direct observations. Broadly speaking, from a social sustainability perspective it examined: (i) the displacement and replacement of local population by new residents and its impact on the identity of the local community; (ii) the number of social networks and people belonging to local associations in the neighbourhood; (iii) the sense of safety of local residents; and (iv) the nature of the media coverage concerning the regeneration process.

An example of the most important findings and indicators used in Cicsene study are summarised in Table 8.4. A first set of selected demographic indicators from the study, including local population trends and migration figures, suggests that the overall local population decreased between 1997 and 2001, partially due to the physical renovation of several buildings and market areas that were informally occupied by immigrants. However, the study maintains that an increasing number of young people (for example, single people and students) have begun to move to the renovated blocks in the area. This suggests a positive change of perception concerning the area but it is unclear whether these newcomers will become permanent residents of the area or whether they will move to other city districts as soon as they are better off. In fact, Cicsene (2002) points out how this increase in young single people could have a detrimental effect on local social cohesion as single people can show low levels of interest in local social life, and little interest in establishing bonds with their neighbours.

By contrast, Table 8.5 highlights the positive impact of regeneration on the local area. Indeed, the percentage of run-down buildings more than halved (from 33.1 to 13.4%) during the observation period. According to a local survey carried out in 2000, fear of crime within the area (26.7% of respondents) converged with Turin's overall figure (26.8%) at the end of the first phase of the regeneration process. Similarly, the media coverage of the regeneration process increased significantly between 1996 and 2000, focusing not only on crime figures but also on the overall improvement of the area, as shown in Table 8.6. Overall, it is clear that this positive media coverage contributed to the improvement of the external perception of the neighbourhood. At the same time, the

Table 8.4   Selected demographic indicators in Porta Palazzo area (1996–2000).

	Number	
Key indicator	1996	2000
Population trend	11 505	10 854
Single people	2 352	2 376
Foreigners	1 442	2 090

Source: Calculated from Cicsene (2002).

Table 8.5   Selected indicators of social change in Porta Palazzo area (1996–2000) with an impact on social sustainability.

	Percentage	
Key indicator	1996	2000
Education*	33.33	33.51
Member of local associations (religious, sport, cultural, etc.)	n/a	42
Run down buildings	33.1	13.4
Fear of crime	n/a	26.7

Note: *Average of high, medium and low level. *Source*: Calculated from Cicsene (2002).

Table 8.6   Media coverage and perception of regeneration process of Porta Palazzo.

	Number	
Key indicator	1996	2000
Media articles concerning the regeneration process*	0	14
Media articles reporting crime*	46	34

Note: *Articles appeared in local newspaper *La Stampa*. *Source*: Calculated from Cicsene (2002).

Cicsene study indicated the need to improve local social networks and to encourage the creation of new associations of residents, an aspect of social sustainability that would seem to have been addressed since the release of the study through, for example, the setting up of associations of women, ethnic communities and other vulnerable local groups. In addition, the average level of education in the area did not improve significantly, highlighting that more efforts were needed in this respect.

However, as pointed out earlier, apart from the Cicsene study, no other major evaluation studies or specific monitoring systems have been set up to systematically measure the social impact of the Porta Palazzo project. According to the current director of the committee, this is mainly due to the large amount of data that would need to be to be collected and analysed, and the lack of human and financial resources allocated for this task at the beginning of the project. Another major obstacle has been the lack of statistical data available at the local and project level and the need for questionnaire surveys, which could only be carried out by trained personnel. In addition, once the project started, the urgency of running daily operations prevented the development of an overall measurement system for the appraisal of the effectiveness of many of the various programmes of the regeneration process.

Nonetheless, it is worth pointing out that several social indicators were used *ex ante* by city authorities within the PSP scheme to identify the areas of the city with specified social qualities that would fall within the operational remit of the newly created Marginal Neighbourhoods Unit. These areas were identified by using five main indicators, including:

1 Percentage of residents aged between 0 and 14;
2 percentage of resident aged over 70;
3 percentage of residents with low educational level;
4 percentage of unemployed and young people looking for first employment; and
5 percentage of workers with low skill level.

As highlighted earlier, once these neighbourhoods or communities were identified, the unit began developing local action plans in cooperation with local residents, and Porta Palazzo was identified as one of the areas to be regenerated at city level. These indicators could therefore be used as a baseline to asses the social impact of the regeneration project.

Another important set of indicators used in Turin and Porta Palazzo's context has been developed by Compagnia di San Paolo (CSP), one of the city's main bank foundations. In Italy, many saving banks have long been the major source of community-focused philanthropy, and were transformed into non-profit charitable foundations by the Amato Law in 1990. Since then, CSP has become a major player in civic, cultural and economic local development, and the co-funding actor of several of Turin's regeneration projects, investing €437 000 000 between 2001 and 2004, and with a €16 500 000 budget from 2006 to 2009 (Ricci, 2009).

As a major funding body for housing and urban regeneration projects, Compagnia di San Paolo carries out three main strands of operations, including:

1 Their own projects, for example reconverting buildings into affordable flats for temporary housing.
2 Partnership projects, including flat-sharing for young people, and mutual help building (*condominio solidale*).

Table 8.7   Criteria used by Compagnia di San Paolo to evaluate housing project proposals.

Criteria	Sub-criteria	Points/weight
Social	Innovative elements Involvement of final users in the planning phase Services open to the neighbourhood Staff training	30
Physical renovation	Overall quality of the renovation project Sustainable building Home automation for elderly/disabled people Room flexibility Accessibility for the disabled	30
Partnership		10
Budgeting	Budget consistency Future financial sustainability	20
Project management	Clarity and completeness of project plan Monitoring/final evaluation plan Communication plan	10

Source: Adapted from Ricci (2009). Reproduced by permission of Antonella Ricci.

3 Grant-making operations for housing and regeneration projects proposed by public and non-profit organisations.

Table 8.7 illustrates how and to what extent social sustainability aspects are taken into account in the evaluation stages of project proposals within CSP's grant-making operations for housing projects. It can be seen how, for example, the evaluation process places significant emphasis (or almost one third of the overall 'points' available) on specific social impacts stemming from the project. These include: (i) the novelty of the approach proposed; (ii) the participation of end users in the planning stages of the proposal; (iii) the extent to which the project provides a service for the area; and (iv) the level of skills upgrading and training opportunities stemming from the project.

CSP's approach to funding urban-regeneration projects highlights the importance of rewarding innovative and experimental ways of dealing with unsolved social problems, and confirms how the participation and engagement of final end users is a fundamental requirement for the delivery of projects providing maximum social benefits. Other important criteria taken into account by CSP during the assessment process are: (i) the establishment of a partnership and the financial soundness of the project, which are fundamental to guarantee the long-term durability of the project once the funding has been invested; and (ii) the envisaged overall management of the project. Nonetheless, Table 8.7 would seem to suggest that the existence of a post-project monitoring or evaluation is not considered to be of crucial importance by Compagnia di San Paolo.

Conclusions

A number of important elements have been at the heart of the success of the regeneration of Porta Palazzo to date. These include: the improvement of the public realm; the fostering of community social life through encouraging resident associations; the renovation of a number of public buildings and private houses through small grants; the physical regeneration of public spaces; and, perhaps most importantly, the opening of a local 'drop in' administrative office in Porta Palazzo, which offered services and advice for local residents. The design and implementation of many of these actions for redevelopment was, to a large extent, possible because of the expertise developed by the City of Turin through close participation in several knowledge-exchange networks of cities in decline since the late 1980s.

In addition, the initial integrated objectives set out at the beginning of the regeneration process were to be achieved by:

- Creating a flexible and autonomous agency;
- promoting public private partnerships;
- seeking political engagement and support at all government levels;
- guaranteeing a transparent process;
- promoting a multidisciplinary, participatory and inclusive process for urban regeneration; and
- providing local actors with methodologies, instruments and competencies to improve local living conditions (Curti, 2007).

Nonetheless, this chapter has shown how the monitoring of the effectiveness of regeneration initiatives in Porta Palazzo has been conducted through external auditing, as illustrated by the example of the 'mid-term' evaluation study commissioned to Cicsene at the end of the Gate Project. This auditing was commissioned externally because the Gate Committee did not collect baseline indicators at the beginning of the project and could not conduct the evaluation of the regeneration process internally.

This highlights the importance of identifying systematic monitoring systems at the planning stages of the regeneration process rather than implementing assessment systems on an *ad hoc* basis. Within this context, the approach of Compagnia San Paolo to evaluating housing and urban regeneration projects to be funded illustrates the importance of establishing *ex ante* assessment systems, which can also be deployed for monitoring purposes. Furthermore, it demonstrates how an increasing number of private- and NGO-sector actors involved in the built environment and urban regeneration can contribute to the development of monitoring systems, which can provide a valuable framework for assessing the critical dimensions of sustainability.

9

The Regeneration of Rotterdam and the 'South Pact'

Introduction

With nearly 600 000 inhabitants, Rotterdam is the second largest city in the Netherlands, and the largest port in Europe. Located on the banks of the River Nieuwe Maas (New Meuse), it is considered the major harbour of the country and the largest one in Europe. Due to its unique geographical location, its stylish modern buildings and its extraordinary economic and cultural attractiveness, Rotterdam is also known as 'Manhattan on the Mass' (URBED & van Hoek, 2007). The municipality covers an area of 319.35 square kilometres (of which 206.44 are land and 112.91 water), has a population density of about 2.850 people per square kilometre and forms a continuous urban area that represents the southern part of the Randstad, the sixth largest metropolitan area in Europe (ESPON, 2007; OECD, 2007).

Until recently, a substantial part of the city's economy revolved around its port, which is the largest in Europe, until it was relocated from the banks of the River Maas to the mouth of the river in the 1960s and 1970s. The river Maas creates both a natural and socioeconomic divide between North and South Rotterdam. Broadly speaking, North Rotterdam boasts prosperous and older neighbourhoods whilst southern areas are characterised by less wealthy neighbourhoods built during the post-war periods to house port workers. The latter form what is generally known as Rotterdam Zuid (South Rotterdam).

Since their development, southern neighbourhoods were left relatively isolated and functioned as first-recipient areas for newcomers to the city because of their affordable rents and lower cost of living. However, several

Urban Regeneration & Social Sustainability: Best Practice from European Cities, by Andrea Colantonio and Tim Dixon © 2011 Andrea Colantonio and Tim Dixon

Figure 9.1   Erasmus Bridge and other iconic development projects in South Rotterdam.
Source: Photograph by Andrea Colantonio (2008).

local and national development plans for Rotterdam devised since the late 1980s opened up new development opportunities for South Rotterdam, which included the waterfront redevelopment of part of the south bank, the extension of the metro and tram systems, and the building of the iconic Erasmus Bridge (see Figure 9.1).

These new development opportunities provided better connections between Southern and Northern neighbourhoods, leading, for example, to the transformation of the abandoned port area of Kop Van Zuip on the south bank of the River Maas. However, these regeneration efforts have not been exempt from criticisms concerning, for example, the fact that the positive impacts of waterfront redevelopment have been confined to spatial enclaves located along the Maas river, and as a result, failing to create 'spill over' benefits for the inland areas of southern municipalities.

This chapter therefore examines how 'South Pact' (Pact op Zuid), the latest regeneration programme embarked upon by Rotterdam municipal authorities, endeavours to comprehensively regenerate the city's southern neighbourhoods in an integrated fashion. It therefore begins with an historical overview of Rotterdam's urban development and the resultant marginalisation of southern areas. The chapter then reviews recent regeneration policies and urban development strategies promoted at national and local level, and concludes with an analysis of how social sustainability issues are being addressed and monitored within the South Pact initiative.

Within the chapter a special emphasis is placed on experimental indicators, such as the Sociale Index, which have been introduced in recent years by the municipality to monitor key aspects of the effectiveness of their urban regeneration policies. Within this context, it is important to highlight that these innovative indicators and monitoring systems will not be examined from an empirical point of view, that is, through the detailed investigation of their operational and practical implications. Rather, the principal aim of the analysis of these indices is to highlight the main methodological and theoretical issues involved in the measurement of social sustainability at city level. For these reasons, this chapter does not carry out an indicator-based analysis of the impact of South Pact regeneration policies on Rotterdam's southern municipalities, but it does examine the key rationale and methods adopted by city authorities to conceptualise the evaluation of their social policies.

Urban development and decline

Rotterdam's place in the urban hierarchy should be understood in terms of its relationship with other large towns and cities nearby (i.e. the Hague, Amsterdam and Utrecht), which as a totality are referred to as the Randstat ('Ringcity'), with some 7.5 m people or nearly half the country's population. In this context Rotterdam has often been seen as a 'working-class' city and relatively less attractive than its neighbours (Cadell *et al.*, 2008). Badly damaged during World War II, the docks in the city were relocated and modernised, which in turn left substantial amounts of dereliction and unemployment. Moreover, there was at this time a large outflow of people to the suburbs and a large inflow of immigrants from the former Dutch colonies and other parts of the world. Nearly 50% of the population are of non-Dutch origins or have at least one parent born outside the country, and recent figures show that Muslims comprise close to 25% of the city's population.

The urbanisation of the south bank of the River Maas dates back to the second half of the nineteenth century when the construction of docks, wharves and warehouses, mostly concentrated in the Kop van Zuid district, began in 1870. Between the nineteenth and the twentieth centuries, South Rotterdam prospered with the expansion of the harbour, which soon became a strategic terminal for ocean-going liners and a vital shipyard at international level. During these years of rapid economic expansion, several buildings and dwellings were built to house the regular flow of new workers employed in the port and in other riverside industries, which led to the formation of a working-class neighbourhood of 50000 inhabitants.

At the beginning twentieth century, subsequent urban expansions of the area were characterised by an increasing specialisation of the district in activities linked to the port functions. As a result, the district slowly became both physically and functionally poorly connected to Rotterdam's city centre. The trajectory of development in the southern areas were also severely impacted by the widespread diffusion of air travel and the containerisation revolution of the 1960s, which led to a substantial decline in passenger traffic between waterfronts and ports across the world and the closure of several piers and liner terminals in Rotterdam. In the Kop Van Zuid area, these innovations rendered most of the existing dock and warehousing facilities nearly useless, and shifted economic development away from the traditional port location (URBED & van Hoek, 2007).

As a result, the southern neighbourhoods entered a period of economic stagnation and social decline, which prompted an exodus of middle-class households and the escalation of social problems. More than ever, the waterfront and port areas began to be characterised by high unemployment, rising crime, low educational achievements, and lack of social cohesion due to the cultural diversity of its inhabitants, mostly immigrants who worked in the port (Dekker & van Kempen, 2004: 111). These conditions, coupled with a general decay of these neighbourhoods, meant that South Rotterdam acquired a very poor image, which rendered the area less attractive for private investment and for middle- to high-income people to move there (URBED & van Hoek, 2007).

From the 1980s onwards, these issues induced Rotterdam's City Council to begin the regeneration for the old port area through a series of wide-ranging programmes of physical and social rejuvenation. Broadly speaking, redevelopment plans followed four basic strategic lines (Legnani, 1996), including: (i) moving the residential functions to the suburbs; (ii) committing the city centre to tertiary activities; (iii) improving urban and physical infrastructure; and (iv) enhancing and expanding port facilities to the estuary of the River Maas, where large areas are not yet urbanised.

Following on from this, and as part of current redevelopment plans, municipal authorities are now trying to reduce the economic and social gap between the 'centre' and the 'periphery' of the city by mitigating the uneven development between the two sides of the city, and cooperating with regional and national authorities, and housing corporations and other private-sector actors to promote the regeneration of southern areas. The policy context of these efforts is reviewed in the next section of this chapter.

Policy context

The Netherlands has a long tradition of urban planning and development policies, predominantly based on decentralised government. Historically, local authorities have always been co-responsible for formulating and implementing urban development plans, with the exception of the 1940s and 1950s when central government assumed executive authority in all spheres of influence of Dutch political life, including functions relating to planning, urban regeneration, land use and housing policies, mainly due to the state of emergency engendered by World War II. However, after a massive post-war urban reconstruction and renewal process, which mainly aimed to improve the housing stocks in major urban areas, local governments regained shared control over urban policies.

Today, urban policies are therefore formulated and implemented at two main levels of government: central government and municipal level. More specifically, on one side, the central government, which is represented by the Ministry of Housing, Spatial Planning and the Environment, is responsible for the national spatial structure and coordinates the implementation of projects of national importance, as stressed by the new Land Development Act and new regulations for the development of building locations. The central government also collaborates with the municipalities and the private sector, and provides the legislative tools for urban development, besides offering the municipalities financial support for five years period programmes. On the other side, municipalities, which have become even more important than the provinces over recent years, formulate their own development programmes (land-use plans and housing plans, for example) and provide economic statements to central authorities and report on results achieved.

At a national level since the 1960s urban policy has endeavoured to curb urban sprawl in favour of compact urban developments in the Netherlands. This has provided additional development opportunities for the regeneration of the inner-city area and for inward investment in central neighbourhoods during the 1980s. In 1994, the 'Big Cities Policy' (GSB – *Grotestedenbeleid*; Priemus *et al.*, 2002; Dekker & van Kempen, 2004) was launched with the specific aim of addressing the problems still affecting the main Dutch cities since the post-war period. This policy emphasised the importance of the 'complete city', that is a city fulfilling the needs of its inhabitants, companies and visitors alike (Van Boxmeer & Van Beckhoven, 2005: 7).

Initially contemplated only as a revitalising policy for the four biggest cities – Amsterdam, Rotterdam, Den Haag and Utrecht – after a few years the Big City Policy also became the key urban policy instrument for medium-sized cities and towns. The policy was based on an integrated and inter-sectoral approach centred around three priority fields, referred to as 'pillars', which included:

1 Physical (urban renewal);
2 economic (employment, business, transport); and
3 social (education, quality of life, safety and social welfare).

This policy was supported by a financial instrument, which is the Investment Budget for Urban Renewal (ISV). Through this tool, budgetary resources were awarded for a period of five years to applicant municipalities who were responsible for formulating their own long-term development plans and were especially rewarded if they were able to create partnerships between public and private actors.

Rotterdam is a municipality and is run by its city council, which takes overall responsibility for the economic, spatial, and social development of the city, although there are also 11 sub-municipalities within the city (Cadell *et al.*, 2008). In the same way that other European cities have tried to build an economy based around the knowledge economy (see, for example, Cardiff in Chapter 6 of this book) Rotterdam has sought to position the city and aim for a more balanced development.

At the city level, Rotterdam has implemented a number of urban regeneration projects since the 1970s. Couch (2003), for example, reported how, in 1974, the city council focused on a major programme of some 11 urban renewal areas focusing on environmental and housing standards improvements in more than 60 000 dwellings, or a quarter of the total city. By the end of the 1980s, especially after the enactment of the Urban and Village Renewal Act in 1985, more than 36 000 dwellings in Rotterdam had been upgraded, alongside the improvement of local environmental conditions in many inner-city areas.

During the 1990s, this monodimensional and piecemeal approach to urban regeneration, emphasising the environmental and physical spheres of regeneration, was abandoned in favour of a more integrated approach to urban redevelopment. Instead the new model was centred around:

- Strategic urban visioning, as exemplified, for example, by the 2030 Spatial Development Strategy for Rotterdam (Gemeente Rotterdam, 2007) developed by local authorities;
- public private partnerships between central government, local authorities and private-sector actors, including, for example, housing corporations such as De Nieuwe Unie, Woningbedrijf Rotterdam, Com.Wonen, Vestia and Woonbron;
- a novel approach to urban renaissance, not limited exclusively to housing rehabilitation and environmental improvement, but also integrating better transport systems, improved urban design and management, increased economic development opportunities and competitiveness, and addressing social problems; and
- the creation of knowledge-broker organisations, such as KEI (Kenniscentrum Stedelijke Vernieuwing – Knowledge, Expertise, Innovation, Dutch Expert Centre Urban Regeneration), which bring together the knowledge and expertise of public and private practitioners and policy makers in urban regeneration in Holland.

In 2005 the City also began a programme of *Kansenzones* (KZ; or opportunity zones), which were based on a local policy aimed at strengthening depressed and deprived areas of Rotterdam through the promotion and encouragement of entrepreneurship. The KZ programme was implemented by the Rotterdam municipal agency, Ontwikkelingsbedrijf Rotterdam (OBR), which has a long history of promoting entrepreneurship amongst both native and local ethnic residents in Rotterdam. The KZ scheme, which is set within the national policy framework *'Grotestedenbeleid'* was focused on the southern part of the city, and was inspired by the work of Michael Porter (see Chapter 4 of this book; Gemeente Rotterdam, 2009b). Initially based around eight zones, three more zones were added later, and all are based in areas that are characterised by high unemployment rate, lack of business and social dislocation. Some €48 m were invested between 2005 and 2008 in the programme, which provided for a 50% subsidy for investments; a special property tax arrangement; Young Starters programme for coaching young entrepreneurs; provision of business-centre space (Business Centre Feijenoord and the Creative Factory); and from 2007 a labour cost subsidy (see Box 9.1 for further details).

These elements are new milestones underpinning one of the most ambitious regeneration programmes in Rotterdam to date, which endeavours to address the regeneration of southern municipalities holistically, as is explained in the next section of this chapter.

The regeneration of South Rotterdam and partnership arrangements

South Rotterdam comprises several neighbourhoods located on the south bank of the river Maas (see Figure 9.2) with nearly 234 000 inhabitants. Traditionally, this city area has been characterised by high unemployment, a poor image, and low educational achievement, which made it difficult to attract private investment or middle- to high-income people to these neighbourhoods (Cadell *et al.*, 2008). In addition, the area is characterised by high levels of crime and population mobility, because people move out of the area at the first opportunity whilst the most disadvantaged with lower incomes and education levels stay behind (Acioly *et al.*, 2007). As a result, some of these neighbourhoods have been classified as city 'hot spots' in terms of their safety record and social problems, and have been included in the list of 40 of the most deprived Dutch neighbourhoods in a recent policy document developed by the Ministry of Housing, Spatial Planning and the Environment. The municipality of Rotterdam has also been forced to take the extraordinary measure of banning 'socially problematic' individuals, for example with crime convictions or unemployed, from relocating to these 'hot spots' from other city areas (see also Box 9.2).

Box 9.1 *Kansenzones* (KZ): Rotterdam

Objectives

To improve the economic climate in designated areas of the city of Rotterdam by lowering the barriers for private investment through an integrated mix of incentives.

Actions

The Rotterdam KZ project is an integrated support scheme, which combines a range of measures to improve the investment climate in 11 areas of South Rotterdam. This includes a 50% subsidy for investments by entrepreneurs and landlords for capital expenditure or renovation of business premises (minimum grant of €2000 up to a maximum of €100 000). Banks can also provide less stringent loan criteria to entrepreneurs receiving such grants. In addition, part of the local property tax is 'given back' to the areas, and the district government and the shopkeepers jointly decide on how to invest this budget to improve the business environment.

Stakeholders

The main stakeholders are City of Rotterdam, Rotterdam City Development Corporation, City Districts of Charlois and Feijenoord, national government, shopkeepers and other entrepreneurs, banks, project developers, property owners and landlords, schools of professional education.

Resources and outcomes

City and national government each invest half of €48 m (2005–2008). In the same period, the municipality received 1400 applications for the KZ subsidy and about half of those were granted.

Further information

http://www.kansenzones.nl

Source: Federal Ministry of Transport, Building and Urban Affairs (2007); Gemeente Rotterdam (2009b); Ramsden (2010).

In 2004, a Neighbourhood Survey was conducted by several housing corporations in cooperation with municipal authorities in South Rotterdam. The survey highlighted: (i) a high level of residents' dissatisfaction with their areas and living environment; (ii) a lack of local identity because individual districts are insufficiently distinguishable from one another; (iii) little differentiation in the available housing stock that consists largely of multi-storey dwellings with a relatively low value, as illustrated in

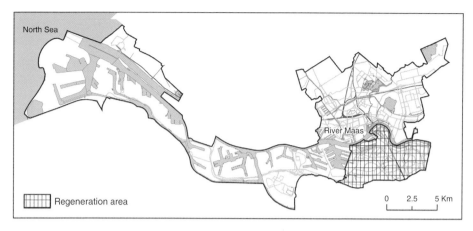

Figure 9.2   South Pact regeneration area. *Source*: Drawn by Venere Stefania Sanna (2009).

Figure 9.3   South Rotterdam. *Source*: Photograph by Andrea Colantonio (2008).

Figure 9.3; and (iv) high unemployment, poor safety and a lack of economic opportunities for increasingly impoverished local communities.

The results of the 2004 Neighbourhood Survey prompted consultations between housing corporations, municipal authorities, five sub-municipalities of South Rotterdam and Rotterdam City Development Corporation, which led to the signing of the 'South Pact' (Pact op Zuid) agreement at the end of 2005. The Pact endeavours to promote the revitalisation of South Rotterdam by intervening in the following three main policy areas (Pact op Zuid, 2006, 2007; Acioly *et al.*, 2007):

1 Creating thriving neighbourhoods by attracting back high- and middle-income residents; generating job opportunities for the unemployed; and promoting higher levels of education and reducing school drop outs amongst local residents.
2 Improving the attractiveness of neighbourhoods by improving the quality of living and the level of satisfaction of local residents with their living environment.
3 Increasing the competitiveness of South Rotterdam as a whole, by fostering local entrepreneurship and generating a safe environment that is able to attract private investment.

It is also clear that the concept of KZ served to inspire the development of the South Pact. As Ditty Blom, programme manager was quoted as saying (Gemeente Rotterdam, 2009b: 15):

When we started the Pact, the Opportunity Zones project was already running. It served as an inspiring example. The power of the Opportunity Zones lies in the notion that governmental organisations, instead of operating on their own, seek cooperation with their local partners from the very start. The Rotterdam South Pact aims at joining many forces. At streamlining the many projects developed by its partners and trying to make optimal use of each other's expertise. The Pact is thus able to operate boldly and efficiently and to really make a difference. The Opportunity Zones project works from the very same idea. The project not only boosts private enterprises, but also aims at enhancing the opportunities of the people living in Rotterdam South.

Partnership arrangements

The Pact op Zuid initiative envisages a joint additional investment programme for Rotterdam South running between 2006 and 2015. Broadly speaking, South Pact can be considered a public private partnership (Pact op Zuid, 2008a) set up to implement a set of extra measures and concerted investments in southern neighbourhoods. Indeed the Pact not only builds on existing initiatives, but also guarantees that measures are intensified and adjusted and geared to one another (Pact op Zuid, 2008b).

Table 9.1   Total investment forecast in South
Rotterdam 2006–2015.

Source	Amount in euros
Housing corporations	850 000 000
Local and national governments	171 000 000
Dutch corporations or public bodies	35 000 000
	1 056 000 000

Source: Pact op Zuid (2007).

The Pact encompasses several private and public actors, including:

- Five housing corporations (De Nieuwe Unie; Woningbedrijf Rotterdam; Com.Wonen; Vestia and Woonbron);
- Three departments of the municipality of Rotterdam (Department for Youth Education and Society, JOS; Department of Sport and Recreation; Department of Town Planning and Housing, dS+V);
- Rotterdam City Development Corporation; and
- Three sub-municipalities of South Rotterdam, including Feijenoord, Charlois and IJsselmonde.

It is forecast that up to 2015 the total investment in the area will be over €1 bn (Gemeente Rotterdam, 2007), as summarised in Table 9.1.

In terms of organisation and implementation, South Pact has a Board of Directors with a chairman and representatives from the municipal departments involved in the programme. The board is responsible for implementing an annual development plan, which is informed by decisions taken by a steering group. The latter is chaired by the Rotterdam alderman responsible for employment, social services and urban development policy, and comprises one representative each from five housing corporations and three sub-municipalities.

In the context of Rotterdam, and more generally of the Netherlands, it is important to highlight the important role that housing corporations play in developing and managing over one third of the national housing stock and an ever bigger proportion of local stock in many Dutch cities. Housing corporations were set up by many municipalities after the promotion of the Housing Act in 1901 to manage social housing in their urban areas. Their annual production of housing units grew from roughly 10 000 houses per year between 1916 and 1925 to some 125 000 houses in 1967 (Aedes, 2007), showing the key role they played in neighbourhood redevelopments in the post-war periods.

Housing corporations grew slowly from almost volunteer-based organisations in the 1910s to 'government branch offices' and key executors of housing policy by the 1970s (Aedes, 2007). However, in the 1980s and 1990s, the government's involvement in social housing shrank because of increasing

debt pressures and financial cutbacks, until 1995, when housing corporations become operationally and financially independent from, but still politically linked to, the Dutch Government. Nowadays, these corporations are
essentially entrepreneurial with social objectives, which are developing into
market-driven social landlords with broad packages of buildings and services geared towards the satisfaction of the needs of not only low-income and
disadvantaged sectors of society but also middle- and high-income groups.

Nonetheless, interviews with key stakeholders revealed how the South
Pact programme does not have an office in South Rotterdam. This may limit
the ability of local residents to identify those Pact officers responsible for
the implementation of specific projects and to actively participate in the
planning stages of project proposals. This is also surprising, given that two
of the fundamental components of the South Pact programme are: (i) the
participation of local residents in the decision-making process of the Pact;
and (ii) their 'indirect' consultation concerning satisfaction with their local
areas through the questionnaire survey included in the Sociale Index (which
is discussed in more detail in the next section of this chapter).

Social sustainability

Rotterdam City is today promoting the integrated regeneration of its
southern neighbourhoods, by addressing social, physical, economic and
cultural concerns simultaneously. South Pact can be defined as a combination of people-based and area-based approaches to regeneration, in which
the local government (people-based aspect) works in cooperation with sub-
municipalities (area-based aspect) to identify a set of policies and programmes aimed a targeting specific groups or sectors of residents living in
the southern neighbourhoods.

At an institutional level, this has meant a restructuring of the modus oper-
andi of several city departments, which now have a designated 'area manager'
responsible for the integrated decision making and intra-departmental management of the regeneration process of southern areas in direct cooperation
with representatives of sub-municipalities or areas involved in the scheme.

As illustrated earlier, Pact op Zuid focuses on three main objectives, each
of which has social sustainability themes embedded in it. First, one of the
main instruments to create thriving neighbourhoods is to encourage social
mixing by attracting back high- and middle-income residents to low-income
settlements in southern areas. It is generally believed that higher income
classes will stimulate the demand for better local goods and services, such
as schools and health care, which will benefit lower income residents.
Wealthier newcomers will also stimulate the demand for better quality
housing, thus increasing the value of local houses. Critics of this approach,

however, point out the risk of gentrification and displacement effects that this strategy may engender in local areas. Furthermore, they criticise the economic rational of the social-mixing approach, arguing that this concept has been promoted by housing corporations, to simply build higher standard houses to diversify and increase the value of their stock.

Second, the attractiveness of neighbourhoods is expected to be improved by strengthening the identity of local districts and by improving their live-ability and the quality of their open spaces (Pact op Zuid, 2008a). At present, many southern areas lack a sense of community due to a high level of cultural diversity stemming from over 160 nationalities and ethnic groups living together. The latter often have limited knowledge of the Dutch language, which poses an obstacle to communication within local communities. In this context, several initiatives have been geared towards the enhancement of social networks and collective identity in South Rotterdam. For example, in the Pedendretch district, a theatre performance initiative entitled 'Monologues and Dialogues' has encouraged foreign local residents to describe the customs of their countries in order to overcome diffidence and break down cultural barriers between local residents.

Third, the main foundations for increasing the competitiveness of South Rotterdam are the promotion of programmes aimed at improving the business skills of local entrepreneurs and the creation of a safe and healthy environment to attract private investment. Thus, an abandoned warehouse has been redesigned to host start-up creative-industry companies; several construction companies building in South Rotterdam are contractually bound to employ 10–15% of their workforce for regeneration projects from within local communities. In addition, the Quaker Oat company, which has a factory in South Rotterdam, has committed itself to offering healthy breakfasts to primary school pupils in three schools in the area.

The achievements of these three objectives is also complemented by several innovative tools also being deployed by Rotterdam City to experiment with new ways of addressing old problems. One of these experiment is '169 *Klushuizen*', summarised in Box 9.2, in which poor quality empty houses are sold to private buyers for a very low price on condition that the buyer carries out the renovation and upgrading of the house and lives there for at least 3–5 years (Gemeente Rotterdam, 2009c). Rotterdam City Development Corporation is also promoting a new home-selling scheme, which allows potential buyers to live for up to two weeks in houses that are for sale across South Rotterdam. The main objective of this experiment is to allow potential buyers to 'experience' the area first hand and decide whether or not to move in.

Together with these new experimental tools, in recent years Rotterdam City has developed several indicator systems to assess and monitor the social development of its neighbourhoods. These include the 'Sociale

Box 9.2   The 169 Klushuizen programme in South Rotterdam

The 'hot spots' approach

In 2002 the newly elected municipal administration identified the nine most dilapidated neighbourhoods across Rotterdam (the so called 'hot spots'), which were characterised by a high percentage of rented homes in decayed and derelict conditions (in some cases 95% of stock) as well as illegal occupation, and an unclean and unsafe public realm. These neighbourhoods had also been abandoned by the middle classes who looked for quieter, cleaner and safer suburban areas.

The 169 Klushuizen programme
The 'Klushuizen' programme (Do-It-Yourself Homes) was therefore set up to attract buyers and higher income first-home buyers back to the so-called 'hot spots'. In the scheme the municipality purchases a large number of rundown buildings that are located in the hot-spot areas of the city and sells these dwellings at a bargain price to enthusiastic young people. The buyers have to carry out the renovation and upgrading of the house, where they need to live for at least 3–5 years. They are assisted by architects and special civil servants responsible for issuing permits and other expert advisors.

   Strategic objectives of the programme:
   - Attract buyers to run-down neighbourhoods;
   - change the neighbourhoods' negative image; and
   - transform the neighbourhoods into trendy and vibrant areas.

   Results achieved in Rotterdam:
   - Some four thousand applicants registered for a DIY home;
   - groups of young creative residents have been attracted to the hot-spot areas selected by the municipality;
   - the freedom of choice and the large degree of the residents' input into the layout of their home resulted in a greater diversity of dwellings;
   - the refurbishment process has produced an increase in the value of dwellings;
   - the programme has prompted a process of social mixing in the these troublesome neighbourhoods;
   - more housing for less money – starters on the housing market get a chance to buy – participants buy their dwelling at cost price instead of at the market value;
   - the partnership between residents and institutional actors is reinforced;
   - the neighbourhood's identity is enhanced; and
   - good example to others (residents, other DIYers, housing associations, (sub)municipalities).

Source: Geemente Rotterdam (2009c).

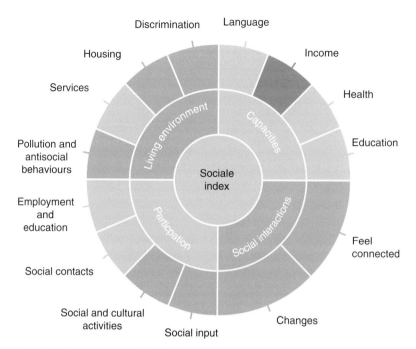

Figure 9.4 The Sociale Index. *Source*: Translated and redrawn by Colantonio from Gemeente Rotterdam (2008). Reproduced by permission of City of Rotterdam.

Index', the 'Safety Index', the 'Travel Guide to South Rotterdam' and the 'Neighbourhood Watch System'.

The 'Sociale Index' (see Figure 9.4) is a composite index launched in 2008, analysing the social qualities of Rotterdam's administrative neighbourhoods. The index collects and aggregates data concerning four main dimensions of Rotterdam's areas and their residents (Leidelmeijer *et al.*, 2007), including: (i) personal abilities (language skills, health, income, education); (ii) living environment (level of discrimination, housing, public facilities, safety, etc.); (iii) participation (going to work/school, social contact, social and cultural activities, etc.); and (iv) 'bonding' (mobility, 'feeling connected', etc.). The index produces a score between 0 and 10, which has four main purposes (Koppelaar, 2009; Leidelmeijer *et al.*, 2007; Gemeente Rotterdam, 2008), including:

- Measuring the social qualities of a place at a given time;
- showing and comparing the differences between 64 of the 80 districts of Rotterdam;
- providing a baseline for the assessment of policies; and
- analysing the strengths and weaknesses of each neighbourhood in terms of the dimensions included in the index.

The index, which is calculated yearly, comprises statistical (30%) and survey (70%) data.

The Sociale Index is relatively new, and no comprehensive evaluation of the pros and cons of this index have been carried out thus far. It is clear, however, that this index embodies the main characteristics of emerging sustainability indicators reviewed in Chapter 3. Indeed, the Sociale Index is a multi-dimensional and hybrid indicator in the sense that it endeavours to aggregate different social sustainability themes together through a mix of qualitative (survey to measure participation and bonding) and quantitative data (official statistics for living environment and personal abilities) analysis. In addition, data for the calculation of the Sociale Index is gathered at neighbourhood level in order to provide an overview of how people live together, participate in local community activities and feel connected with each other (RIGO, 2007).

It is worth noting that the Sociale Index is often used in conjunction with the 'Safety Index', which is another important indicator launched in 2003 by the municipality in order to assess the safety of it districts and identify possible 'hot spots'. As in the Sociale Index, the Safety Index combines a number of objective data (number of crimes committed, number of people reporting crime to the police, etc.) and subjective data (perceptions of safety, etc.). The index produces a score of between 1 and 10, which indicates the safety level of a given area. The index, which is calculated yearly, includes statistical and survey data.

A considerable number of neighbourhoods in South Rotterdam were classified as 'socially problematic' and 'unsafe' in a monitoring survey that Rotterdam City carried out in the 2003–2006 period. (Acioly *et al.*, 2007). Some of them have been included in the national list (composed by the Dutch Ministry of Housing and Spatial Planning and Environment) of neighbourhoods that need special policy attention. In these areas, the municipality of Rotterdam pursues a 'no-tolerance' approach towards drugs trafficking and illegal housing, which also includes preventive screening of people who enter these areas labelled as unsafe or 'hot spots' (see also Box 9.1 and 9.2). The improvement of safety in these hot spots is measured and published as the 'Safety Index', which not only monitors the safety situation of unsafe areas but allows policy makers to adjust city-wide policies when the achieved results are deemed unsatisfactory.

A third important monitoring element of the social sustainability of South Pact areas, is the 'Travel Guide' or *Reisgids* to South Rotterdam, which is an illustrative guide concerning the socioeconomic characteristics of Rotterdam's southern neighbourhoods (Gemeente Rotterdam, 2009a). The first *Reisgids* was developed in 2008 (Pact op Zuid, 2008c) by higher education institutions in collaboration with South Pact officers in order to improve information concerning southern municipalities and enhance the image of

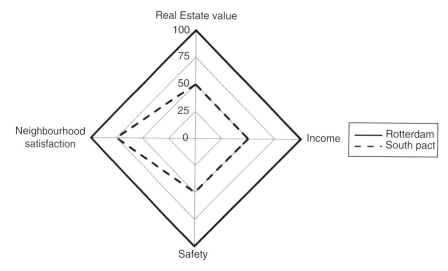

Figure 9.5 Travel Guide Monitoring System. *Source*: Translated and adapted by Colantonio from Pact op Zuid (2008c). Reproduced by permission of Pact op Zuid.

local communities. Contrary to its name, the Travel Guide is not a guide-book intended to entice tourists to visit the city in the traditional sense. Rather, the guide endeavours to narrate a journey through statistical data that might be useful to propelling forward and sharpening up government policy and activities. It is a journey of numbers and statistics, a visual jour-ney leading past districts and neighbourhoods, a voyage through the experi-ences of professionals and local residents (Pact op Zuid, 2008c: 11).

The guide combines photographic material, personal narratives and statis-tical data, which together provide a comprehensive image of the social and economic progress in South Pact neighbourhoods. According to the authors, the *Reisgids* focuses primarily on stories of success and failure of projects, and on the experience of local residents, entrepreneurs, organisations and municipal departments working together for the first time. From a data-analysis perspective, the Travel Guide provides snapshots of each neigh-bourhood through the visualisation of web diagrams (see Figure 9.5), which compare each neighbourhood in terms of: (i) income; (ii) security/safety; (iii) house values; and (iv) community satisfaction with the average for Rotterdam City. The 'Rest of Rotterdam' is represented in each web diagram as the benchmark (index = 100%), whilst the data of the first travel guide produced in 2008 offers a baseline for the measurement of the progress of South Pact because data was collected in 2006 or earlier, that is, before the beginning of South Pact.

The less publicised monitoring elements of South Pact is, the 'Neighbourhood Watch System', which is a monitoring system deployed

internally and confidentially by several city departments to assess the negative socioeconomic evolution of specific city areas. The system looks at
elements such as houses to be demolished, squatter houses, unemployment,
people on social benefits, crime rate, etc., which signal the possible social
deterioration of an area and trigger 'alarms' when specific values hits minimum thresholds, indicating that action is required.

The neighbourhood watch system is currently being used internally by
the municipality of Rotterdam, so, due to its confidentiality, it proved difficult to gather more in-depth information on this system during the fieldwork conducted in Rotterdam. There can be little doubt, however, that this
is an additional monitoring initiative, which is intended to inform social
and urban regeneration policies in South Rotterdam in an effective fashion.

As pointed out in the introduction, the in-depth analysis of these indices
and their results is outside the scope of this chapter. However, it is clear that
Rotterdam and South Pact can be considered to be at the forefront of measuring the social sustainability of urban regeneration in Europe, despite the fact
that municipal authorities are still facing the old dilemma of whether to use
people-based indicators or area-based metrics in order to assess their interventions in South Rotterdam. As mentioned earlier, the southern areas
exhibit a high degree of mobility amongst local residents, which prevents
the effective assessment of the impact of municipal policies in the social and
public realm. For example, many local residents benefit from area-based initiatives before becoming better off and moving out of the area. This makes it
difficult to trace the effectiveness of local projects on people's socioeconomic
conditions. In addition, the improvement of the social qualities of a place
and related social change can take generations to fulfil. It is therefore important that the assessment of social policies is carried out in the medium and
long term, together with yearly monitoring.

Conclusions

The South Pact of Rotterdam is an ambitious integrated programme of trans-
disciplinary and cross-departmental regeneration initiatives, involving public and private actors. It is also important to note that the South Pact is
effectively a charter that adopts a holistic and integrated approach to housing, sociocultural facilities, health education, training, economic investment and entrepreneurship. In this sense the development of the KZ
programme was key to underpinning the South Pact (Gemeente Rotterdam,
2009b), and is an example of a zonal approach to private sector stimulation
(in a similar way to the waiving or reduction of tax and social security
charges in the French *Zones Franches Urbaine* for example (Federal Ministry
of Transport, Building and Urban Affairs, 2007).

The South Pact programme is still in its infancy, and it is difficult to forecast how the economic downturn, which began in 2008, will impact on the investment programme. There can be little doubt, however, that the city has invested in developing effective and comprehensive systems of monitoring indicators, ranging from the 'Sociale Index' to the 'Safety Index'. These have become essential tools for the assessment of urban development and regeneration policies. Nonetheless, the maintenance of non-routinely collected data sets and the yearly conducting of questionnaire surveys may have significant cost implications for municipal financial resources. For this reason, from 2010 onwards the Statistical Office of the City of Rotterdam is planning to publish the 'Sociale Index' every two years rather than on a yearly basis. Thus, it is important that alternative cost-effective methodologies are developed to conduct local surveys, for example with the involvement of local communities and educational organisations, or that readily available data is identified and used as proxy variables for 'soft data' to be included in the index. Furthermore, it is essential that indices providing aggregated and potentially superficial social representations of places, are not manipulated for political purposes or used in ways that could lead to the, stigmatisation, of city areas.

The chapter has also highlighted the importance of the private sector in urban regeneration, and shown that private-sector actors holding and managing significant amounts of housing stock, such as the Dutch housing corporations, can play a major financial and operational role in urban regeneration, which goes beyond mere housing maintenance. High-quality housing and services provision, which has been used as a tool to encourage social mixing in South Rotterdam, can help reduce the stigma and bad reputation of degraded neighbourhoods. However, it is important that the economic rationale underpinning social mixing is embedded in the pursuit of broader social objectives in order to avoid the re-casting of older gentrification policies in 'new clothes', and to minimise the displacement of less able sectors of society.

10

Leipzig East and the Socially Integrative City ('*Soziale Stadt*') Programme

Robin Ganser

Introduction

The Eastern areas of Germany or the '*Neue Bundesländer*' (new regions), of which Leipzig is a part, are still facing major challenges of urban regeneration due to their unique history throughout the twentieth and early twenty-first centuries.

For example, in 1990, the City of Leipzig was faced with a difficult inheritance: the quality and quantity of apartments offered on the housing market was very poor and some 25 000 apartments were uninhabitable. At this time the region also witnessed large-scale housing development, but the renovation of old properties was impeded by a complicated legal situation regarding property ownership and restitution claims in the wake of German reunification (www.leipzig.de/int/en/stadt_leipzig/stadtentw/wohnen). Before reunification the city was also affected by a lack of resources for urban regeneration, which led to the dereliction of '*Gründerzeit*' quarters, dating from the Wilhelminian era, and large-scale edge-of-city 'slab' building projects in order to make up for the loss of urban fabric. More than 85 000 apartments from that era have been fully or partially refurbished and renovated since 1991. As a result, only about 20% of the nineteenth-century architectural fabric is currently in need of refurbishment. At the same time, an 'overlap' of developmental and social issues is hindering the development of less-favoured districts whilst refurbished '*Gründerzeit*' quarters are enjoying increasing popularity as attractive residential areas.

Urban Regeneration & Social Sustainability: Best Practice from European Cities, by Andrea Colantonio and Tim Dixon   © 2011 Andrea Colantonio and Tim Dixon

Leipzig makes a highly interesting case study of urban regeneration in Germany not only due to its unique history but also because the city has always been at the forefront of testing the latest urban-regeneration concepts. Hence, Leipzig has been coined an 'urban laboratory' for regeneration. In this context it is also common knowledge that recent lord mayors of Leipzig as well as deputy mayors all had a specific interest in urban regeneration – some of them subsequently moving on to take over this portfolio as secretary of state in Berlin.

This chapter therefore focuses on Leipzig East (*Leipziger Osten*) as a case study, which covers several suburbs east of the city centre. The chapter begins with an overview of the policy context, covering the transition from 'redevelopment' to 'regeneration' in Germany, culminating in the emergence of the Socially Integrative City. The chapter then goes on to examine the regeneration of Leipzig East in more detail, in terms of its funding structures and partnership arrangements, before examining how social sustainability has been promoted, and how it has been measured and monitored. The chapter concludes with a review of the lessons learned for social sustainability and how important 'integration' has been in terms of not only institutional responses and governance/community structures but also in terms of physical scale in the area and the city as a whole.

Policy context

From redevelopment to regeneration

Modern legislation and linked funding programmes targeting urban regeneration were introduced in Germany as early as 1971 (*Städtebauförderungsgesetz*; StBauFG) and were integrated in mainstream planning law in the 1980s. Urban regeneration has come a long way since then. The initial purpose of the so called 'urban development aid legislation' was to provide a planning instrument that not only allowed responsible public planning bodies to draft a detailed planning framework at the local level but also gave them implementation powers in order to ensure urban restructuring. This includes wide ranging compulsory purchase powers. The spatial focus of this planning instrument – which is still used today – is on urban areas that suffer from specified structural deficiencies such as failing infrastructure, dereliction, unfit housing, etc. In this context the technical term '*Sanierungsgebiet*' (redevelopment area) was introduced to label the formally designated area that was to be targeted with regeneration measures. A distinction is made between redevelopment in order to overcome deficits of physical substance (buildings, infrastructure, etc.) and redevelopment with the aim of reinstating or, if necessary, changing the specific urban functions of the area (e.g. provision of certain types of housing, services, infrastructure, etc.).

As regeneration activity regularly requires large public-funding commitments the urban development aid legislation also introduced an instrument to recoup betterment. In this context the difference between land values before the start of redevelopment and after its completion is calculated in order to establish the economic impact of the redevelopment measures (BauGB, 2004, section 152 *et seq.*). Land owners are required to pay an adjustment fee which is directly linked to this increase in land value. On the other hand, land and property owners are given the opportunity to tap into subsidies in order to improve private buildings according to the objectives set for the redevelopment area.

The usage of this planning instrument requires a formal council decision and the exact delineation of redevelopment area boundaries, which have to be based on a preliminary analysis of the area and its structural deficiencies. A core strength of the planning instrument is (Jacoby *et al.*, 2008) streamlining of the redevelopment process due to local planning authorities being vested with wide-ranging planning, controlling and enforcement powers and the direct link between planning instrument and funding streams furthers swift implementation. An additional benefit in this context is the minimisation of speculation with land values as the local authority controls the redevelopment of the land – if necessary by means of compulsory purchase on the basis of a Legally Binding Land-Use Plan (section 30 BauGB, 2004).

Right from the inception of redevelopment areas, social issues were legally defined as part of the material considerations that have to be addressed in the planning process. However, the interpretation of social considerations in the 1970s was – in part – quite different to today's planning philosophy. The legislation places the main emphasis on the following two social issues: First, the planning authorities are required to inform owners, leaseholders and other stakeholders as early as possible and to discuss with them the proposed redevelopment area. Second, the authorities are required to develop a 'social plan' the core purpose of which is to ensure adequate re-housing and avoidance of unintended financial hardship due to redevelopment measures. This, of course, was directly linked to the planning paradigm of the early 1970s, which favoured wholesale clearance and redevelopment of urban quarters rather than developing endogenous potentials and careful restructuring while preserving existing neighbourhoods and communities. Current ideas of social enablement, education and furthering neighbourhood spirit, etc., are not catered for by this planning instrument, which is clearly focused on physical interventions to date.

Redevelopment Areas are still an important planning instrument today and are incorporated in Chapter 2 of the Federal Building Code – an act of parliament providing the legal framework for Planning and Building: '*Baugesetzbuch*' (BauGB). It comprises all the legislation that is relevant for urban regeneration and redevelopment. This is also referred to as 'Special

Urban Planning Legislation'. According to the statutory objectives, urban redevelopment areas are designated for the purpose of substantially improving or transforming an area in order to alleviate urban deficits. In this context the focus still is on physical issues, which is reflected in the legal definition of 'deficits' (section 136 BauGB, 2004).

While redevelopment areas still prove very effective in remedying physical shortfalls, the planning instrument comes with the following implementation problems, which led to the development of alternative planning instruments (Jacoby *et al.*, 2008). Core issues are negative land values, which may lead to problems with regard to calculating and recouping betterment from landowners – or in some cases rendering this impossible when the increase in land value is not sufficient to absorb private investment in the scope of redevelopment measures.

Another obstacle of the instrument is the necessity of relatively complex management and controlling activities as well as required know how. In particular, smaller planning authorities with less specialised personnel may be overwhelmed by the tasks at hand.

Additionally, local authorities face a comparatively high economic risk due to the necessity to provide match funding up front, which can only be recouped later in the process – and only providing that the issue of negative land values, mentioned above, does not arise of course.

The core strengths of redevelopment areas – wide ranging planning, controlling and enforcement powers – may also turn into one of the core hindrances for the implementation of this instrument. This is regularly the case when private sector stakeholders are reluctant to join public private partnership schemes where the public sector has almost complete control of the redevelopment projects, which in turn means that – theoretically – private interests can easily be overruled in the process. Private-sector participation is therefore dependent upon the fine balance between the public sector bearing the main economic risks but also gaining much influence on redevelopment outcomes. If the former is attractive enough private investment can be attracted – if the latter dominates, the chances are that it will be difficult to lever in private funding. Some of these problems have been addressed by allowing local authorities to delegate powers to a redevelopment corporation, which can be a private entity with specific know how and relevant experience.

Nonetheless it became clear that redevelopment areas with their focus on physical regeneration and a strictly area-based approach were not geared to dealing with the multiplicity and complexity of problems that many local authorities were facing after the reunification of the Eastern and Western parts of Germany. These issues not only comprised dereliction, overheated housing markets ins some parts and failing demand in other regions and poor infrastructure, but to also the necessity of increasing the competitiveness, particularly of Eastern '*Bundesländer*', and of improving education levels in disadvantaged urban areas as well as ensuring an equal quality of life in the whole of Germany. Therefore a range of new formal planning instruments and funding programmes was developed. These included '*Stadtumbaugebiete*' (Urban Regeneration Areas), which were introduced in the scope of the 2004 planning reforms. Regeneration areas can be designated either as complementary to redevelopment areas or instead of them, and address a wider set of issues, which include failing property markets. In this context legal provision is made to subsidise the demolition of substandard and/or vacant properties (Battis *et al.*, 2007). It is important to note in this context that a strategic approach to demolition is adopted, which can entail the demolition of properties on the urban fringe in order to preserve and regenerate inner city quarters with buildings of historic or heritage value.

A key difference to redevelopment areas is therefore noticeable in that less rigorous tests are applied when checking whether the designation is justified. This is understandable as regeneration areas are less powerful and usually less obtrusive planning instruments – giving planning authorities less control but at the same time more flexibility. The latter also relates to the indicators that signify that the presuppositions for designating a regeneration area are present. After all, the purpose of regeneration areas is to create long-term sustainability, which in turn implies that designated areas do not necessarily suffer from physical dereliction or the other statutorily defined structural deficits. In fact, it is conceivable that regeneration areas include precautionary measures in order to avoid structural problems or to tackle them early in the process. Furthermore, the instrument relies on a consensual approach and the use of legal agreements between public- and private-sector stakeholders. The latter is seen as a strength of this instrument (Jacoby *et al.*, 2008) as it avoids one of the potential problems of redevelopment areas (i.e. perceived overly strong influence of the public sector) and thereby promotes public private partnerships.

Additional benefits of regeneration areas include a lower economic risk for the local authority mainly due to the fact that public acquisition of land and buildings (based on section 85, subsection 1, No. 7 BauGB, 2004) is usually not necessary in the context of this consensual approach to regeneration. Although the planning powers and therefore local authority influence on regeneration is rather limited when compared with redevelopment areas, public-sector funding is nonetheless available.

The main strengths described before can potentially turn into a great weakness, however. On the one hand, the principle of consensus can lead to prolonged discussions and negotiations between different public and private stakeholders. This can influence the overall duration of the planning process as well as of the implementation of regeneration measures. On the other hand, there are no robust enforcement or default powers that would enable local authorities to safeguard and streamline implementation.

Although regeneration areas' main statutory objectives are still focused on structural physical improvements, social issues have also gained more importance. In this context improvements of the living and working environment are amongst the core objectives. However, the investigation and improvement of social sustainability issues is still clearly limited in this context.

The socially integrative city

The new planning instrument of '*Soziale Stadt*' (Socially Integrative City – also known as Social City) was also introduced as part of the 2004 planning reforms because it had become apparent that – in addition to physical and economic regeneration – particular emphasis has to be placed on the resolution of social problems (section 171e BauGB, 2004; www.sozialestadt.de/programm). In this context the planning instruments described above were only of limited use mainly because the criteria that triggered the employment of these instruments were too narrowly defined. For the implementation of this new instrument, therefore, a different set of criteria was defined, which mainly focused on social issues: namely 'severe disadvantages' with regard to the social structure and/or the economic situation of the residential and working population in areas of 'special (re)development need' (DIFU, 2008). As a rule of thumb the 'Socially Integrative City' areas are usually far larger than 'Redevelopment Areas'. This is mainly due to the fact that, on the one hand, the criteria for their designation are broader and, on the other hand, the social problems, the resolution of which are at the heart of this planning instrument, require the coverage of a wider area as opposed to planning tools, which are focused on physical redevelopment, which usually relates to clearly defined, spatially limited areas.

In a similar way to the other planning instruments, the designated Socially Integrative City areas can tap into a special funding programme. The funding programme strives to foster and to promote future-oriented urban development in districts with acute needs and social sustainability is at the heart of this programme. The unique spatial, cultural economical and environmental setting and its interrelationship with social issues provide a compulsory starting point for regeneration considerations and local objectives.

The programme seeks to tap into the existing social capital and to empower residents by providing them with better education, skills base, and knowledge. It also seeks to promote the image of each district, to foster the sense of place, and to increase local residents' personal identification with their neighbourhoods. In order to achieve this, the programme works on the premise of spatially grounded social interaction and active resident

participation (BMVBS, 2008). Across the whole of Germany some 500 neighbourhoods in around 320 cities and communities were designated as Socially
Integrative City programme areas (BMVBS, 2008).

The management of the complex programme – within the setting of the
German planning system, which is characterised by its tiered, federal structure – created an increased demand for opportunities of knowledge exchange,
cooperation across city and '*Länder*' (regions) boundaries, and to coordinate
public-relations campaigns. All levels of government and administration are
involved: federal, regional, municipal and neighbourhood. In due course the
Federal Ministry of Transport, Building, and Urban Affairs (Bundesministerium für Verkehr Bau und Stadtentwicklung; BMVBS), represented by the
Federal Office for Building and Regional Planning (Bundesamt für Bauwesen
und Raumordnung; BBR), employed the German Institute of Urban Affairs
(Deutsches Institut für Urbanistik; DIFU) to provide scientific advice and
guidance throughout the first phase of programme implementation.

From the outset the 'Socially Integrative City' programme was devised as
a 'learning system' the policy objectives and implementation of which
could be adapted – based on experiences from pilot projects and applied
research results. This idea makes sense particularly when considered in
the context of the planning system in the German federal state where traditionally the individual regions, sub-regions and local authorities have a
certain degree of freedom when implementing and further developing planning instruments. In fact the competition between different concepts and
implementation approaches are a strong point of this system, which very
often leads to innovation that is adapted and adopted from one region to
another in due course. The organisational structure incorporates bottom-
up as well as top-down elements, thereby practically mirroring the German
planning system.

Strategic elements of programme implementation are bundling of funding
streams and pooling of personnel and other resources, local empowerment
and participation, as well as the creation of tailored organisational structures
at the local level – including the neighbourhood level. Further to this, the
designation of Socially Integrative City areas has to be based on an in-depth
analysis of spatial context, strengths and weaknesses and an integrated regeneration strategy document, which is coordinated with other planning documents. Furthermore, programme implementation depends on monitoring
systems, which cover material- and process-related considerations.

Similar to regeneration areas, the criteria that define the presuppositions
of the formal designation are more flexible than for redevelopment areas. In
fact, in some cases the designation is also justified as a preventative measure
(BMVBS, 2008). This can be particularly helpful to avoid a problematic social
structure due to selective segregation, which usually leads to stigmatisation
of neighbourhoods or entire urban quarters.

Strategic fields of activity with particular social emphasis include the promotion of social stability and homeownership, as well as diversification of social services (BMVBS, 2008). The former highlights that a positive link between ownership and responsibility as well as buy-in into the neighbourhood is expected – an idea that was already reflected in the English right-to-buy schemes. In this context, recent research suggests that homeownership does not automatically result in positive development. In fact, for some households on the margins of affordability, this dream can turn into a nightmare with the possibility of mortgage arrears, negative equity and even the repossession of properties (Jones, 2007). It is apparent that homeownership does not always provide a sense of social security and it may therefore be assumed that related positive effects on social well-being and neighbourhoods are also not guaranteed.

According to BMVBS (2008) schooling and education issues have continually grown in importance in conjunction with labour-market integration, whereby particular emphasis is placed on the transition from education to professional life.

Another core programme area is the integration of ethnic minorities and migrants. This endeavour coincides with the National Integration Plan, a federal government initiative launched in 2007. Socially Integrative City integration strategies at the neighbourhood level include promotion of German as a foreign language, education, fostering an ethnic economy, improving opportunities for migrants to participate and contribute, and heightening the intercultural awareness of local government and social services. In general, it appears to be easier to achieve local integration if neighbourhood projects are supported by a coherent, city-wide integration policy (BMVBS, 2008).

Although quality of life is at the heart of the Socially Integrative City – promotion of a healthy lifestyle and sports only plays a subordinate role in the programme. However, health promotion is gaining importance in the context of implementation. This is due to various factors, including the cooperation between the Federal Ministry of Transport, Building and Urban Affairs and the Federal Ministry of Health, which began in 2007. District-based health promotion strategies include the formation of health networks, the development of target-group specific health-promotion services and infrastructure such as healthcare centres, health shops and health clubs (BMVBS, 2008). In this context it appears particularly important to improve the cooperation between health and planning authorities – which in the past was virtually nonexistent.

All of the above planning instruments have been used in Leipzig. In this context some instruments have been used in parallel or in sequence and the boundaries of designated areas are not always congruent. Both can help to address the identified regeneration issues – making sure that the spatial coverage as well as programme-specific regeneration objectives are appropriate.

Case study area Leipzig East – urban development and decline

'*Leipziger Osten*' (Leipzig East) encompasses several suburbs to the east of Leipzig's city centre (see Figure 10.1). It is home to a population of 27 000 and covers an area of 347 hectares. The area is part of the city-wide redevelopment and regeneration activities and is covered by several statutory redevelopment and regeneration designations.

This mainly residential area is characterised by dense, late nineteenth-century block structures and large-panel construction development stemming from the German Democratic Republic (GDR). The latter is generally of comparatively low structural quality (see Figures 10.2 and 10.3).

Historically, the area was known as the 'graphics quarter' due to the dominance of publishing companies and printing works and the residents were mostly 'working class'. During World War II the area suffered considerable damage, from which the industrial sector never recovered. During the GDR regime only limited resources for reconstruction and maintenance of the built environment were available, which led to further physical decline.

Since the late 1970s, pre-fabricated substitute housing has been built, and some nineteenth-century housing stock was modernised. Urban regeneration received a boost after reunification when particular emphasis was placed on inserting new physical and social infrastructure as well as establishing new open and green spaces in formerly heavily built-up neighbourhoods, thereby transforming brownfield and derelict sites by means of 'soft' land uses (see Figures 10.4 and 10.5).

Following on from German reunification, the official designation of urban redevelopment and regeneration areas covering parts of the '*Leipziger Osten*' initiated a comprehensive process of regeneration (www.leipziger-osten.de). However, this became increasingly difficult from the late 1990s due to worsening fiscal conditions and declining demand for rehabilitated housing, and so Leipzig East lost out to more attractive city districts and to the suburbs.

The main problems of Leipzig East are caused by the wider 'shrinkage' of Leipzig as a consequence of:

- Sharp decline in birth rate;
- substantial out-migration to the western '*Bundesländer*'; and
- suburbanisation processes.

This caused a downturn in housing markets and a movement away form the area towards the more affluent parts of the city. In the same way, poorer households moved into the area, which gives a present-day demographic structure of an ageing population but also one characterised by a high proportion of children and adolescents. Among less-well-off new arrivals

Figure 10.1 Overview of regeneration and redevelopment designations in Leipzig. *Source:* Leipzig (2009).

Figure 10.2 GDR large-slab construction. *Source*: Photograph by Robin Ganser (2008).

FIGURE **10.3** Wilhelminian era building blocks – partially refurbished. *Source*: Photograph by Robin Ganser (2008).

Figure 10.4 New green infrastructure (parks and footpath networks). *Source*: Photograph by Robin Ganser (2008).

Figure 10.5 New green infrastructure (new play areas for different age groups) in Leipzig East. *Source*: Photograph by Robin Ganser (2008).

were a large number of migrant households and ethnic German immigrants from Eastern Europe, and the proportion of migrants in Leipzig East is higher than the average for the city as a whole. Due to segregation and social disintegration, therefore, the social structure of Leipzig East – especially the neighbourhood of Volkmarsdorf – generates serious problems (www.volkmarsdorf.de). Social infrastructure has also been hit badly with the closure of schools because of a lack of funding and/or demand.

The key local regeneration objectives can be categorised under the following headings (Stadt Leipzig, 2008a):

- Economy, employment and infrastructure;
- physical regeneration and open spaces, environment, housing and living environment; and
- social cohesion and social/cultural infrastructure.

These objectives recognise the redevelopment potential of the area, which is close to the city centre with a direct public transport route (tram and buses) to the central railway station, and also offering good access to the motorway.

Funding structures

The history of funding of redevelopment and regeneration activities in Leipzig East clearly highlights that the integration and/or 'bundling' of different funding streams is a very complex task but can help to achieve the overall objectives. For example, in 1999 the funding for the designated '*Sanierungsgebiete*' (redevelopment areas) accounted for the bulk of the overall funding. In many cases such redevelopment was carried out in public private partnership and public funding was used to lever in private investment.

Between 2000 and 2005 these funds – mainly employed for physical redevelopment – were reduced proportionately to the achievement of redevelopment objectives (Stadt Leipzig, 2008c). The split in the context of these 'classic' funding instruments is based on 30% public and 70% private contributions. The former are shared by local authority, '*Bundesland*' (region) and federal level in equal parts.

Between 1999 and 2001, some €6.8 m were also received through the Socially Integrative City programme. While the funding split is similar to the classic planning instruments mentioned above, the most important difference is the possibility of funding up to 30% of 'non-investive' measures (i.e. funding of activities such as training, education, self-help, establishing networks) rather than physical redevelopment, which is crucial for the problems faced by Leipzig East.

The funding period 2000 until 2006 saw €9.9 m of ERDF investment in Leipzig East. As part of the same programme the city of Leipzig has applied for approx. €4.5 m to be spent in Leipzig East between 2007 and 2013. It is important to point out in this context that 50% of all ERDF funding must be spent on improvements of the public realm. This of course is vital for a healthy and attractive living and working environment and therefore contributes to social well-being. However, this limits the flexibility of utilising the funding and therefore the range of projects to which it can contribute. Several complementary funding streams can also be used as appropriate (e.g. 'heritage conservation funding').

Partnership arrangements

An integrative approach was taken with regard to funding: different funding streams were combined to achieve the identified objectives. In this context the local authority – through an 'Advisory Council for Integrative District Development', composed of representatives from politics, clubs and associations and administrative authorities – continuously assessed the availability of funding and whether the eligibility criteria of individual programmes fitted the objectives of the identified redevelopment and regeneration areas in Leipzig. Wherever possible, 'bundling' of several funding streams was sought in order to maximise the positive effects in the designated areas (BMVBS & Stadt Leipzig, 2008).

The organisational structure at the local level aims to resolve the dichotomy between streamlined administration and direct control of implementation, on the one hand, and high flexibility and bottom-up development of project ideas, on the other hand.

At the local strategic level the department for regeneration and housing takes the lead and coordinates the interdepartmental cooperation. Of particular importance are departments for economic development, social issues, youth, culture and planning. Core responsibilities at this level are the identification and acquisition of appropriate funding as well as the coordination of statutory planning instruments thereby setting a formal framework for implementation. An important platform for topical discussions in this context is the thematic forum for integrated urban development.

In parallel to this, thematic task groups are formed by the departments mentioned above and other stakeholders including the private sector. All relevant stakeholders – including the public, city departments and the private sector – meet in the so called Forum Leipzig East, which provides a platform for dialogue, cooperation and recommendations. It works both ways, top down and bottom up.

Additionally, at the neighbourhood level – a neighbourhood management is established. The latter is crucial for outreach work including grass-roots project development, on the one hand, and communication with city departments, on the other hand. It also has a central role for project implementation.

Social sustainability

Integration of policy and planning documents, organisational structures as well as funding streams and procedures are at the heart of the 'Socially Integrative City' programme. This is clearly reflected in the case study of Leipzig East, and the Integrated Development/Action Concept ('*Integriertes Entwicklungs/Handlungskonzept*') is of crucial importance for the success of social sustainability in urban regeneration (DIFU, 2002). This planning document is based on a thorough analysis of the spatial and socioeconomic context of identified regeneration areas. It includes a clear set of objectives and clearly linked measures in order to address the identified social and physical/structural problems.

Focal points – social sustainability in Leipzig East

In order to fully understand the integrated approach, which specifically aims to improve social sustainability in the scope of regeneration in Leipzig East, it is helpful to take a closer look at some of the core projects and regeneration measures.

A lot of emphasis is placed on community empowerment and improvement of the employment situation. In this context an employment development commissioner provides a direct contact promoting employment opportunities at the neighbourhood level (Stadt Leipzig, 2008b). The commissioner cooperates with companies to develop new work and training options in the neighbourhood and to find new partners to finance education of potential employees. Another responsibility is the development of employment projects in the so called 'second labour market', whereby job seekers can update their skills, etc., in state-funded schemes that mirror the real-world labour market until they can fill a position in the latter. Further to this the commissioner helps local businesses with recruitment and provides advice for start-ups and offers guidance for the personal development of employees, school leavers, teachers and parents on the latest vocational-training opportunities. Additionally concepts for integrating immigrants into the labour market are developed. All of this is based on a cooperative approach with various administrative bodies and private-sector partners (e.g. labour agencies, trade associations).

Several projects aim to use the creative and cultural potential in order to improve the image of Leipzig East and to (re)install a sense of place as well as identification of the community with their neighbourhood. Under the headline 'East Lights' – making reference to the sun-rise in the East – a platform for festivals, cultural activities, clubs, etc., was launched in 2003 (Stadt Leipzig, 2008b). One of the main benefits and attractions was the mix of cultures and intercultural activities in this context (Stadt Leipzig, 2008b). In this context a city-wide integration policy seems to be of great importance for neighbourhood-based integration schemes to work. The city department for culture took the lead in these projects but neighbour-hood management, local clubs and community organisations were the main actors in developing ideas and implementing these cultural projects.

Another focal point of regeneration in Leipzig East was concerned with the quality of life of children. Projects comprised physical regeneration such as refurbishment of youth centres, increased capacity and quality of kinder-gartens/crèches, improvement or new build of play areas and sports facili-ties as well as advice for kindergarten teachers and parents, organised activities, establishment of youth festivals and clubs, etc.

An important element of social sustainability appears to be empower-ment by means of establishing and/or strengthening social networks. No less than 13 permanent and 29 temporal community networks are at the heart of this effort (Stadt Leipzig, 2008b). These are based on or complemented by 16 established community meeting points – some of them including advisory functions (Stadt Leipzig, 2008b).

Did the particular emphasis on social sustainability have a positive effect? Were there tangible results? These questions regularly crop up in academic and practice-related discussions as it is much more difficult to assess the results of 'non-investive' regeneration measures. Because of this it is very often more difficult to ensure political and financial support for such projects – particularly when they compete with physical regeneration where clear out-puts such as new infrastructure or a beautifully designed public space are immediately and obviously visible.

The relevant stakeholders were aware of these problems, which is why detailed monitoring activities were introduced from the outset.

Monitoring social sustainability

The case study of *'Leipziger Osten'* is interesting with regard to indi-cator-based monitoring and controlling in two different ways: on the one hand, it provides valuable insight into the monitoring carried out in the context of the ongoing regeneration process while, on the other hand, a new monitoring approach combined with an *ex ante* project evaluation toolkit have been developed on the basis of lessons learned from Leipzig East.

The analysis of the ongoing monitoring shows that the following four levels are covered (Stadt Leipzig, 2008b):

1 Sub-regional level with a focus on sub-regional migration.
2 City-wide level with a focus on:
   - Context of housing market development and regeneration;
   - employment and income levels;
   - demographic development;
   - residential completions and (re)development of existing dwellings;
   - residential vacancies;
   - migration within the city;
   - supply of residential units and expected population movements;
   - rental prices; and
   - real estate market (sites).
3 District level with a focus on:
   - Completions, demolition, existing buildings;
   - migration;
   - demography;
   - unemployment; and
   - residential vacancies.
4 Neighbourhood and/or project level with different foci depending on specific problems addressed as part of the projects.

Monitoring results from sub-regional to district level are published in an annual monitoring report. The analysis of monitoring results of these levels (e.g. comparisons of different levels) is uncomplicated as the monitoring is integrated and coordinated across these levels. More effort is required when more detailed information is needed as the monitoring results of individual projects and neighbourhoods are neither coordinated nor documented centrally (Stadt Leipzig, 2007).

Since 2003 an additional set of indicators has been introduced, which is specifically geared to monitoring urban redevelopment and regeneration measures. The administrative regulations '*Städtebauliche Erneuerung*' (urban renewal) of the Saxony region require local authorities to monitor the effectiveness of intervention measures such as designations of Redevelopment Areas or Socially Integrative City areas (Stadt Leipzig, 2008a, b, c; VwV StbauE, 2008).

The purpose of this 'topic-specific' monitoring is, on the one hand, to supply information for funding bodies as to the programme implementation so that on this basis the funding frameworks can be improved continuously at national and '*Bundesland*' (regional) level (DIFU, 2003). On the other hand, this monitoring tool is vital for the controlling and review of

204 Urban Regeneration & Social Sustainability

the 'integrated development concept'. In this context it is also of great value to justify the current and future needs for regeneration funding in the political realm at the city level.

Surveys, evaluations and the experiences of field workers and other stakeholders confirm that much has changed for the better in the programme area Leipzig East. This applies particularly to how residents perceive the situation in their neighbourhood. There has been a range of feedback, including the assertion that much has been accomplished in improving the living environment in the neighbourhood where certainly projects targeting the improvement of the physical environment, among other issues, have made profound visible impact ensuring better integration into the city. In parallel to this the quality of life and the atmosphere in the neighbourhood has improved not least due to improved green and social infrastructure.

Conclusions

The comparison of the core planning instruments for urban redevelopment and regeneration showed that the shortcomings in the context of tackling social issues have been addressed to a large extent by the designation of Socially Integrative City areas and the linked funding programme. However, there still appears to be a mismatch in social regeneration needs and allocated funding. The emphasis on physical regeneration is too strong – as can be seen in Leipzig East, the need for 'non-investive' measures, such as funding for clubs, cultural activities, education, etc., is far greater. It is therefore safe to argue that the link between the proportion of physical regeneration (currently 70%) and of 'non-investive' measures (currently 30% of overall regeneration funding) is problematic. In a worst-case scenario this can either lead to a situation where physical work that is not strictly necessary is undertaken in order to justify 'non-investive' measures or to a situation where not enough 'non-investive' funding is available to meet regeneration needs. Both cases are equally undesirable. A solution could be more local flexibility in funding allocation, which has to be justified on the basis of monitoring results (see also monitoring conclusions below).

Leipzig East provides a good example of gradually building up self-reliant structures and nurturing inter-cultural understanding. With the start of programme implementation, the Leipzig municipality created an organisational and management structure that encompassed all relevant levels, including city-wide departments, the intermediary district level and the neighbourhood level. It is clear that the vertical as well as horizontal integration of organisational structures, planning documents and funding were vital to the success of regenerating Leipzig East.

A monitoring system that is equally vertically integrated and covers the most important regeneration objectives proved vital in several ways: first it was needed to monitor the achievement of objectives and control the implementation of planning instruments, projects and funding, and, second, it helped to justify the investment in social measures, which are not immediately visible but vital for the long-term social stability of the district. In addition, monitoring has provided a basis for the review of planning documents and informed the decision making of public and private stakeholders.

It appears that in order to achieve social sustainability objectives flexible as well as long-term funding perspectives are vital: for example, it would be severely detrimental to establish a neighbourhood management centre and then lose the funding for it just when local residents have learned to trust the new structures (DIFU, 2006a, b).

Soft end land uses were also decisive in changing the image of the district. The establishment of new green spaces (both public and private) as well as cultural events in the district helped immensely. They are focal points of community life today.

Leipzig East is also a good example of successful 'preventive action'. The local authority acted early in order to stop a downward spiral highlighted by socioeconomic indicators. This helped to prevent social unrest and intercultural clashes in the district. It appears to be an approach that should be promoted widely as it will be more effective and also more cost efficient than retrospectively salvaging a situation of social unrest and low levels of well-being (DIFU, 2007).

With regard to the overall programme implementation – not only for Leipzig East – but for the whole of Germany several core areas for improvement of social sustainability have been identified by BMVBS.

In this context it is postulated that important progress in the fields of training, education and participation of residents has to be more closely linked to micro- and macro-scale economic development (BMVBS, 2008). This appears to be essential in order to tackle overriding structural problems such as long-term unemployment and low household income.

The limited duration of the Socially Integrative City programme and the statutory requirement to gradually reduce public subsidies – makes sustainment strategies very important. In Leipzig East the long-term sustainability appears to work for most projects, there are, however, problems of gap funding particularly with regards to neighbourhood-management schemes.

Interdepartmental cooperation and coordination should be strengthened further at both federal and regional level. In doing so, particular efforts must be made to continue work in the fields of school and education, integration of immigrants, health promotion and local economy (BMVBS, 2008).

Despite evidence of considerable advances in the harmonisation of funding programmes at federal and regional level there still appears to be room for improvement. Inter alia this applies to compatibility in terms of content, funding periods, application procedures. Furthermore, provision of comprehensive information concerning the possibilities of pooling various resources remains a desirable objective (BMVBS, 2008).

It has become increasingly clear that monitoring systems and evaluations in the municipalities are prerequisites for positive impacts and required quality control. Further development of these instruments by commissioning state-wide evaluations, elaborating indicators for monitoring systems, etc., are therefore postulated (BMVBS, 2008).

In addition to the topics mentioned above, the need for more scientific analysis and research are recognised particularly in the fields of area designation and defining the right spatial boundaries, neighbourhood management and local partnerships (BMVBS, 2008).

In this context the value of international comparative studies should definitely be considered as well as the importance of effective dissemination of research results. While the former can help to think 'outside the box' and to reach more innovative solutions, the latter is indispensable to link academia, planning practice and politics.

Part III

Best Practices in Urban Regeneration:
Concluding Perspectives

11

Towards Best Practice and a Social Sustainability Assessment Framework

Introduction and context

It is clear from the previous sections of this book (the theoretical analysis of social sustainability carried out in Part I, and the review of the urban regeneration projects in Part II) that the social dimension is often treated as a 'poor cousin' when it comes to assessing and monitoring its success or failure in urban-regeneration projects. Despite the existence of several examples of best-practice measurement within cities (for example, Cardiff, Leipzig and Rotterdam) there is a paucity and dearth of tangible examples of formalised and integrated systems or frameworks for measuring social sustainability. This reflects both an issue over the cost and complexity of collecting data on relevant indicators and also the wider issue of which indicators should be included in such systems in the first place. In many instances, therefore, there is an inherent bias towards measuring environmental sustainability, and more research is needed on the social dimension of integrated sustainable urban regeneration.

Part II of this book has also shown how municipal authorities have begun to experiment with the use of composite indices, such as *footprint*™ (Cardiff) and 'Sociale Index' (Rotterdam), which integrate different social dimensions together to measure and monitor the social evolution of places. On the one hand, such indices can provide powerful concise tabulated or visual indications concerning the social qualities of places and their evolution over time. On the other hand, aggregated indices may run the risk of providing superficial social representations of places and communities, whose social performance is summarised and compared through single numerical values.

Urban Regeneration & Social Sustainability: Best Practice from European Cities, by Andrea Colantonio and Tim Dixon   © 2011 Andrea Colantonio and Tim Dixon

Low scores in such indices, for example, could lead to the 'stigmatisation' of some areas through over-simplistic comparisons.

Within this context, however, it is worth pointing out how the mobility of individuals at rural–urban level, between cities, and within city areas has increased significantly over the last few years, leading to the generation of highly mobile and transient communities. This increased mobility has spurred a debate as to whether 'people-based' indicators are preferable to area-based metrics in order to assess the social sustainability impacts of urban-regeneration policies. At present, there is no conclusive empirical evidence on the issue and the debate is likely to continue for several years to come.

In addition, the selection of social targets and objectives for urban-regeneration projects relies on system values and political objectives rather than scientific criteria. This selection process should therefore be carried out with the participation of local residents and political representatives elected locally. However, target values (e.g. affordable housing, educational infrastructure) can also stem from national or regional legislation or regional and national programming documents. Also, as shown in the regeneration of La Mina, it is becoming common practice in EU cities to set objectives and thresholds for neighbourhood regeneration that are 'in tune' with surrounding communities of the regeneration area or the city as a whole in order to avoid sharp social and spatial divides between city areas. In this sense, a key challenge for urban regeneration is to deliver neighbourhoods that integrate and connect well (from both the spatial and social point of view) with surrounding communities, and that are linked to the city's overall vision and development plans.

Another important best practice in terms of social sustainability assessment is the allocation of resources for monitoring at the planning stages of the project. The regeneration project of Porta Palazzo has shown how the monitoring of the social impacts of regeneration is often hampered by the:

- Lack of forward thinking and the selection of a monitoring system at the planning stages of the project proposal;
- large amounts of data to be collected and analysed; and
- lack of clear and legally-binding post-project monitoring agreements amongst stakeholders.

Another major obstacle is the lack of statistical data routinely collected by city statistical offices at the local and project level. This highlights the importance of allocating financial and human resources for *ex post* monitoring of the regeneration process at the early, planning stages of project proposals, following, for example, the best practice provided by the Leipzig case study.

Against this background this chapter therefore aims to: (i) highlight best practice in socially sustainable urban regeneration, with a particular focus on igloo's footprint SRI system; and (ii) propose a broad Social Sustainability Assessment Framework (SSAF) applicable to urban regeneration of EU cities. These aims are both now examined in more detail. In highlighting igloo's best practice the reader is also referred to Chapter 6 and Appendix 5 for more details.

Best practice in social sustainability monitoring systems: igloo's SRI system

Background

There is a growing body of evidence to suggest that sustainable property investment can generate superior returns or at the very least 'future proof' investments (UNEPFI, 2009). Such investments, which can form the focus for regeneration projects, can create economic benefits for both occupiers and investors. These benefits can include:

- Additional brand value and reputation benefits;
- enhanced capital growth and rental income;
- lower operating costs;
- improved tenant retention; and
- lower depreciation costs in comparison with non-sustainable buildings.

In this sense an increasing focus on a 'triple bottom line approach' has led to a broad definition of sustainable property being developed by the UK Green Building Council as (UKGBC, 2008; Dixon, 2009):

> Buildings which (1) are resource efficient (physical resources, energy, water, etc.); (2) have zero or very low emissions (CO_2, other greenhouse gases, etc.); (3) contribute positively to societal development and well-being; and (4) contribute positively to the economic performance of their owners/ beneficiaries and to national economic development more generally.

In theory RPI can be implemented throughout the property lifecycle; for example (Dixon, 2009):

- Developing or acquiring properties designed with environmentally and socially positive attributes (e.g. low-income housing or green buildings).
- Refurbishing properties to improve their performance (e.g. energy efficiency or disability upgrades).
- Managing properties in beneficial ways (e.g. fair labour practices for service workers or using environmentally friendly cleaning products).
- Demolishing properties in a conscientious manner (e.g. reusing recovered materials on-site for new development).

Table 11.1   Ten principles of responsible property investment.

1   *Energy conservation*: Green power generation and purchasing, energy efficient design, conservation retrofitting
2   *Environmental protection*: Water conservation, solid waste recycling, habitat protection
3   *Voluntary certifications*: Green building certification, certified sustainable wood finishes
4   *Public-transport-oriented developments*: Transit-oriented development, walkable communities, mixed-use development
5   *Urban revitalisation and adaptability*: Infill development, flexible interiors, brownfield redevelopment
6   *Health and safety*: Site security, avoidance of natural hazards, first-aid readiness
7   *Worker well-being*: Plazas, childcare on premises, indoor environmental quality, barrier-free design
8   *Corporate citizenship*: Regulatory compliance, sustainability disclosure and reporting, independent boards, adoption of voluntary codes of ethical conduct, stakeholder engagement
9   *Social equity and community development*: Fair labour practices, affordable/social housing, community hiring and training
10 *Local citizenship*: Quality design, minimum neighbourhood impacts, considerate construction, community outreach, historic preservation, no undue influence on local governments

Source: UNEPFI (2008).

The perceived benefits of investing in such projects (see Chapter 4) have also led to the development of ten principles for Responsible Property Investment (RPI), which are shown in Table 11.1.

Demand for sustainable property is therefore growing and the appetite from institutional investors for urban-regeneration projects, particularly in the UK, has also grown (UNEPFI, 2009; Dixon, 2009). For example in the UK, a number of commercial property investors have led by example through their commercial property activities, including PRUPIM, igloo, Hermes, Land Securities, British Land and Hammerson, and in Australia they include Investa, Lend Lease Mirvac and MPT (Dixon *et al.*, 2007; Newell, 2008; UNEPFI, 2008; Dixon, 2009).[1]

igloo Regeneration Fund

igloo was established in 2002 and was the UK's first regeneration fund. Its primary focus is mixed-use urban-regeneration projects in towns and cities throughout the UK, and the fund has a strong SRI focus. It is jointly managed

---

[1]   In the USA favourable real estate yields and property borrowing conditions, declining green building costs, increasing technical sophistication and rising confidence in green property performance have led to the 'first generation' of sustainable real estate investment offerings. Initial institutional forays into green real estate have so far typically taken place in the context of additions to established portfolios (Tobias, 2007), and examples include the Multi-Employer Property Trust and the Liberty Property Trust (Dixon, 2009).

by Morley Fund Management and igloo Regeneration Ltd (UNEPFI, 2008). As of 31 December 2007, the fund had a gross asset value of £113 m comprising 22 assets and the portfolio of projects has a completed development value of around £2.5 bn. Currently the fund has a £130 m capital commitment with 68% held in direct projects and 32% in joint ventures. The fund is open only to those with more than £5 m to invest and is targeting a further £50 m of new equity for 2010 (igloo, 2010a).

The underlying fund structure is an unregulated English Limited Partnership and the fund's life runs until December 2016. The fund has the ability to gear to 60% loan to value and, as at the end of Q3 2009, it was 18% geared. The fund is managed by Aviva Investors and governed by a General Partner board made up of directors from Aviva Investors, Barclays and igloo Regeneration Limited (igloo, 2010a).

The fund's origins lie in the fact that Morley identified an under-pricing opportunity for financial returns in the UK urban-regeneration market (because such areas were erroneously perceived as being high risk, low return; UNEPFI, 2008). However, research (see Chapter 4) suggested that this was not so and that in fact returns could be higher in such areas.

igloo Regeneration therefore invests in sustainable communities, and its buildings are designed to be environmentally sound. It also focuses on regenerating communities in the 20 biggest cities in Britain to promote new jobs, new income, new homes and commercial space Their flagship projects are in Cardiff, Leeds, London, Manchester and Nottingham and the projects are assessed continuously for their social impact, including acquisition, construction and post-occupancy. There is also a Socially Responsible Investment Committee to enforce the SRI goals of the company (2010b).

igloo's footprint system

The United Nations has referred to igloo as the 'world's first sustainable property fund' (igloo, 2010a). This reflects igloo's approach to delivering mixed-use schemes that are well designed and environmentally sustainable, and each scheme adheres to the standards defined in igloo's pioneering Sustainable and Responsible Investment (SRI) policy, *'footprint'*.

igloo's investment policy is guided by the belief that it can deliver not only benefits for the fund through stable and long-term investment opportunities but also for the local community by maximising the regeneration impact. The SRI policy, therefore, seeks to realise these benefits by:

- Selecting sites which are accessible and have the potential to contribute to the overall regeneration of the urban area;
- carrying out a thorough process of 'contextual analysis' focusing not only on the historic and present-day fabric of the area but also on its economy, culture and liveability;

- managing a meaningful process of engagement with stakeholders and focusing not only on the local community but also on other communities of interest; and
- taking a long-term view of the project and looking at how management and community structures can work together over time to deliver long-term benefits to the local community.

As we saw in Chapter 6 (see also Appendix 5) the four key themes against which projects are assessed comprise:

1 Health, happiness and well-being;
2 regeneration;
3 environmental sustainability; and
4 urban design.

All present challenges in measurement but perhaps one of the most challenging is the first. igloo suggest that three basic premises have informed the development of this dimension (igloo, 2010b):

1 Celebrating the city in terms of culture and civilisation;
2 contextualising the regeneration project in its local place; and
3 promoting happiness but not at any cost (i.e. recognising the need to develop strong social bonds and promote environmental sustainability).

As suggested in Chapter 6, there is a strong social dimension to all of the above themes or dimensions of sustainability and the igloo system with its four-stage review 'screening – assessment – monitoring – post-occupancy' enables a robust and qualitative/quantitative measurement to be conducted based on a range of benchmark scores. *footprint* is also audited by an independent audit reporting to an audit committee led by Jonathan Porritt, the first chair of the UK Government's Sustainable Development Commission.

For igloo (igloo, 2010a, b) a key advantage of its SRI policy is that it can deliver higher returns through its *'footprint'* policy, by delivering sustainable buildings that integrate communities and manage estates over the long term, as well as delivering well-designed places for people to work, live and play. *'footprint'* also enables the company to align its interests with the public sector, through public–private partnerships such as Blueprint and Isis. A measure of its success is that it wins 80% of the projects it tenders for and 50% of its projects are acquired off the market, which reduces transaction costs (UNEPFI, 2008).

igloo recognises the long-term nature of regeneration and the whole process can take 5–10 years to come to fruition, with value enhancement flowing in some 4–7 years into the project when values can increase by as much

Table 11.2 igloo's projected IRRs.

	Fund geared	Fund ungeared	Fund benchmark (IPD benchmark; UK universe)
December 2011	16.0%	14.3%	10.9%
December 2016	13.3%	11.9%	9.4%

Source: UNEPFI (2008). Reproduced by permission of UNEPFI.

as 20–80% of the values of surrounding areas. Returns are therefore based on a combination of land value uplift, development profit, rental income and capital growth (market based and regeneration based). Essentially, igloo is seeking to minimise its risk by maintaining balanced exposure to investments and developments and with strong focus on medium- and long-term returns to 2011 and 2016, respectively. In the case of Roath Basin the company has a 12.5% p.a. priority real return. (UNEPFI, 2008). Table 11.2 gives details of projected internal rates of return (IRRs) for its projects.

The social sustainability assessment framework

Background

Despite the examples of best practice that we encountered during the course of the research, including igloo's *'footprint'* system, it is clear that the field is relatively undeveloped in terms of theoretical and analytical constructs.

As part of the research that formed the basis for this book, therefore, we also developed a simplified social sustainability assessment framework (SSAF) that stems from the literature review, the results from the case-study analysis, and the latest EU sustainable-development policy. The framework, which is illustrated in Figure 11.1, offers a model for the appraisal of urban development projects in EU cities against social sustainability criteria at multiple levels, including:

- Theoretical;
- policy; and
- practical.

Broadly speaking, it is important to point out that the framework applies mainly to urban areas of the EU and other developed countries because urban and social issues of developing countries will differ significantly from those of developed countries. The framework is therefore presented in the sections below.

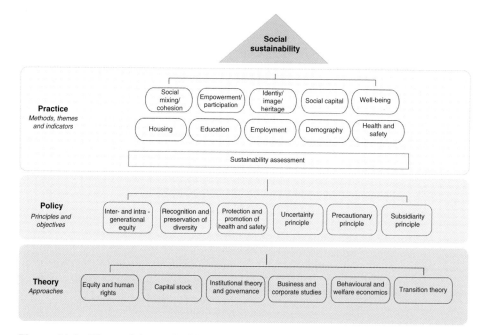

Figure 11.1   The social sustainability assessment framework. *Source*: Colantonio, see also Colantonio and Dixon (2009).

Purpose of the framework

The SSAF can take different shapes and fulfil different purposes, which vary according to project, spatial scale, local social and cultural contexts, and political priorities. Broadly speaking, the purpose of this framework is to:

1 Provide practical and simplified guidance to identify, assess and measure key broad social impacts of single development projects;
2 rank *ex ante* project proposals according to their consideration of social sustainability themes;
3 monitor *ex post* the social sustainability performance of projects against baseline indicators; and
4 identify areas for improvement of project proposals in terms of particular social sustainability aspects.

Approaches to social sustainability theory

As briefly introduced in Part I of this book, several theoretical and methodological approaches to the study of social sustainability can be identified. These include, for example:

- *Capital stock*, e.g. social capital, environmental capital and ecological foot-prints, etc. (Coleman, 1988; Putnam 1993; Wackernagel & Rees, 1996).
- *Equity and human rights*, e.g. poverty studies and unequal development (Sen, 1985, 1992; Sachs, 2001).
- *Institutional theory and governance*, e.g. participation and stakeholder analysis (Chambers, 1992; Healey 1992).
- *Business and corporate studies*, e.g. triple bottom line, corporate social responsibility, etc. (Elkington, 1994).
- *Behavioural and welfare economics*, e.g. capabilities approach, well-being, health and happiness perspectives (Sen, 1993; Nussbaum & Glover, 1995; Layard 2005).
- *Transition theory*, e.g. institutional theory and system analysis (Rotmans *et al.*, 2001, Loorbach & Rotmans, 2006).

Throughout these perspectives there has been an examination of different aspects of the 'social' dimension of development, but the exact positioning of this varies depending on the perspective adopted. For example:

- The equity and human-rights approach emphasises the inter- and intra-generational aspect of the benefits of development;
- advocates of the capital stock perspective focus on the importance of human relationships (social capital) and its impact on development or the physical carrying capacity of planet earth (environmental capital) and how these capitals are shared amongst individuals and societies across the globe;
- institutional theorists highlight the importance of participation in the governance mechanisms underpinning development;
- the business approach calls for a more ethical and proactive role of the private and corporate sectors in improving the social qualities of communities and places where they operate;
- behavioural and welfare economy scholars have recently pointed out that both the preconditions and the finality of development should be to increase people's happiness and quality of life; and
- transition scholars have recently focused on the elements required to foster a systemic societal shift from the current unsustainable development model toward a more sustainable one.

Policy: Principles and objectives

It can be argued that some aspects of the theoretical approaches to sustainability have been incorporated into national and international sustainable development (SD) policies in varying degrees. Figure 11.2 shows, for example, several examples of how social sustainability research approaches have led

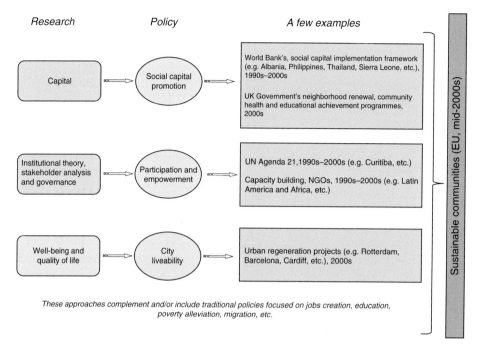

Figure 11.2   Examples of research approaches and policy linkages.

to the promotion of specific SD policies. These include, for example, the promotion of social capital by the World Bank; capacity building programmes promoted by the UN, and urban development policies geared towards the enhancement of quality of life and happiness in several EU cities. In addition, more recently, the Lisbon European Council held in 2000 also launched the idea of the social dimension as an integral part of sustainable development, paving the way for the Bristol Accord and the EU Sustainable Communities Agenda in 2005.

Sustainability objectives and guiding principles therefore constitute the backbone of most sustainable-development policies. They are interlinked together, providing both the platform informing policy development and the criteria against which the effectiveness of policies, programmes and plans should be assessed and monitored. In the context of social sustainability assessment in EU cities, several objectives and principles are essential for the appraisal process. These include definitions provided by the International Association of Impact Assessment and the glossary of the European Union (http://europa.eu/scadplus/glossary/subsidiarity_en.htm).

Intragenerational equity   The benefits from the range of planned interventions should address the needs of all, and the social impacts should not fall disproportionately on certain groups of the population, in particular children and women, the disabled and the socially excluded, certain generations or certain regions.

Intergenerational equity   Development activities or planned interventions should be managed so that the needs of the present generation are met without compromising the ability of future generations to meet their own needs.

Recognition and preservation of diversity   Communities and societies are not homogenous. They are demographically structured (age and gender), and they comprise different groups with various value systems and different skills. Special attention is needed to appreciate the social diversity that exists within communities and to understand what the unique requirements of particular groups may be. Care must be taken to ensure that planned interventions do not lead to a loss of social diversity in a community or a diminishing of social cohesion.

The protection and promotion of health and safety   Health and safety are paramount. All planned interventions should be assessed for their health impacts and their accident risks, especially in terms of assessing and managing the risks from hazardous substances, technologies or processes, so that their harmful effects are minimised, including not bringing them into use or phasing them out as soon as possible. Health impacts cover the physical, mental and social well-being and safety of all people, paying particular attention to those groups of the population who are more vulnerable and more likely to be harmed, such as the economically deprived, indigenous groups, children and women, the elderly, the disabled, as well as the population most exposed to risks arising from the planned intervention.

Uncertainty principle   It must be recognised that our knowledge of the social world and of social processes is incomplete and that social knowledge can never be fully complete because the social environment and the processes affecting it are changing constantly, and vary from place to place and over time.

Subsidiarity principle   It is defined in Article 5 of the treaty establishing the European Community. It is intended to ensure that decisions are taken as closely as possible to the citizen and that constant checks are made as to whether action at community level is justified in the light of the possibilities available at national, regional or local level. Specifically, it is the principle whereby the union does not take action (except in the areas which fall within its exclusive competence) unless it is more effective than action taken at national, regional or local level.

Practice

There are several sustainability appraisal methods, which differ in terms of purpose, stakeholders involved, complexity, understanding of the impacts generated and spatial and temporal framework in which they can be used. In addition, some methods are more technical and/or more participative than others.

Some examples which prove useful from a social sustainability point of view, include stakeholder decision/dialogue analysis, social cost-benefit analysis and social multi-criteria decision analysis. However, the choice of method will depend on: (i) understanding and measurability of the impacts; (ii) the desired level of participation in the appraisal process; and (iii) technique to deal with the tradeoffs associated with integrated approaches. In many cases, for example, the latter are dealt with by assigning weights to several aspects, values, objectives or alternatives related to the project. These weights are decided by the researchers/consultants carrying out the assessment process after they have analysed the data available, as highlighted, for example, by monitoring systems developed by the Rotterdam municipal authorities (see Chapter 9).

For the purpose of the SSAF framework we suggest a practical scoring system/composite index for social sustainability assessment, founded on the metrics related to social sustainability themes and indicators, which have been identified as part of our research. Table 11.3 lists the main social sustainability themes that have emerged in the literature review and the case studies. It can be seen how ten main themes are consistently identified in our case studies as essential to foster socially sustainable urban regeneration in different EU urban milieus.

These ten dimensions provide the assessment areas linked to a scoring system, which awards points ranging from 1 to 5 depending on the inclusion of specific items in the regeneration project The scoring system can be applied *ex ante* to evaluate project proposals through the application of checklists, or *ex post* through the evaluation of performance indicators, which have been selected to monitor the overall progress of the project for each area. Thus, a score of 5 for a given checklist item means that the project includes elements that comprehensively address a specific issue or criterion (e.g. affordable housing, job creation and so on). Similarly, at the monitoring stage, if a project indicator is performing very well (for example reaching or going above pre-fixed targets) a score of 5 could be assigned to that specific monitoring area.

Table 11.4 proposes a checklist for the application of the scoring system to evaluate *ex ante* project proposals, whilst Table 11.5 reports a 'bank' of possible indicators that could prove useful for assessing and monitoring project performance. The selection of the checklist items and monitoring indicators will be subjective but can be conducted with the general public

Table 11.3 Main social sustainability objectives of regeneration schemes (explicitly mentioned in project documents or the interviews conducted during the fieldwork).

City theme	Sant Adriá de Besós, Barcelona	Cardiff	Rotterdam	Turin	Leipzig
Housing and environmental health	✓	✓	✓	✓	✓
Education and skills	✓	✓	✓	✓	✓
Employment	✓	✓	✓	✓	✓
Health and safety	✓	✓	✓	✓	✓
Demographic change (ageing, migration and mobility)	✓	✓	✓	✓	✓
Social mixing and cohesion	✓	✓	✓	✓	✓
Identity, sense of place and culture	✓	✓	✓	✓	✓
Empowerment, participation and access	✓	✓	✓	✓	✓
Social capital	✓	✓	✓	✓	✓
Well-being, happiness and quality of life	✓	✓	✓	✓	✓
Equity	X	X	X	X	X
Human rights and gender	✓	X	X	✓	✓
Poverty	✓	X	✓	X	X
Social justice	X	X	X	X	✓

(for example, asking local residents or project recipients to take part in the evaluation and scoring exercise).

From an interpretational point of view, the scores obtained in each row of both Table 11.4 and Table 11.5 are totalled and then the average is calculated. As with other similar point-scoring systems, the higher the number of total points the better the overall rating. More specifically if the score obtained ranges between 1 and 1.80 the performance of the specific social sustainability key theme being assessed (e.g. demographics, education and skills, etc.) is very poor; 1.81 to 2.60 indicates poor performance; 2.61 to 3.20 suggest barely acceptable performance, whilst scores ranging from 3.41 to 5 indicate a good to very good performance or a positive impact, as summarised in Table 11.6.

The scores can also be represented more graphically in a 'radar' diagram, which visualises the overall position of each dimension and identifies areas that are underperforming and need improvement. For example the radar

Table 11.4 Example of social sustainability checklist items to be expanded and tailored to local social and built environment contexts.

Social sustainability themes / Assessment value	Very negative (points = 1) [A]	Negative (points = 2) [B]	Neutral (points = 3) [C]	Positive (points = 4) [D]	Very positive (points = 5) [E]	Comments	Totals [Average of A+B+C+D+E]
1 Demographics (migration, ageing, etc.)							
1.1 The scheme takes into account the existence of current demographic trends							
1.2 The project envisages the development of adequate infrastructure and services for the integration of newcomers, especially if international immigrants							
1.3 The project envisages the development of adequate social infrastructure and services for the elderly							
1.4 The project envisages the development of adequate social infrastructure and services for young people							
2 Education and skills							
2.1 The project envisages the development of good educational facilities in the area capable of catering for residents and newcomers							
2.2 After-school and youth-development programmes are planned as part of the scheme							
2.3 There are special educational programmes or services targeted to most disadvantage groups							
2.4 There are training skills programmes for minority groups and women							
3 Employment							
3.1 The scheme will create local jobs							

3.2 The project proposes a satisfactory balance of independent businesses/ commercial chains

3.3 Priority for the allocation of productive and commercial spaces in the area is given to companies with proven effective CSR and SRI policies

3.4 Project developers have reserved a local labour quota

3.5 A proportion of newly created businesses will be locally controlled or owned

3.6 Business support services for local businesses and micro-enterprises is available

3.7 There are programmes aiming to attract back local business managers, who have moved out of the area but could provide examples of successful role models for the community

3.8 The project promotes a sound jobs/housing balance

3.9 The project generates job opportunities for local graduates

4 *Empowerment, participation and access*

4.1 Education, health and social services have been involved in planning services for the increased population

4.2 The engagement of existing residents has been appropriate for the type and scale of the project

4.3 Local residents, including traditionally marginalised or under-represented groups, have been or will be involved in project selection, design, implementation and monitoring

Table 11.4 *(cont'd).*

Social sustainability themes Assessment value	Very negative (points = 1) [A]	Negative (points = 2) [B]	Neutral (points = 3) [C]	Positive (points = 4) [D]	Very positive (points = 5) [E]	Comments	*Totals* *[Average of* A+B+C+D+E]
4.4 The scheme aligns with community goals and objectives							
4.5 There is evidence that residents or neighbouring community members feel that the project will be beneficial for the area							
4.6 Possible concerns of community members have been taken into account							
4.7 Offices of project developers or project businesses (e.g. regeneration agency, local development agency) will be located in the regeneration area to encourage local participation and consultation							
4.8 The project supports or offers programmes and initiatives to build individual and community leadership capacity							
5 Health and safety							
5.1 The scheme includes the building of health and wellness infrastructure to cater for local and additional population							
5.2 The project provides safe, pedestrian-friendly streets							
5.3 The project envisages minimisation plans for noise, air and visual pollution if necessary							
5.4 There is an adequate ratio between healthy eating shops and fast-food chains in the area							
5.5 Local police forces have been consulted on safety needs of the area and contributed to the design of the project							

Table 11.4 (cont'd).

Social sustainability themes Assessment value	Very negative (points = 1) [A]	Negative (points = 2) [B]	Neutral (points = 3) [C]	Positive (points = 4) [D]	Very positive (points = 5) [E]	Comments	Totals [Average of A+B+C+D+E]
6.13 Provision for information technology to be incorporated into dwellings is guaranteed							
6.14 The are plans to retrofit existing buildings							
6.15 The needs of less able people are catered for							
6.16 Adequate parking or storage areas (cars, motorbikes, and cycles)							
6.17 Affordable housing percentage is in line with local and national regulations							
7 Identity, image and heritage							
7.1 The scheme contributes to a community sense of place and identity (e.g. through spaces for performing arts, museums, festivals, farmers' markets and local craft fairs, etc.)							
7.2 The project contributes to a sense of community pride (e.g. by hosting pioneering programmes, landmark buildings, jewel parks, etc.)							
7.3 The project protects or enhances buildings and areas of significant cultural or heritage value							
7.4 The project supports commercial free public spaces							
7.5 The project supports adequate multi-faith infrastructure							
7.6 Local residents have been consulted on the demolition or movement to a different location of buildings of historic and cultural importance for the area							

8	*Social mixing, inclusion and cohesion*
8.1	Public spaces encourage social interaction in the community, especially amongst the different house tenures and household types
8.2	A broad social impact assessment has been conducted by project promoters to assess whether specific groups will bear disproportionate burdens or accrue disproportionate benefits in environmental, social or financial terms
8.3	The project promotes inter-cultural understanding and envisages programmes or projects that encourage interaction between people of varying ages, incomes, ethnicities and abilities
8.4	The scheme forecasts informative 'training' workshops for newcomers concerning the social qualities of the area
9	*Social capital*
9.1	The project works with and supports community organisations and networks
9.2	The project supports the creation of local associations
9.3	The scheme provides adequate spaces to gather for meetings, connection and celebration
9.4	The project will generate a community that integrates and connects well (from both physical mobility and social points of view) with the surrounding community

Table 11.4 (cont'd).

Social sustainability themes Assessment value	Very negative (points = 1) [A]	Negative (points = 2) [B]	Neutral (points = 3) [C]	Positive (points = 4) [D]	Very positive (points = 5) [E]	Comments	Totals [Average of A+B+C+D+E]
10 Well-being							
10.1 The projects entails the development of amenities located within 500 m or 15-minute walk of the scheme, including:							
Leisure							
Arts and culture							
Parks							
Sports							
Recreation							
10.2 The project encourages creative activities							
10.3 The project aims to improve standards of life and provide residents with enhanced personal development opportunities							
10.4 The scheme includes good shopping facilities, especially environmental ones							
10.5 The project includes the development of restaurants and night-life facilities able to cater for all age groups							

Source: Elaborated by Colantonio from case-study analysis and several sources, especially East Thames Housing Association (2006) and Hammer (2009).

Table 11.5 Example of indicators used to measure aspects of social sustainability.

Criterion/indicator Impact value	Very negative (points = 1) [A]	Negative (points = 2) [B]	Neutral (points = 3) [C]	Positive (points = 4) [D]	Very positive (points = 5) [E]	Comments	Totals [Average of A+B+C+D+E]
1 Demographics (migration, ageing, etc.)							
• Percentage of population above 65 years old							
• Percentage of population below 15 years old							
• Number of community centres for the elderly							
• Proportion of long-term residents							
• Percentage of newcomers							
• Percentage of ethnic minorities							
• Birth rate							
• Mortality rate							
• Number of marriages							
• Number of divorces							
○ Satisfaction with current facilities for elderly							
○ Satisfaction with current facilities for young people							
○ Satisfaction with current facilities for less-represented groups							
2 Education and skills							
• Number or percentage of educational facilities within 500 metres or 15-minute walk							
• Percentage of children enrolled in schools outside the area							
• Percentage of children in schools maintained by the local education authority achieving certain standards							
• Number of pupils per teacher							
• Number of after-school and youth-development programmes							
• Number of training programmes for disadvantaged or traditionally marginalised groups							

Table 11.5 (cont'd).

Criterion/indicator Impact value	Very negative (points = 1) [A]	Negative (points = 2) [B]	Neutral (points = 3) [C]	Positive (points = 4) [D]	Very positive (points = 5) [E]	Comments	Totals [Average of A+B+C+D+E]
• Number of training programmes for women and minority groups							
• Number of skill-development centres							
• Number of training opportunities provided by local authority or available free							
3 Employment							
• Number of jobs created (per 1000 square metres)							
• Unemployment rate							
• Percentage of new enterprises still operating after 3 years							
• Percentage of low-skill jobs generated (e.g. labour)							
• Percentage of medium- to high-skill jobs generated (e.g. managerial)							
• Percentage of independent jobs							
• Percentage of jobs in chain stores							
• Percentage of jobs in businesses with CSR or SRI policies							
• Average rent to income ratio							
• Anti-poverty benefit uptake							
• Anti-poverty campaigns to increase uptake							
• Deprivation index if available							
• Percentage of children and people over 60 that live in households that are income deprived							
• Previous investment per capita on social infrastructure							
• Percentage of social-benefit claimants							

4 *Empowerment, participation and access*
- Proportion of registered electorate voting in national elections
- Proportion of registered electorate voting in local elections
- Number of local residents or their representative associations involved in the design of the scheme
- Number of local residents or their representative associations involved in the implementation of local programmes and projects
- Number of local residents or their representative associations involved in the monitoring of the project
- Number of local associations
- Percentage of households with internet access at home
- Number of initiatives or attention centres for the elderly
- Number of initiatives and attention centres for ethnic minorities or immigrants
- Number of public internet access points
- Existence of local libraries and information centres
- Number of administration forms available for download from local authority official website
- ○ Percentage of adults who feel they can influence decisions affecting their local area
- ○ Percentage finding it easy to access key local services
- ○ Percentage who feel well informed about local affairs

Table 11.5 (cont'd).

Criterion/indicator Impact value	Very negative (points = 1) [A]	Negative (points = 2) [B]	Neutral (points = 3) [C]	Positive (points = 4) [D]	Very positive (points = 5) [E]	Comments	Totals [Average of A+B+C+D+E]
○ Proportion of those able to express and articulate their needs							
5 *Health and safety*							
• Proportion of a population within a 15-minute walk or 500 metres of a health facility							
• Number of hospital beds per 1000 residents							
• Number of patients per doctor (general practitioner; GP)							
• Incidence of specific disease							
• Visits to doctors (general practitioners; GPs) or other medical care							
• Estimated proportion of drug-related incidents							
• Number of antisocial behaviour incidents in the area							
• Number of minor crimes per 1000 inhabitants							
• Number of serious crimes per 1000 inhabitants							
• Number of neighbourhood police officers per 1000 inhabitants							
• Number of built-environment initiatives to improve local security (e.g. improved lighting system, etc.)							
○ Percentage who feel 'fairly safe' or 'very safe' outside after dark							
○ Percentage who feel 'fairly safe' or 'very safe' outside during the day							
6 *Housing and environmental health*							
• Percentage of built-up area							
• Population density							

- Percentage of non-decent/unfit homes
- Average price for a house per square metre
- Total number of new housing completions
- Occupancy levels
- Affordable dwellings as percentage of new housing completions
- Average price per square metre for an apartment/median household income
- Annual social housing rents to median household income
- Ratio of owned/rented housing
- Ratio of converted buildings
- Ratio of retrofitted buildings
- Percentage of newly built housing that follows main environmental and design protocols, standards and certifications (LEED, BREAM, Secure by Design, etc.)
- Percentage of construction-related green infrastructure (e.g. installation of energy-efficient/water-saving devices, use of recyclable/durable construction materials)
- Percentage of design-related green infrastructure (e.g. optimisation of natural lighting and ventilation, provision of sun shades, balcony)
  - Percentage of residents satisfied with their home(s) and neighbours
  - Percentage of residents who do not feel resentful towards higher income newcomers who may own better houses

7 *Identity, image and heritage*
- Proportion of long-term residents

Table 11.5 (cont'd).

Criterion/indicator Impact value	Very negative (points = 1) [A]	Negative (points = 2) [B]	Neutral (points = 3) [C]	Positive (points = 4) [D]	Very positive (points = 5) [E]	Comments	Totals [Average of A+B+C+D+E]
• Percentage of households owning their accommodation							
• Percentage of households renting their accommodation							
• Number of projects or programmes contributing to the enhancement of buildings and areas of significant cultural or heritage value							
• Number of commercial free public spaces							
• Number of adequate multi-faith places							
○ Percentage of people who have moved out of the area							
○ Percentage of residents who would like to improve the neighbourhood image							
○ Percentage of residents who feel the area is changing for the better							
○ Percentage of residents who feel they 'belong' to the neighbourhood/community							
8 *Social mixing, inclusion and cohesion*							
• Number of events and cultural activities encouraging interaction between people of varying ages, incomes, ethnicities and abilities							
• Number of associations encouraging interaction between people of varying ages, incomes, ethnicities and abilities							
• Number of public spaces frequented by residents of varying ages, incomes, ethnicities and abilities							
• Number of informative 'training' workshops for newcomers concerning the social qualities of the area							
• Percentage of class or schools attended exclusively by pupils from ethic minorities							

- Percentage of schools attended by pupils from different income or background households

9 *Social capital*

- Number of groups, organisations, or associations operating in the area
- Number of voluntary organisations in the neighbourhood
- Number of local residents' regular meetings and gatherings in public buildings or spaces
- Numbers of social networks
  - ◇ Percentage of residents who feel the level of trust has improved/worsened/stayed the same since the beginning of the regeneration project
  - ◇ Percentage of neighbours who look out for each other
  - ◇ Percentage of residents who have done a favour for a neighbour
  - ◇ Percentage of residents who have received a favour from a neighbour
  - ◇ Percentage of residents who trust their neighbours
  - ◇ Percentage of residents who see or speak to friends at least once a week
  - ◇ Percentage of residents who have at least one close friend who lives nearby
  - ◇ Percentage of residents who see or speak to a relative at least once a week
  - ◇ Percentage of residents who have at least one relative who lives nearby

Table 11.5 (cont'd).

Criterion/indicator Impact value	Very negative (points = 1) [A]	Negative (points = 2) [B]	Neutral (points = 3) [C]	Positive (points = 4) [D]	Very positive (points = 5) [E]	Comments	Totals [Average of A+B+C+D+E]
10 Well-being							
• Access to open space – average journey time for residents/employees by foot (minutes)							
• Access to leisure facilities – average journey time for residents/employees by foot (minutes)							
• Access to retail facilities – average journey time for residents/employees by foot (minutes)							
• Access to entertainment facilities – average journey time for residents on foot (minutes)							
○ Percentage who feel the level of living of this community may be characterised as: Wealthy/Well-to-do/Average/Poor/Very poor							

Note: ○ Indicates qualitative data to be gathered through perception survey. *Source:* Elaborated by Colantonio from case-studies analysis, interviews and a variety of sources, including Eurostat (2001), Egan (2004), Hemphill *et al.* (2004), EP (2007), NEF (2007), and Chan and Lee (2008).

Table 11.6 Scoring system for interpretation of results.

Description	Range
Very poor	1.00–1.80
Poor	1.81–2.60
Barely acceptable (or neutral)	2.61–3.40
Good	3.41–4.20
Very good	4.21–5.00

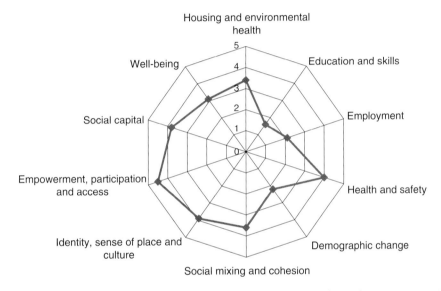

Figure 11.3 Example of the visualisation of the scoring system for project assessment.

diagram reported in Figure 11.3 indicates a project scoring very highly in terms of softer social sustainability themes, such as empowerment, identity and social mixing, but could be improved from the point of view of social and economic infrastructure, e.g. employment and education facilities.

If necessary these scores can also be aggregated into a composite index, similar to the 'Sociale Index' used in Rotterdam, for example, which can then provide an overall idea of the social sustainability performance of a given project or a place. The weight and aggregation methodology of the various sub-dimensions will depend on the context where the assessment is being carried out and the social objectives prioritised in the regeneration scheme.

Theme/dimension	SSAF score	Result*	Traffic-light system**	Aggregated scores (equal weights)
Housing and environmental health	3.4	Good		
Education and skills	1.6	Very poor		
Employment	2.1	Poor		
Health and safety	4	Good		
Demographic change	2.2	Poor		3.2 Barely acceptable
Social mixing and cohesion	3.6	Good		
Identity, sense of place and culture	3.9	Good		
Empowerment, participation and access	4.5	Very good		
Social capital	3.8	Good		
Well-being	3.1	Barely acceptable		

Figure 11.4   Examples of categories of performance to be used in social sustainability assessment. *Notes*: *See Table 11.6; **Elaborated from Table 11.6, where 1–2.3 = red(dark grey) 2.4–3.6 = yellow(mid grey); 3.7–5 = green(light grey).

Finally, the overall score can also be linked to categories of performance (for example, gold, silver, and bronze) or a 'traffic light' assessment system, where the red colour could signal areas needing attention or an overall unsatisfactory result, whilst the yellow and green colours relate to areas that may need attention or are performing satisfactorily, respectively. This is illustrated in Figure 11.4, which presents the score of Figure 11.3 in a different way.

Conclusions

igloo's success in regenerating important parts of the urban fabric in the UK is a testament to the way in which it approaches urban regeneration projects. The company's SRI policy has won praise for its integrated approach to sustainability and our focus on the policy as an example of 'best practice' is also mirrored in work elsewhere (UNEPFI, 2008; IPF, 2009). Part of igloo's popularity and potential is also highlighted by the fact that its Blueprint agreement (i.e. the joint venture PPP – see Chapter 4) has been characterised as a form of Urban Development Fund, akin to the new JESSICA model (King Sturge, 2009).

In a more generic sense, the assessment framework and the scoring system suggested in the social sustainability assessment framework (SSAF) offers, in our view, a practical method to broadly assess and compare the social sustainability performance of regeneration projects. The framework has a number of advantages:

- The framework provides simplified and linear guidelines on the main themes and principles of sustainable urban regeneration, which can be readily put into practice by policymakers and practitioners alike.
- The sub-themes in each social sustainability assessment dimension are flexible and can be adapted to contingent contexts.
- The framework can be based on a normative model to assess the distance from sustainable urban development objectives and prescriptions.

By the same token the SSAF also has several disadvantages:

- The framework could be deemed over simplified because the interactions between social sustainability themes at present are not fully taken into account in the assessment process.
- The dearth of readily available indicators (especially those measuring soft social sustainability aspects) may limit the full operationalisation of the framework.
- The assessment process is based on the traditional assessor–assessed relationship because it relies upon expert-based indicators and checklists, which have limited stakeholders participation in the selection process.

Essentially the assessment framework is a work in progress and so further research is needed to test it on urban regeneration projects to assess its strengths and weaknesses and to identify ways of improving the model. Nonetheless, in framing the SSAF our intention has been to highlight and emphasise the key ways in which social sustainability can be explored and measured in urban-regeneration contexts.

12

Conclusions

Introduction

This book has contended that social sustainability concerns how individuals, communities and societies live with each other and set out to achieve the objectives of development models that they have chosen for themselves, also taking into account the physical boundaries of their places and planet earth as a whole. Broadly speaking, in the social sustainability debate, from both policy and practice perspectives, traditional 'hard' social sustainability themes, such as employment and poverty alleviation, are increasingly being complemented or replaced by emerging 'soft' and less measurable concepts such as happiness, well-being and sense of place. This is adding complexity to the analysis of the concept of social sustainability, especially in terms of its operational definitions and the integration of its sub-dimensions at the assessment stage.

International comparisons are, of course, subject to caveats. It is clear that, for example, there is no single European model of urban regeneration and transferability in differing contexts is often difficult. Moreover, in qualitative research of this nature there is often a matter of judgement involved in identifying common themes (Cadell *et al.*, 2008). Nonetheless, we do believe that there are key common themes that emerge strongly from the research we have conducted and that an international comparison enables us to develop more innovative solutions for social sustainability in urban regeneration. The analysis of five case studies carried out as part of the research project, shows how urban regeneration projects can

Urban Regeneration & Social Sustainability: Best Practice from European Cities, by Andrea Colantonio and Tim Dixon   © 2011 Andrea Colantonio and Tim Dixon

generate potential outputs and outcomes at least in the following ten social sustainability dimensions and policy areas:

1 Demographic change (ageing, migration and mobility);
2 education and skills;
3 employment;
4 health and safety;
5 housing and environmental health;
6 identity, sense of place and culture;
7 participation, empowerment and access;
8 social capital;
9 social mixing and cohesion; and
10 well-being, happiness and quality of life.

These are critical areas for the social sustainability of local communities and neighbourhoods, and it is of fundamental importance to assess the potential direct and indirect impacts that urban regeneration project proposals are likely to generate on them.

In addition, social sustainability can relate to different spatial and functional levels, including:

• Household or business;
• community or neighbourhood;
• city;
• regional or national; and
• international.

Urban regeneration can play a key role in achieving sustainability at several of these levels, through trans-disciplinary and cross-departmental activities. Stakeholders and financiers involved in regeneration should also take into account at which level a project or a programme is likely to generate an output or outcome from a social sustainability perspective.

Promoting socially sustainable communities means tackling areas that have become distressed or deprived. It is clear that the five case-study areas in this book all share elements of underachievement economically, socially and environmentally in comparison with other neighbouring parts of their cities. The remainder of this chapter, therefore, begins by setting the context and comparing and contrasting the characteristics of our case-study areas before moving on to review the policy approaches to promoting socially sustainable outcomes. The chapter then reviews best approaches and practices to implement and monitor social sustainability and reviews the PPPs and emerging urban regeneration delivery vehicles that have formed the basis for successful regeneration. Finally we discuss the future of urban regeneration and how regeneration projects can best capture the social dimension as we move out of recession.[1]

Setting the scene: from distressed urban areas to regenerated urban areas?

As we have seen, promoting social sustainability is fraught with difficulties, not only in terms of how communities engage with the regeneration process and how social sustainability is actually measured, but also in terms of the starting point for regeneration. For some critics, regeneration is often seen as a euphemism for 'gentrification' (Shaw, 2009). This is true when displacement or exclusion occurs, and so the concept of 'exclusionary displacement' (Marcuse, 1985) is also important here: if people are excluded from a place they might have lived or worked in or otherwise occupied had the place not been 'regenerated' then accusations of 'gentrification' are hardened, prompting the view that neo-liberal policy dogma has overridden a socially sustainable vision (Swyngedouw, 2007). In a sense, regenerated areas may become victims of their own success: if deprived or distressed areas are the subject of regeneration then the new jobs and improved infrastructure may in fact create an upward spiral, which causes increased house prices and therefore displacement (Figure 12.1).

Against this, what are the consequences of not regenerating an area? The case studies we have examined all possess some of the characteristics associated with 'distressed' or 'deprived' areas (LUDA, 2003; Jacquier *et al.*, 2007). These have been well documented in other literature (see for example OECD, 1998; LUDA, 2006) and are summarised in Table 12.1.

For example, Cardiff, Turin and Rotterdam have all suffered economic decline as a result of changing trade and industry restructuring over varying periods of time. Without intervention the resultant distressed or deprived areas in such cities can enter a spiral of decline with areas suffering on multiple levels because of the interrelationship between economic and structural change, demographic and sociocultural change, social polarisation and segregation and environmental problems (LUDA, 2003, 2006).

Nonetheless, if we are to avoid criticism of gentrification we need to ensure that regeneration projects have both community and local residents' inputs and participation from the outset. This argument accords with Shaw's (2009) view, which places an emphasis on 'reinvestment', the retention of

---

[1]   Although our case studies did not focus explicitly on the recession, because they were examined during a period which preceded its most substantive impacts, we believe that it is important to place our findings in context, and outline how the recession could potentially impact on cities, neighbourhoods and the social dimension of sustainability.

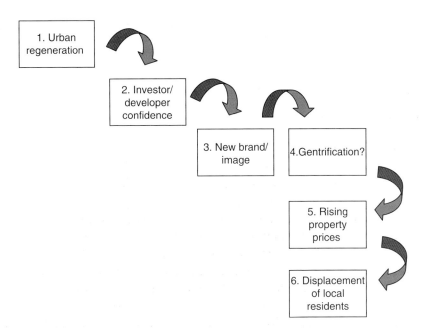

Figure 12.1   A spiral of success?

Table 12.1   Factors creating distressed or deprived urban areas.

External factors	Internal factors
Global economic restructuring	Population change
Deficient welfare policies	Demographic and social change
Sociocultural transformation	Social capital resources
Political and ideological transformation	Local economic development
Sectoral government policies	Effectiveness of local services
Planning approaches and legacies	
Patterns of racial discrimination	

Source: OECD (1998).

the specific character of a neighbourhood, and 'gradual improvement' underpinned by solid financial support. A community in this sense comprises people, places and institutions (Jacquier *et al.*, 2007). For example, we need to understand that communities are geographical places with a social construct and social product and with key identifying features (i.e. *'dasein'* or 'genius loci'). People will also be key because they live and work in the place and form individual and collective characteristics about a place which over the longer term helps develop human, social and cultural capital, or what Jacquier *et al.* (2007) refer to as *'mitsein'* (being and living together). Finally, institutions are also important because they regulate relationships among people, between people and place and between themselves, thus contributing to being and living together in the same community. Effectively, the interaction of these three components (i.e. places, people and institutions) constitutes a 'local culture', perhaps akin to an ecosystem in 'unstable balance' or 'dynamic imbalance' (in system terms). Empowering local communities in such areas, and in ways that create an integrated vision, will need to include consultation, joint deliberation and decision making, alongside the co-production of goods and services (Jacquier *et al.*, 2007), and some of these are perhaps characteristic of both the Turin and La Mina case studies.

Also key to several of these regeneration projects is the treatment and inclusion of the ethnic, immigrant communities that form part of the overall community. These areas have often been associated with unsafe neighbourhoods and urban violence, either because they are places where crimes are committed or because people find shelter in the area after crimes have been committed (Jacquier *et al.*, 2007). The most successful programmes of regeneration are those that recognise the importance of promoting cultural diversity. A recent European Commission report (EC, 2009) suggests that the average non-national population in the EU Member States is about 5.5% of the total population. The report also goes on to suggest that immigrant workers bring a wide variety of skills and experience to their new country and there are often new market opportunities for them to exploit within their local community. Although EU funding has been used very effectively by cities in supporting new ethnic businesses, on the negative side, however, there are greater hurdles for immigrants in entering the labour market, due to language and culture differences. Training and employment packages, therefore, should be a fundamental part of the regeneration programme.

This view also implies that 'integration' is important. Historically, a lack of integration is perhaps part of the reason for some of the key problems associated with regeneration in both Barcelona (including neighbouring areas such as Sant Adriá de Besós) and Cardiff. In Sant Adriá de Besós, for example, for several years the regeneration of La Mina area had been treated in a relatively piecemeal way, whilst in Cardiff the regeneration of Roath Basin was a relatively late addition to a pro-city-centre regeneration policy agenda. In Leipzig, in contrast, the Socially Integrative City concept has helped integration at both a physical and institutional (as well as at community) level. Indeed, the strength of national planning systems is a key characteristic of the South Pact programme in Rotterdam in conjunction with a strong PPP, and in this example, the innovative use of 'opportunity zones', which was tied into Dutch national policy, has played an important role at city level. In this sense we are moving very much to a view of regeneration as part of 'integrated sustainable urban development' (ISUD), a theme that is discussed in greater depth later in this chapter.

An overemphasis on physical regeneration can also cause problems and raise issues over community, as we saw in Leipzig. Getting the balance right in terms of 'non-investive' and 'investive' measures, therefore, is also very important. That is not to say that infrastructure in terms of transport, schools, hospitals and the building blocks of community are not important: in fact, in Roath Basin (Cardiff), South Pact (Rotterdam) and La Mina (in Sant Adriá de Besós) all suffered because of relative isolation and physical disconnection. Rather, the mix of such measures needs to carefully consider the spatial context and has to be focused on the right people and in the right way so that sustainable outcomes for local residents are achieved. This raises further issues about how socially sustainable policies can be formulated, as reviewed in the next section of this chapter.

Socially sustainable urban regeneration policy

The case studies in this book have shown how, at present, urban social sustainability policies are:

1 *Experimental* because the pursuit of emerging policy agendas such as social mixing have not been grounded on empirical evidence and it proves difficult to assess the results of early programmes;
2 *local* as communities and neighbourhoods have re-emerged as key arenas for the achievement of sustainable development; and
3 *fragmented and contested* because of the multiple stakeholders who have become involved in regeneration and the pursuit of sustainability.

In addition, social sustainability policies are influenced by the existence of several urban cycles in the functioning and management of cities. These include *political cycles*, coinciding with the lifecycles of municipal governments, lasting normally four years each; *macroeconomic cycles*, which can last between 10 and 20 years; and *social and environmental cycles*, which can take up to a generation to complete. The existence of these cycles should be taken into account in the evaluation of project impacts and policy outcomes. For example, evidence from the case studies of Turin and La Mina suggests that the beginning of new urban-regeneration programmes often coincides with the instalment of new local and national governments, or a change in national or international public policy. From a social point of view, the outcomes of a project or plan may outlive the life span of a political administration or take a generation before beginning to manifest themselves. As a result, the correct evaluation of the social output or outcome of urban regeneration should not solely adopt a short-term perspective (e.g. a yearly evaluation), but should take into account

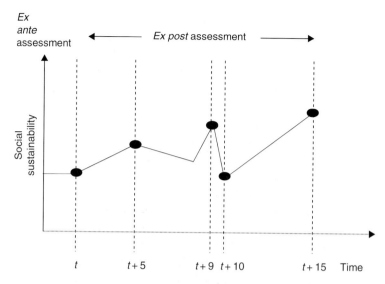

Figure 12.2   Timescales for measuring social sustainability.

medium- to long-term inter-generational changes. Social sustainability policies that are embedded within integrated sustainable urban-develop-ment programmes also need to recognise that at some point there will need to be an exit strategy when public funding ends, but that also politi-cal changes at a local level can impact on outcomes. Gaining relatively short-term payback can also be gained through the use of Operational Programmes, which put development actions and outcomes within a mid-term planning framework (EC, 2009).

As Bell and Morse (2008) point out, however, different systems may require different time scales for measuring sustainability. This also has implications for the measurement of social sustainability. Figure 12.2 shows in simple terms that the point at which we measure social sustainability, and over what time scale, will determine whether we see an improvement or not. If we have a project that measures social sustainability every 5 years, for example, after an initial *ex ante* assessment at time, *t*, then intervening patterns of variation will be missed. Thus, for example, an assessment at time, *t* + 10 will give a lower result than at *t* + 9, even though there is an overall upwards trend in social sustainability from time *t* to *t* + 15.

There is also an issue over the spatial scale at which a regeneration project is drawn: are we talking about the focus for a project at a neighbourhood level, a group of neighbourhoods or a city scale? If we are, for example, reviewing and assessing change in an integrated way then surely this implies that we must link and embed our measurements of the programmes of regeneration within a holistic, city-level analysis?

There can be little doubt, however, that EU programmes such as URBAN I and II, and knowledge-exchange networks such as REGENERA, have been a crucial driver for regeneration projects in EU cities, introducing a competitive process for the allocation of limited financial resources in urban regeneration. Furthermore, they have placed considerable emphasis on the importance of partnership working, through encouraging the inclusion of relevant private and NGO actors in the design, management, implementation and evaluation of programmes.

These programmes have been even more effective when local regeneration development projects were linked to city-wide development plans. Indeed, this has frequently been a key requirement of major national and EU funding bodies and helped attract financial resources. Similarly, the promotion of linkages between the objectives of local project and city-wide development plans have helped avoid the repetition of mistakes linked to property- or retail-led regeneration models promoted in the 1980s, in which the benefits of regeneration failed to spread outside the area being regenerated.

The success of the URBAN approach to policy (EC, 2009) marks a substantial shift away from the 'mono-policy' approaches of single projects towards city-wide visions of regeneration. There are five main dimensions or features of this policy that can be identified (EC, 2009: 25):

1 A move away from individual sectors towards wider integration within the local or regional economy;
2 decentralisation and a shift from government to governance (i.e. the tendency of central governments to confer certain responsibilities to lower levels of government, such as provinces, regions, cities, city districts and neighbourhoods (referred to as 'decentralisation'), together with the privatisation of governmental tasks, this involves the participation of a large number of different policy partners, third sector and NGO organisations and individuals (governance);
3 an increasing focus on empowering the inhabitants of cities and specific neighbourhoods;
4 a shift from universal policies to more focused, area-based policies; and
5 growing attention paid to the effectiveness of policies.

What we can also conclude from the five case studies is that integrated sustainable urban development is critical to a successful outcome. Projects that approach urban regeneration in a holistic way are more likely to succeed (for example Leipzig). In this respect an integrated plan for sustainable urban development comprises a system of interlinked actions, which seeks to bring about a lasting improvement in the economic, physical, social and environmental conditions of a city or an area within the city (EIB, 2010;

URBACT, 2010). The key to the process is 'integration', meaning that all policies, projects and proposals are considered in relation to one another. In this regard, the synergies between the elements of the plan should be such that the plan as a whole adds up to more than would the sum of the individual parts if implemented in isolation. In turn this implies vertical integration amongst the various levels of government and other stakeholders involved in governance and horizontal integration amongst the various sectors of public action.

Whilst it would be difficult to argue that all the case studies represent the purest form of ISUD, they do exhibit some degree of integration, with perhaps Leipzig and Turin the leading exemplars. Although it is sometimes difficult to make direct comparisons internationally, several other important characteristics were highlighted in our case-study work as being important critical success factors:

- *Strong brand and identity*: the most successful urban-regeneration programmes promoted a strong brand and identity. In some cases these were linked to the competitiveness agenda (for example Cardiff and Sant Adriá de Besós) whilst in other cases sports or media-based events had assisted promotion (for example Turin and Sant Adriá de Besós). In turn this had led to increased inward investment to the areas in question. It is crucial, however, that regeneration projects include the development of adequate infrastructure and services for the integration of newcomers and external investors by organising, for example, workshops and networking events. Similarly, it is of fundamental importance for municipal authorities to have plans in place (for example 'decanting' and subsequent relocation back to the existing community) to minimise the involuntary displacement effect that higher income people may have on local communities in terms of housing and local economic activities and services.
- *Local community participation*: local community participation and empowerment are essential if programmes of regeneration are to be successful. This includes the inclusion of non-administration actors such as residents and local businesses and also focuses attention on developing strategies and neighbourhood associations to activate and empower residents through social-service providers, associations and NGOs (Franke *et al.*, 2007; EC, 2009). Neighbourhood funds and budgets are being used successfully in German and Dutch urban policy for example (EC, 2009).
- *Partnership models*: finding the right blend or mix of public and private partnership is vital to consider. In some cases there was a strong and equal basis for a PPP, but in other instances most activity was underwritten by the public sector. This is true of both local and regional partnership arrangements. Incorporating both local knowledge and private-sector

skills is vital in such arrangements. As the investment gap in Europe's cities widens, new and innovative methods of financing urban regeneration will be also be required.

- *Planning policies and governance models*: strong national, regional and city-level planning polices, which are integrated and robust, are also fundamental to success. Examples that have worked well include the Socially Integrative City in Leipzig and La Mina in Sant Adriá de Besós. It also implies that planners should examine a neighbourhood's horizontal and vertical ties (Warren, 1963), where vertical ties comprise the relationship with outside entities and horizontal ties reflect the strength of social networks and overall social fabric within and between the neighbourhoods (LUDA, 2006). Experience also shows that urban-regeneration policies are more successful when they are linked with strategic land-use policies; equal-opportunity policies; environment policies and demographic policies (EC, 2009). Vertical cooperation through local, regional and national bodies is also vital to promote sound and effective governance (for example the way in which the 'opportunity zone' concept in Rotterdam was tied into national and local policies.

Best approaches and practices to implement and monitor social sustainability

Conventionally there has been no shortage of *ex ante* evaluation in urban regeneration (LUDA, 2006; EC, 2009).This is not unexpected given that scarce public resources are allocated on the basis of competing demands. For example, pre-project analysis has been a general feature of URBAN programmes, and follow-up analysis adopted in mid-term evaluations. In essence, good quality *ex ante* evaluation supports rational decision making as it can assess whether proposed solutions are in accordance with expected results and impact (Kazmierczak *et al.*, 2007). However, the main deficiencies have been in relation to *ex post* ('downstream') monitoring.

Most of the best practices to promote socially sustainable urban regeneration have been discussed in the previous chapter.[2] Nonetheless, here it is important to reiterate how vision, leadership and a sound managerial approach to regeneration are essential components to deliver socially sustainable urban regeneration. Regeneration plans for a local neighbourhood

---

[2] At the time of writing Building Research Establishment (BRE) in the UK had just released a new radar system of scoring master plan developments in the UK, called Greenprint (Fisher, 2010). This *ex ante* system covers eight areas that impact on sustainability (including climate-change resources, transport, ecology, business, place making, community and buildings) and is being trialled internationally.

become even more effective if they are linked to city-wide development plans and vision. They can also help attract further funding and generate self-sustaining projects.

In addition, image and branding are crucial for the social regeneration of city areas. Indeed, neighbourhoods undergoing urban regeneration have often acted as recipient areas for low-income newcomers to the city because of their affordable rents and lower cost of living. Regeneration projects are therefore trying to improve the image of these places in order to attract new inward-investment in social, economic and green infrastructure, as well as middle- to high-income people to these neighbourhoods. It is crucial, however, that regeneration projects include the development of adequate infrastructure and services for the integration of newcomers and external investors by organising, for example, workshops and networking events. Similarly, as we suggested earlier in this chapter, it is of fundamental importance for municipal authorities to have plans in place to minimise the involuntary displacement effects that higher income people may have on local communities in terms of housing and local economic activities and services.

From a monitoring perspective, this book has shown how difficult it is to measure universally the 'softer' aspects of social sustainability, such as well-being, happiness and neighbourhood satisfaction arising from urban regeneration. At present the only effective way to measure these dimensions of social sustainability is through the use of surveys and other qualitative research techniques such as interviews and focus groups, which can prove expensive in the long term. As a result, there is a need for more investment in new and cost-effective data gathering procedures and methodologies. The statistical offices of local and national governments and EU institutions should invest in developing innovative methods and optimised procedures, which involve, for example, local residents and bipartisan organisation such as universities, in order to gather data in the field in a cost-effective way.

This book has also demonstrated that an increasing number of private- and NGO-sector actors involved in the built environment and urban regeneration have developed monitoring systems (for example, igloo's *footprint*™ system and Compagnia di San Paolo's housing projects evaluation system), which appear to provide a valuable framework for assessing the critical dimensions of sustainability in a robust and effective way. There can also be little doubt that the experience gained through PPPs between local authorities and frontrunner actors in the sustainability arena can contribute to the implementation of state-of-the-art cross-disciplinary and cross-sectoral assessment and monitoring systems, which can also integrate Socially Responsible Investment policies, Third Sector metrics and social-monitoring indicators developed by local authorities.

The igloo model of social sustainability measurement is intriguing because it taps into a dimension that is very challenging to measure. As we saw in

Chapter 6, the idea of 'health, happiness and well-being' has recently been added by igloo to their *footprint* system. For igloo the promotion of 'health, happiness and well-being' is informed by the bringing together of three premises (igloo, 2010: 12):

- A focus on 'celebrating the city' and ensuring that the positive contribution that cities make to people's lives is promoted.
- An emphasis on context or understanding the regeneration project in the scope of the wider neighbourhood, with an understanding of the impact each intervention will have on neighbourhood well-being.
- Promotion of happiness but not at any cost, in that a regeneration project should seek to create opportunities for people to live fulfilling and happy lives based on an understanding of the human condition and basic needs, and bounded by a strong social contract and the need to live within environmental constraints.

In terms of measurement this means minimising environmental risk (through safe roads and the promotion of cycling); promoting a healthy urban environment through high-quality indoor environmental quality; positive choices and active lives, including fresh food, leisure and recreation, and healthy and inclusively designed homes (for all age groups). Community opportunities should also be encouraged through sociable space networks, communal spaces and virtual spaces. Finally, the well-being of those in the community can also be assessed through five key dimensions:

1 *Aspirations*: working with local people to explore the proposed changes to their neighbourhood.
2 *Environmental quality*: quality, safety and security of the local environment and public realm.
3 *Access to employment*: access to a range of diverse job opportunities.
4 *Housing standards*: access to affordable, quality housing that meets decency standards and fitness criteria as a minimum.
5 *Public services*: quality of core services such as education, health and welfare.

This, of course, raises the question of how well-being and happiness are defined. A recent report (NEF, 2010) suggested that 'place happiness' (pH) captured three core aspects of well-being to which the built environment can contribute:

1 *Personal well-being*, which is based on people's experience of life in relation to their physical and psychological well-being;
2 *social well-being*, which is focused on people's experience of life in relation to their community; and

3 *economic and material well-being*, which is based on people's life experience in relation to conditions and circumstances and their physical
surroundings.

The report also suggested that regeneration projects should also capture
'place sustainability' (pS), which is based on resources used during construction and across the project's lifetime. This builds on other thinking within
the urban policy agenda. For example LUDA (2006) referred to a conceptual
framework for assessing urban policy outcomes as a 'Diamond Quality of
Life' with five dimensions for 'quality of life', including: (i) sociocultural
conditions; (ii) economic conditions; (iii) urban structure; (iv) environmental conditions; and (v) community and institutional capacity. Essentially
there is therefore a trend away from maximising purely financial return as a
measure of success. As NEF (2010) pointed out, investment in areas will not
always improve the economic well-being of the residents and well-being
itself is not always associated with increased wealth. In this sense we can no
longer rely purely on markets or the profit motive (if ever we could) to produce sustainable outcomes. There is also a related issue here over how such
'softer' concepts can and should be measured. As the NEF (2010: 59) report
pointed out:

> Where attempts to measure effects on individuals, communities, or the
> environment are made, it is often the case that inadequate indicators and
> poor or under-resourced data collection methods obscure the real impact –
> positive and negative – of development projects … if sustainable well-
> being is to be the overarching objective … then such a transition will
> need to be supported by a measurement framework that can capture the
> wider social, environmental and economic impact that projects are
> having.

This implies, as far as social sustainability is concerned, a much more
robust data-collection system linking with indicators that tie in with a
project's goals and outcomes. Moreover, downstream evaluation in the
post-occupancy phase of a project is vital, and should be linked with the
collection of *ex ante* baseline data. In this sense a systematic review of
impact is also essential. Therefore, if a project is underpinned by both
public and private partnership arrangements then the basis for measurement also needs to reflect both social and economic value. The research
on which this book is based also raises further questions for research, such
as how can we adopt a more integrated approach to measurement? and
how might the frameworks we have outlined translate into practice in
other national contexts?

Public–private partnerships and emerging urban regeneration delivery vehicles

Single task *ad hoc* agencies and public–private partnerships (PPPs) are beneficial vehicles to deliver self-sustaining and socially sustainable urban regeneration projects. In addition, a well-resourced and integrated approach to regeneration supported by diversified and continuing funding is crucial to deliver sustainable communities and avoid piecemeal interventions. There is also evidence from the empirical work in this research that the location of the regeneration agency offices in the areas being regenerated have beneficial effects, because they can guarantee a forum for discussion and transparency, helping reduce mistrust towards city authorities, which often characterises these areas.

In addition, interviews conducted as part of the research process highlighted the widespread belief amongst policy makers and practitioners that current EU 'grant-based' public funding instruments in support of urban areas, such as the Structural Funds and Cohesion Fund, are likely to be gradually abandoned in favour of new, 'non-grant' funding mechanisms and vehicles (e.g. Urban Development Funds, EIB JESSICA programme) after the current 2007–2013 Structural Funds programming period. These new funding mechanisms and instruments will increasingly be based on the integration of private and public financial resources and managerial skills. As a result, cities that have fostered the development of PPPs for sometime may present a competitive advantage in terms of development opportunities, in comparison with cities and municipal authorities that have thus far attracted and benefited only from traditional public funds.

Fundamentally, urban regeneration has frequently been about the profit motive as far as developers and investors have been concerned. However, as we have seen in this book, this will no longer suffice. First and foremost, ISUD is focused on a model of regeneration that places emphasis on people and places in the context of communities. Those private sector partners that will succeed in this brave new world will be those who recognise the importance of their role in communities and city-wide visions for the future. Perhaps we are also seeing some signs of a 'blended value' concept emerging in regeneration as the social dimension gains more traction. This concept recognises that all organisations (whether for-profit or not) create value that consists of economic, social and environmental value components, and that investors simultaneously generate all three forms of value through the provision of capital to organisations. The outcome of all this activity is 'value creation' and this value is non-divisible and is, therefore, a blend of economic, social and environmental elements, forming what is called 'blended value' (Emerson, 2003). Essentially, therefore, the concept of blended value recognises the importance of social entrepreneurship and places emphasis on non-economic value.

As we enter a period of restraint and retrenchment in pubic spending, however, and a challenging investment gap in European cities (created by low liquidity and confidence), new concerns will also present challenges for policy makers and other key stakeholders seeking to maintain a strong social dimension to their future urban vision.

The future of urban regeneration: Moving out of recession and retaining the social dimension

Over the last 10 years a common methodology for sustainable urban development has begun to take shape and has been promoted, following the emergence of a European 'Acquis Urbain', which builds on the experience gained in supporting integrated and sustainable urban development (EC, 2009). This methodology is also in line with the policy principles and recommendations laid down in the Leipzig Charter on Sustainable European Cities (EU Ministers, 2007). The 2004 Rotterdam 'Acquis Urbain' is based on the following cornerstones (Ministry of Kingdom and Interior Relations, 2005):

- The development of city-wide visions that go beyond each project and are embedded in the city-regional context;
- the integrated and cross-sectoral approach (horizontal and vertical coordination);
- the new instruments of urban governance, administration and management, including increased local responsibilities and strong local and regional partnerships;
- financing and investing with lasting effects, concentration of resources and funding on selected target areas;
- capitalising on knowledge, exchanging experience and know-how (benchmarking, networking); and
- monitoring the progress (*ex ante*, mid-term and *ex post* evaluations, and indicators).

Some of this thinking is indeed at the heart of ISUD, and at the heart of some of the case studies that we have examined in this book. Despite this agreed methodology, however, European cities face new challenges. Although there is a general trend in Europe towards ageing populations, it is expected that urban areas in Europe will face substantial population increases as migration continues to be a powerful force for change, although in other EU member states some cities will face depopulation. A recent

Table 12.2 'Barcelona principles' for promoting city recovery and reinvestment.

1	Provide proactive and collaborative leadership at the local level
2	Make the case for public investment
3	Robust long-term economic strategy
4	Purposeful short-term action
5	Investment attraction and readiness
6	Relationships matter and need increased attention
7	Effective public works and major investments
8	Stay close to the people
9	Stay open to the world
10	Build national–local alliances

Source: Clark (2009). Reproduced by permission of OECD. Barcelona Principles (p13–14) of Clark, G.

EC report (EC, 2009: 48) suggested that there would be several broad and specific challenges for European cities:

- The integration of migrants into the labour force and society;
- adaptation of infrastructure;
- social disparities and social polarisation;
- increased ecological pressures in the region as a whole, due also to urban sprawl;
- environmental problems in certain areas; and
- a reinforcement of regional disparities in the economic growth potential.

These challenges also broadly reflect the European regional challenges to 2020 that were identified in a recent report: globalisation, demographic change, climate change and energy systems (EC, 2008).

In the short term, however, European cities also face the prospect of emerging from the current economic recession, which is the worst economic crisis for decades. Some cities have already responded with recovery plans (for example London), and others have formed new alignments and collaborations with higher tiers of government (for example Bilbao; Clark, 2009; UCLG, 2009). A recent OECD LEED paper (Clark, 2009) identified 10 principles ('Barcelona Principles') to guide further action (Table 12.2). This suggests that in order to remain competitive, cities will need to develop along four frontiers, by creating:

- New economic strategies which promote differentiation, based on a city's unique assets.
- New investment strategies and tools, which may no longer be based on conventional PPP models but on new private sector co-investments that are more adaptable and based on shared goals rather than a single transaction.

Table 12.3 Recovery matrix for cities and neighbourhoods.

	Economy (firms *and* labour market)	Society (people)	Place/environment
Short term	Filling the gap in credit for firms (e.g. Lyon – sale and leaseback of land)	Debt advice and support	Public–public financial instruments
(a) Credit	Bringing forward public investment and expenditure (e.g. Spanish local authorities)	Tax and rate cuts	Take advantage of lower land and property prices
(b) Recession	Short-term working arrangements (Germany, Duisburg)	Minimum income support	Protect/bring forward key regeneration projects
	Subsidising existing jobs and sectors	Advice and support for housing, heating, transport, basic services	Protect basic services
	Creating temporary jobs and training (Intermediate Labour Markets, UK; Work Integration Coops, Germany; Type B Coops, Italy)	Integration policies	Delay, cut back non-essentials
		Building resilience and insulation from recession	Environmental pilots
Long term (positioning the city in the face of long-term global shifts)	Creating the conditions and investing in sustainable activities (e.g. green, health care, education, knowledge, culture)	More equality	Sustainable building, transport, energy, water and waste
Examples: Transition Cities, Slow Cities, Mayors Covenant, WWF One Planet Living	Training in the skills required for sustainable activities	Shifts in consumption and saving patterns	
	Support for innovation in these activities	Shifts in use of time and work–life balance	

Source: Sato (2010). Reproduced by permission of URBACT.

This may also mean long-term joint ventures, which are not simply based on land value uplift.
- New partnerships with higher tiers of government so that flexible and adaptive policies can be developed for city-level recovery.
- A renewed focus on making public-sector delivery more efficient, with a drive for improved service quality at lower costs.

It is clear that city-level responses are dependent on a complex mix of factors, which include size, economic composition, location and global positioning, social composition and culture, global connectivity, media and cultural identity, migration policies and position in the urban hierarchy (Clark, 2009; Sato, 2010). Similarly, understanding a neighbourhood's response can only be seen in the context of its position in the 'urban value-added chain' (Jacquier, 2005).

Cities (and their neighbourhoods) will need, therefore, to plan both for short-term pressures and longer term changes that will aid recovery, and will need to cope with complex social and economic changes (Young Foundation, 2009a; Sato, 2010; Table 12.3). For example, the Young Foundation (2009a) suggested that the 'resilience' of communities needs to be strengthened through family, informal and institutional networks and that people and communities need 'insulating' from the recession through local food and energy schemes, time banking and other forms of social banking. Moreover, the concept of 'social innovation' or new ideas, institutions, or ways of working that meet social needs more effectively is also seen by some as critically important to cities' success (Murray, 2009; Young Foundation, 2009b).

The economic crisis has also thrown up fresh challenges for the European Social Model itself, and perhaps provides a fresh opportunity to tackle social cohesion and social progress in different ways. As a recent Notre Europe report put it (Rubio, 2009: 4–5):

> While the general goal of Lisbon remains valid (to convert Europe into a socially-inclusive, sustainable, knowledge-based economy), some of the dogmas and causal assumptions inspiring Lisbon interventions so far have been seriously challenged over the last few months – the exclusive focus on supply-side reforms, the lack of attention paid to income inequalities, the assumption that technological innovation is enough to promote a move towards a low carbon economy and, last but not least, the belief that growth automatically leads to an improvement of social conditions.

This has produced new thinking on how cities and deprived neighbourhoods can contribute to the recovery (Sato, 2010). The juxtaposition of banking crisis, recession and global economic shift presents major challenges, and it is likely that consumption-driven sectors based around financial services and retail will no longer have the attraction they once did for investors. It is also doubtful as to how long we will continue to accept that cities are both 'engines of growth and jobs' but, at the same time, continue to contain substantial areas of deprivation. As Sato (2010) pointed out, even before the economic crisis, inequality had risen and many of the new jobs created in Europe were low paid, temporary or casual. In fact some 20% of those in poverty in the EU are in work, which has huge cost implications for cities in terms of social services, health, education and community polarisation.

Within this context European Structural Funds and financial engineering tools such as JASPERS (Joint Assistance in Supporting Projects in European Regions), JEREMIE (Joint European Resources for Micro to medium Enterprises), JESSICA (Joint European Support for Sustainable Investment in City Areas) and JASMINE (Joint Action to Support Micro-finance Institutions in Europe) must continue to provide valuable additional financing opportunities for urban regeneration and related activities. This will be vital as climate change will present new challenges for city finance, prompting moves towards greener forms of taxation and also additional pressures on existing city finances. Additional pressure could also result from adaptation and mitigation policies, as well as rises in the price of fossil-fuel energy sources thus placing further strictures on already over-burdened budgets (OECD, 2009). A recent Work Foundation (2009) report based on more than 40 case studies not only suggested that those cities that are more reliant on local sources of taxation may be more prone to recessionary impacts, but that lack of flexibility over funding is a constraint in the short and medium term. Moreover, innovative forms of finance such as Tax Increment Financing (TIF) may become more attractive as this can allow cities to finance infrastructure investment by borrowing against future increases in tax revenues (APUDG, 2010; see Chapter 4).

For some, however, the recession has, in fact, provided a rationale for challenging the mainstream discourse of sustainability and regeneration. For example, Evans *et al.* (2009) suggested that a more 'organic' model of urban regeneration, based on bottom-up community action should replace what they consider to be the essentially private-sector led, 'commodity-based' model, which, for them, has frequently failed to deliver on social sustainability. Nevertheless, today more than ever, there is surely a need for integrated thinking at a city and urban regeneration level, and this must place social sustainability as a vital element in the move towards an integrated and sustainable urban future. There are, indeed, great opportunities as we face the challenges of today: the growth areas in employment in the future will be in green jobs and, if the public purse permits, also in health and education. There is an increasing probability therefore, as Sato (2010) suggested, that we will see cities as 'gardens for growth' rather than as 'engines for growth' in the future, with a greater emphasis on smart growth and more sustainable outcomes. The challenge of achieving social sustainability will remain, however.

Appendices

Appendix 1:   Interviews conducted as part of the research process and fieldworks

1.1   Background and in-depth interviews conducted in the UK

Interviewee and role	Date	Type of interview
1 Chief Executive Officer, regeneration company	October 2007	Formal
2 Chief Executive Officer, developer	December 2007	Formal
3 Head of Research, institutional investor	December 2007	Formal
4 Research & Development Manager, CSR consultancy	November 2007	Formal
5 Director, Underserved Markets, CSR consultancy	November 2007	Formal
6 Associate Director – Development, developer	November 2007	Formal
7 Consultant, CSR consultancy	November 2007	Formal

1.2   Case-study interviews

City	Interviewee and role	Date	Type of interview
Turin, Italy	1 Deputy Mayor for Urban Development and Integration of Turin	April 2008	Formal
	2 Architect, Turin City Council	April 2008	Formal
	3 Representative, Municipal Police, City of Turin	April 2008	Formal
	4 Representative, 'The Gate' and Spina 3 Projects Committees	April 2008	Formal
	5 Senior Officer, Progetto Periferie, Turin City Council	April 2008	Informal

Urban Regeneration & Social Sustainability: Best Practice from European Cities, by Andrea Colantonio and Tim Dixon   © 2011 Andrea Colantonio and Tim Dixon

1.2   (*cont'd*)

City		Interviewee and role	Date	Type of interview
	6	Senior Office, Spina 3 project	April 2008	Formal
	7	Senior Funding Officer, Bank Foundation	April 2008	Formal
	8	Senior Officer, The Gate Committee	April 2008	Formal
	9	Professor of Architecture, Turin-based university	April 2008	Informal
	10	Professor of Geography Turin-based university	April 2008	Informal
Sant Adriá de Besós/ Barcelona, Spain	1	Representative, La Mina Consortium	April 2008	Formal
	2	Architect, La Mina Consortium	April 2008	Formal
	3	Project Manager, developer	April 2008	Formal
	4	Senior Social Officer, La Mina Consortium	April 2008	Formal
	5	Senior Social Officer, La Mina Consortium	April 2008	Formal
	6	Senior Social Officer, La Mina Consortium	April 2008	Formal
	7	Councillor, Sant Adriá de Besós City Council	April 2008	Formal
	8	Women Association representatives, La Mina	April 2008	Formal
	9	Sociologist, La Mina Consortium	April 2008	Formal
	10	Representative, Community Participation Division, Sant Adriá de Besós City Council	April 2008	Formal
	11	Representative, Institute of Territorial Studies, Generalitat de Cataluna and Universitat Pompeu Fabra	April 2008	Informal
	12	Lawyer, Catalan Government	April 2008	Formal
	13	Project Manager, B_Tec	April 2008	Informal
	14	Professor of Human Geography, Barcelona-based university	April 2008	Informal
Cardiff, Wales	1	Project Manager, developer	May 2008	Formal
	2	Representative of Welsh Government	May 2008	Formal
	3	Planner, County Council	May 2008	Formal
	4	Representative, Welsh Design Commission	May 2008	Formal
	5	Partner, developer	May 2008	Formal
	6	Architect, design company	May 2008	Formal
	7	Representative, design company	May 2008	Formal
	8	Senior Lecturer of Urban Planning, Cardiff-based university	May 2008	Informal
	9	Manager, Cardiff Harbour Authority	May 2008	Formal
Leipzig, Germany*	1	Abteilungsleiterin/Stadt Leipzig	July 2008	Formal
	2	Sachbearbeiterin/Stadt Leipzig	July 2008	Formal

1.2   (*cont'd*)

City		Interviewee and role	Date	Type of interview
	3	Quartiersmanager/Volkmarsdorf	July 2008	Formal
	4	Stadträtin (SPD)/Stadt Leipzig	August 2008	Formal
	5	Baudezernent/Bgm/Stadt Leipzig	August 2008	Formal
	6	DIFU	August 2008	Informal
	7	Stadt Leipzig	July 2008	Informal
	8	Fachreferentin/Stadt Leipzig	July 2008	Informal
Rotterdam, the Netherlands	1	Representative, South Pact	July 2008	Formal
	2	Social Officers, Municipal Authority	July 2008	Formal
	3	Representative, Housing Corporation 1	July 2008	Formal
	4	Representative, Housing Corporation 2	July 2008	Formal
	5	Two Development Officers, Municipal Authority	July 2008	Formal
	6	Planner, Ministry for Housing and Spatial Planning	July 2008	Formal
	7	Academic, The Hague-based university	July 2008	Informal
	8	Academic, Rotterdam-based university	July 2008	Informal
	9	Development Officer, Statistical Office	July 2008	Formal

Note: *Interviews by Robin Ganser.

Appendix 2: Vancouver's quality of life and social sustainability indicators

Demographic background information	Affordable appropriate housing	Civic engagement	Community and social infrastructure	Education	Employment	Local economy	Natural environment	Personal and community health	Personal financial security	Personal safety
Population	30%+ Income on shelter	Voter turnout	Social service professionals	Education levels	Unemployment/employment rates	Business bankruptcies	Air quality	Low-birth-weight babies	Community affordability	Young offenders
Foreign born	Vacancy rates	Women in municipal government	Private health care expenditures	Literacy levels	Quality of employment	Consumer bankruptcies	Urban transportation	Teen births	Families receiving EI/social assistance	Violent crimes
Visible minorities	Core housing need	Newspaper circulation	Subsidised child-care spaces	Adult learning	Long-term unemployment	Hourly wages	Population density	Premature mortality	Lone-parent families	Property crimes
Language spoken at home	Substandard units	Volunteering	Social assistance allowance	Education expenditures	Labour force replacement	Change in family income	Water consumption	Work hours lost	Incidence of low income families	Injuries and poisonings
Population mobility	Changing face of homelessness	Charitable donations	Outdoor recreation areas	Classroom size		Building permits	Wastewater treatment	Suicides	Children living in poverty	
New immigrant group	50%+ Income on shelter		Public transit costs	Student/teacher ratio			Solid waste	Infant mortality	Government transfer income	
Aboriginal population	Rental housing starts		Social housing waiting lists	Post-secondary tuition			Ecological footprint		Economic dependency ratio	
Migration	Monthly rent		Rent-geared-to-income housing	Spending on private education			Recreational water quality		Government income supplements	
Household									Household income	
Renters and owners										

Source: City of Vancouver (2005).

Appendix 3: The evolution of sustainable development metrics initiatives by governmental and institutional organisations

Initiative	Organisation/year	Brief description	Spatial scale	Inclusion of social sustainability themes
Human Development Report Indices	United Nations Development Programme (UNDP), early 1990s	Human Development Index, Human Poverty Index	International, national	The indices have a focus on the basic need theme of social sustainability
CSD Indicators for Sustainable Development	United Nations, 1995	50 core indicators part of a set of 96 indicators. The framework contains 15 themes, which are no longer explicitly categorised into four pillars of sustainable development	International, national	Social indicators include: (i) poverty; (ii) governance; (iii) health; (iv) education; and (v) demographics
Well-being assessment	IUCN – The World Conservation Union and the International Development Research Centre (IDRC), mid-1990s	It is based on the Well-being of Nations survey, introducing the 'Egg of Well-being' formed by the Ecosystem Well-being Index (EWI) and Human Well-being Index (HWI)	National	HWI focuses on: (i) health and population; (ii) wealth; (iii) knowledge and culture; (iv) community; and (v) equity. Aggregation uses several techniques (unweighted averages, weighted, and lowest value)
Genuine Progress Indicator and Index of Sustainable Economic Welfare	Redefining Progress and Herman Daly, mid-1990s	Indicators that attempt to improve the Gross National Product measurements including environmental and social values	National	Social sustainability aspects include: (i) crime and family breakdown; (ii) household and volunteer work; (iii) income distribution; (iv) changes in leisure time; and (v) lifespan of consumer durables and public infrastructure. Their aggregation method is still being developed

Appendix 3: (cont'd)

Initiative	Organisation/year	Brief description	Spatial scale	Inclusion of social sustainability themes
Urban Audit	Eurostat and DG REGIO, piloted 1997–2000	A collection of 336 variables collected in nine statistical fields, divided into 25 domains. The data gathering is carried out every five years	(i) Core city; (ii) larger urban zone; and (iii) district	These are not sustainability indicators strictly speaking. The statistical fields related to social issues are: (i) demography; (ii) social aspects; (iii) civic involvement; (iv) training and education; (v) travel and transport; and (vi) culture and recreation
Policy Performance Index	Jochen Jesinghaus on behalf of the European Commission, 1999	Policy Performance Index is proposed as an aggregation process of several indices in different policy fields. The indices are chosen and weighted according to consensus and international standards	National	The initiative evaluates the relevance that different stakeholders assign to each value. It has not been tested yet. Could be controversial in how group consensus is built (UNCSD, 2001)
City Development Index	Habitat, 2001	Formed by five indices: (i) infrastructure; (ii) waste; (iii) health; (iv) education; and (v) city product	Metropolitan	Three indices measure aspects of social sustainability, but relevant issues are left out. The overall aggregation considers all the indices to have the same weighting
Eurostat Sustainable Development Indicators	Eurostat, 2001	Indicators are divided into 10 themes. There are level I, II and II indicators for each theme	Regional, national	The main focus on social sustainability is on poverty and social exclusion, ageing society, and governance

The Sustainability Dashboard	Consultative Group on Sustainable Development Indicators, IUCN, early 2000s	Information panel formed by three dials labelled as 'Environmental Quality', 'Economic Performance' and 'Social Health'	National	The indicators and aggregation on Economic Performance and Social Health are very general and basic. The Social Health Index is based on the UNDP's Human Development Index (UNCSD, 2001)
Sustainable Communities Indicators – Egan Review	Egan Review, UK, 2004	50 indicators, 30 of which are 'objective', or statistically based, and 20 of which are 'subjective', based on surveys and questionnaires	Regional; sub-regional; neighbourhood community	First attempt to develop indicators explicitly to monitor the sustainable communities approach as set out in the Bristol Accord. Indicators are grouped in eight themes linked to the eight characteristics of sustainable communities described
EU Sustainable Communities Indicators	The European Regional and Business and Economic Development Unit (ERBEDU) and the Centre for Urban Development and Environmental Management (CUDEM), Leeds Metropolitan University, UK, 2007	These are EUROSTAT and Urban Audit Indicators mapped against the eight characteristics of sustainable communities. Each theme is subdivided into a number of sub-themes	City region; city; neighbourhood	The initiative calls for the EU statistical services (Eurostat and Urban Audit) to collect data that monitor progress within individual communities, whether they be neighbourhoods, towns, cities or metropolitan regions

Appendix 4: Main CSR * and social capital initiatives, tools and techniques

Initiative/tool/technique	Organisation/website	Brief description/comment
The Sustainability Assessment Model (SAM)	British Petroleum (BP) and Genesis Limited (UK division), with the University of Aberdeen	The Sustainability Assessment Model (SAM) follows a Full Cost Accounting (FCA) approach that considers the full life-cycle of a project and identifies all its internal and external costs and translates them into monetary values. The limitations of this model stem from the lack of an operational definition of sustainability. The question of substitutability between several forms of capital and the extent to which an organisation can be held responsible are also unclear (Baxter et al., 2002)
SA 8000	Social Accountability International (SAI)	SA 8000 is promoted as a voluntary, universal standard for companies interested in auditing and certifying labour practices in their facilities and those of their suppliers and vendors. It is designed for independent third-party certification
Equator Principles	http://www.equator-principles.com	The Equator Principles is a framework for financial institutions to manage environmental and social issues in project financing. The principles are intended to serve as a common baseline for the implementation of individual, internal environmental and social procedures and standards for project financing activities across all industry sectors globally. The principles were developed and adopted by the International Finance Corporation (IFC) and 20 of the world's leading banks, and quickly became a global market standard for project finance
Global Sullivan Principles	Leon Sullivan, http://www.thesullivanfoundation.org	Corporate codes of conduct designed to increase the active participation of corporations in the advancement of human rights and social justice at the international level
Global Reporting Initiative (GRI)	http://www.globalreporting.org	Sustainability Reporting Guidelines set a globally applicable framework for reporting the economic, environmental, and social dimensions of an organisation's activities, products, and services. It is the most widely used and internationally recognised standard for corporate sustainability measurement and reporting

Dow Jones Sustainability Index	http://www.sustainability-index.com	Dow Jones Sustainability Index (DJSI) is described as the first global index tracking the financial performance of the leading sustainability-driven companies worldwide. Company questionnaire is designed to assess opportunities and risks deriving from economic, environmental and social activities of companies. Inclusion in the Index is a competitive process; selection is considered a mark of distinction for companies that want investors to see them as sustainability leaders
KLD Social Indices	KLD, http://www.kld.com	Indices for investors who integrate environmental, social and governance factors into their investment decisions. Examples of such indices include: Domini 400 Social Index; Dividend Achievers Social Index; Global Climate 100 Index; Large Cap Sudan Free Social Index
FTSE4Good	http://www.ftse.com/ftse4good/index.jsp	The FTSE4Good Index Series was created by FTSE, a UK-based financial index company, in response to the increasing interest in SRI. Its inclusion criteria measures the performance of companies that meet globally recognised corporate responsibility standards. The visibility and reputation of FTSE4Good provides companies with a powerful vehicle to communicate their CSR achievements. It is widely used by investors and asset managers, especially in Europe, and increasingly in Asia
Smart Growth Network	http://www.smartgrowth.org	The Smart Growth Network (SGN) was formed in response to increasing community concerns about the need for new ways to grow local communities while boosting the economy, protecting the environment, and enhancing community vitality. Its focus is on community engagement and development, with emphasis on integrative solutions to a mix of community issues, such as traffic, housing, jobs, sprawl and environment. Smart Growth has gained attention recently; it provides an alternative to single-issue focus; and engages companies and stakeholders in productive problem solving. It is widely used by companies that seek to build strong community bonds. Numerous states and municipalities have endorsed the approach in their development strategy
Global Citizenship 360	The Future 500 or The Conference Board	Strategic planning process to measure corporate performance against the major standards, align with corporate strategic objectives, prepare GRI Report-Builders and other reports, and build team and corporate commitment
One Report	http://www.one-report.com/	Web-based tool to submit data easily using a GRI framework to over 20 social-investment organisations and research and rating institutions, such as Calvert and Accountability

Appendix 4: (cont'd)

Initiative/tool/technique	Organisation/website	Brief description/comment
Amnesty International Human Rights Principles for Companies	Amnesty International, http://web.amnesty.org	Amnesty International has produced an introductory checklist of human rights principles to assist multinational companies in the following areas: (i) company policy on human rights; (ii) security; (iii) community engagement; (iv) freedom from discrimination; (v) freedom from slavery; (vi) health and safety; (vii) freedom of association and the right to collective bargaining; (viii) fair working conditions; and (ix) monitoring human rights
Balanced Scorecard	Robert Kaplan and David Norton, http://www.balancedscorecard.org	Developed in the early 1990s, the balanced scorecard is a management system (not only a measurement system) that enables organisations to clarify their vision and strategy and translate them into action. This approach provides a clear prescription as to what companies should measure in order to 'balance' the financial perspective. Other types of scorecards include stakeholder and key performance indicator scorecards
Sustainability Balanced Scorecard	Möller and Schaltegger	A modification of the Balanced Scorecard that shows a greater focus on environmental reporting. The sustainability balanced scorecard (SBSC) is consistent with the environmental and social strategies of the company. In addition it is a prerequisite and includes a non-market perspective (such as environmental or social impacts of a firm's operations) in order to influence management's decision making
The Corporate Responsibility Index	Business in the Community, http://www.bitc.org.uk	Management and benchmarking index/tool that assesses the extent to which corporate strategy is integrated into business practice throughout an organisation. It provides a benchmark for companies to evaluate their management practices in four key areas of corporate responsibility and performance: (i) community; (ii) environment; (iii) market place; and (iv) work place
BRE Sustainability Checklist for Developments	BRE	The BRE Checklist provides practical tools and indicators to measure the sustainability of developments (both buildings and infrastructure) at site or estate level
SEEDA Sustainability Checklist	The South East England Development Agency (SEEDA)	The SEEDA Checklist is designed to be used by those involved in planning or building sizeable developments from estates to urban villages and regeneration projects

Tool	Source	Description
Social Capital Assessment Tool (SOCAT)	World Bank, http://www.worldbank.org	Multifaceted instrument designed to collect social capital data at the household, community and organisational levels. It is an integrated quantitative/qualitative tool. An important feature is the detailed information about structural and cognitive social capital that is collected at the level of the household, which is crucial to link social capital information with poverty and household welfare outcomes
Social Capital Question Bank	Office for National Statistics (ONS), UK, http://www.statistics.gov.uk/socialcapital/	This tool is based on the ONS survey matrix developed in 2001, and contains related questions from 15 major government and non-government surveys. It uses the same themes as the original matrix and allows users to see the actual wording of questions. The matrix is divided into accessible, interactive blocks linked together through the matrix grid
Social Capital Impact Assessment (SCIA) and Social Capital Building Toolkit	The Saguaro Seminar at Harvard University, USA	SCIA can be used to analyse the impact of the implementation of a programme or project on social capital. The building toolkit outlines and illustrates some effective ways to build social capital among individuals and groups. It includes examples about supportive settings, venues and activities for building social capital, and when possible some 'smart bets' or best guesses about its different purposes and outcomes
Social Capital as a Public Policy Tool	Policy Research Initiative, Canada	Launched in January 2003, this tool is intended as a reference tool for measuring social capital for use by the public policy research community within the Government of Canada. It presents various methodological options for adopting a social capital approach in the context of developing and evaluating public policy and government programmes
Social Capital Indicators	The Siena Group at OECD	Indicators proposed by the Siena Group for social statistics based on a module of standardised questions

Note: *Socially Responsible Investing (SRI) is also included in CSR. *Sources:* The Future 500 (2007), The Accounting for Sustainability Group (2006), RICS (2007), and listed websites.

Appendix 5:   Assessment of igloo's SRI policy objectives

Themes	Key policy issues	Performance assessment checklist
Health, happiness and well-being	Supporting healthy living	Minimising environmental risks
		Healthy internal and external microclimate
		Access to leisure routes and recreation spaces
		Access to health facilities and services
		Making fresh food available
	Creating opportunities for community	Creating sociable space networks
		Public realm vibrancy and intensity
		'Third' places and living rooms
		Communal, non-consumptive spaces
		Virtual spaces and broadband access
		Social contract for residents
	Changing lives and realising potential	Relationship of the scheme with its context
		Partnerships to deliver improvements
		Focus on five key 'well-being' themes
		Assessment of each scheme's impact
Regeneration	Location and connectivity	Proximity to amenities
		High degree of accessibility
		Permeability of streets
		Area's formal regeneration status
	Contextual analysis	Analysis of local context
		Regeneration, environmental-sustainability and urban-design themes
		Starting point for engagement and scheme concept
	Engagement process	Consultation process (present/discuss proposals to identify/prioritise concerns)
		Recording, documentation and accessibility
		Concerns and aspirations
		Partnership working (involve all key stakeholders in decision making)
		Community and stakeholder satisfaction
	Neighbourhoods and liveability	Amenities and services (shortfalls in basic provision within walkable distance; anticipate demand changes over time)
		Housing choice and access (respond to needs/ aspiration as identified by council/market research/engagement process)
		Local environmental quality (improve and maintain quality of public realm and reinforce civic pride)
		Neighbourhood management structures
	Community and stewardship	Social integration/diversity (provide amenities that promote social interaction)
		Community development (encourage diversity, opportunities for self-expression, social/ economic networks)

		Long-term stewardship (establish appropriate structures to encourage community decision making)
		Community-led decision making
		Commitment and partnerships
	Economic diversity and independence	Characterising the economy
		Lettings policy
		Facilitate access to employment
		Support of goods and services
		Culture of partnership and cooperation
Environmental sustainability	Energy systems	Low-carbon energy strategy
		Microclimate and urban grain
		Energy and carbon management
		Efficient design, specification and construction
		Low-carbon energy supply
	Car dependency	Low-carbon transport strategy
		Parking standards and car ownership
		Public transport quality and connectivity
		Encourage cycling/walking (e.g. cycle hire)
		Living and flexible working patterns
		Vehicle technology and fuels (e.g. car clubs)
	Waste minimisation	Waste-minimisation strategy
		Provide recycling services and promote systems to facilitate recycling
		Encourage participation through marketing (raising awareness)
		Promote waste minimisation
	Food supply	Market assessment and lettings policy
		Food miles and regional sourcing
		Organic and fair-trade products
		Identifying proactive retailers
		Reconnecting producers and consumers
		Affordable fresh produce
	Construction process/ materials	Environmental performance
		Material specification (low in toxicity)
		Waste arising
		Local and regional sourcing (sustainably sourced and natural in origin)
		Creative reuse (recycled or reused)
		Lifecycle utility
	Water cycle (management of water resources)	Encourage stakeholder participation
		Encourage water saving in areas of scarcity (e.g. water metering)
		Rainwater and waste-water systems
		Ecological design and management
Urban design	Permeable street network	Permeability and connectivity with urban fabric

Appendix 5: *(cont'd)*

Themes	Key policy issues	Performance assessment checklist
	Public realm and enclosure of space	Create recognisable hierarchy of streets Provide public pedestrian routes and thoroughfares Urban grain and relationship to nodes of activity Building line and enclosure Creation/animation of public realm Provide open and green space Provide street furniture and public art Sound management strategy
	Density and mix of uses	Gross densities/plot ratios (minimum 60 units/ha for houses; 7600 m²/ha commercial; plot ratios exceed 2 for both commercial and residential) Urban location and street hierarchy Horizontal and vertical mix of uses (great mix on high streets/local centres) Placing of tall buildings Access requirements Privacy distances (not <20 metres for single aspect units and 15 for dual
	Quality, diversity and distinctiveness	Architectural diversity Design competitions CABE design review (iconic buildings will be submitted to CABE for review) Heritage and building reuse Tall buildings subjected to assessment based on CABE/English heritage guidance
	Biodiversity by design	Contextual analysis Ensure valued natural green spaces/protected habitats/species; continuous canopy on street trees to define streets; habitat mosaics on roofs, facades, courtyards Green infrastructure plan Energy and microclimate Management and stewardship Wider benefits

Source: Adapted from igloo (2010).

Appendix 6: List of comparative baseline basic indicators for La Mina neighbourhood (2001)*

Population structure		La Mina	Sant Adriá de Besós	Barcelona	Catalonia
Total population		9 185	33 076	2 068 387	6 133 992
Population in relation to Sant Adriá de Besós		27.77%	100.00%	—	—
Population density inhabitant/km²		15 568	8 704	14 894	191
Population by sex	Female	49.73%	49.24%	52.55%	51.18%
	Male	50.27%	50.76%	47.45%	48.82%
		100%	100%	100%	100%
Population by age	Children (0–14)	19.67%	15.33%	12.03%	13.95%
	Young People (15–24)	17.68%	14.69%	13.83%	14.70%
	From 25 to 64 years of age	50.26%	54.79%	54.21%	54.13%
	Over 65	12.39%	15.18%	19.94%	17.22%
	Percentage of population over 65	62.98%	99.03%	14.87%	12.34%
	Percentage of population over 85	6.55%	9.44%	11.43%	10.09%
Birthplace		9 185	33 076	2 131 378	6 090 040
	Born in %	66.84%	64.23%	64.85%	68.40%
	Born in the rest of %	31.69%	33.16%	31.86%	28.78%
	Born abroad %	1.47%	2.61%	3.29%	2.82%
Resident Foreign Population		141	921	35 049	98 035
	European origin	34.04%	26.28%	27.66%	30.98%
	African origin	43.97%	29.75%	19.86%	35.76%
	Asian origin	7.09%	8.14%	16.14%	8.53%
	American origin	14.89%	35.83%	36.34%	24.73%
Population ethnically gypsy, approximate %		30%			
Education					
No. of educational centres		3	17		
	Nurseries	1	5		
	State schools	0	1		

Appendix 6: (cont'd)

Population structure		La Mina	Sant Adriá de Besós	Barcelona	Catalonia
Nursery and Primary Education	Private schools	1	4	807	3.007
	State schools	1	7	301	1.795
	Private schools	0	4	506	1.212
Secondary Education	State schools	1	3	255	729
	Private schools	1	5	121	509
		0	2	134	220
			3		
No. of students at educational centres 2000/2001		608	4 727		
Nurseries		60	320	63 531	205 991
Nursery education		122	858	106 069	349 530
Primary education		267	1 854	111 056	358 182
Secondary education		159	1 695		
School-age population, obligatory (6 to 16)		1 450	3 895		
School registration rate, obligatory		28.28%	78.72%		
Level of studies (population over 10 years of age)		8 153	30 106	1 967 010	5 539 012
Can neither read nor write %		12.72%	6.19%	1.40%	1.74%
Primary school incomplete %		30.19%	22.67%	16.28%	15.97%
Primary		35.35%	33.87%	30.53%	35.68%
O Levels		13.76%	16.30%	14.87%	15.88%
Professional training 1 %		4.46%	7.18%	6.11%	6.29%
Professional training 2 %		1.68%	4.27%	4.95%	4.41%
A levels %		1.26%	5.78%	12.36%	10.02%
Ordinary degree %		0.38%	2.26%	6.62%	5.21%
Higher degree %		0.20%	1.48%	6.88%	4.80%
Illiteracy rate %		12.90%	6.26%	1.44%	1.73%
No. women		706	1 237	20 761	69 743

Higher level studies among population over 24 %	No. men	331	628	6 805	26 684
		0.27%	1.93%	8.83%	6.08%
School absenteeism rate	No. women	3	223	61 548	120 998
	No. men	13	224	73 875	145 024
Students per neighbourhood					
Primary Schools		8%	1%		
Secondary Schools		10–12%	1%		
		30%	1%		
School failure rate					
Work					
Active Population					
Active population of in relation to Sant Adriá de Besós					
Economically active rate					
Active population by sex					
Women					
Men					
Active population young people %					
Population of 16 years and over by sex					
From 16 to 24 years women					
From 16 to 24 years men					
From 25 to 44 years women					
From 25 to 44 years men					
45 years and over women					
45 years and over men					
Working population					
Working population in relation to Sant Adriá de Besós					
Employment rate %					
Female employment rate %					
Employment rate of people of 45 years and over %					
Working population by sex					

Appendix 6: (cont'd)

Population structure		La Mina	Sant Adriá de Besós	Barcelona	Catalonia
Resident occupied population by sector	Female				
	Male				
	Services %				
	Building industry %				
	Industry %				
	Agriculture %				
Occupied population by professional situation	Companies with wage earners				
	Companies without wage earners				
	Members of co-operatives				
	Family benefits				
	Fixed employment				
	Sporadic employment				
	Other situations				
Recipients of unemployment benefit 1999					
Recipients of benefits by age and sex	Between 16 and 25 women				
	Between 16 and 25 men				
	Between 26 and 44 women				
	Between 26 and 44 men				
	Over 45 women				
	Over 45 men				
Recipients of benefits as % of total registered as unemployed	Men				
	Women				

Unemployment

Unemployment claims pending
Registered unemployed
Unemployment rate registered %
Long-term unemployment rate
Claims as a percentage of the total %

Registered unemployment by sex

Female
Registered female unemployment of the total %
Registered female unemployment rate %
Male

Unemployment according to level of studies

Without studies
Primary studies
School leaving certificate
Professional training
O Levels
A Levels
Ordinary degrees
Higher degrees

Unemployed by age

Over 45
Men
Women
From 25 to 44
Men
Women
From 16 to 24
Men
Women

Youth unemployment as a percentage of the total %

Appendix 6: (cont'd)

Population structure		La Mina	Sant Adriá de Besós	Barcelona	Catalonia
Registered youth unemployment rate					
Unemployment by sector	Agricultural sector				
	Industrial sector				
	Construction sector				
	Services sector				
	Unskilled				
Companies					
No. of companies	Industry				
	Construction				
	Service sector				
	Retail services				
	Professionals and artists				
No. of wage earners					
No. of professionals and self-employed workers					
Company size (medium size)	Service companies				
	Industrial companies				
	Construction companies				
	Companies with more than 50 workers %				
Small- and medium-sized companies with more than 50 workers %					
5 main business sectors %	First				
	Second				
	Third				
	Fourth				
	Fifth				

Gross domestic product at 1991 market prices — GDP / GDP per inhabitant

Distribution of gross added value per sector % — Agriculture / Industry / Construction / Services

Income 1996
Gross family income available (millions of pesetas)
Gross family income per habitant (millions of pesetas)
Gross family income per habitant
Poverty index
Social services
Death rate
Life expectancy
Number of non-contributory pensions — For illness / For retirement

Old people — One person households (people over 65)
No. places in old people's homes
Day centres for old people
No. of requests for places in homes
No. of requests for places in homes on waiting lists
No. of requests for day centres
No. of requests for day centres on waiting lists

Appendix 6: *(cont'd)*

Population structure	La Mina	Sant Adriá de Besós	Barcelona	Catalonia
Jobseeker's allowance 1999				
No. cases (families)				
No. of people included (that form part of the family unit)				
No. of users of restart schemes				
No. of users of training opportunities				
No. of users of psychological social services				
Requests female %				
Requests male %				
Recipients of social benefits 1999				
No. of emergency payments (subsistence, housing and transport)				
No. of housing benefits (debts, benefits for new rents or furnishing)				
No. of school subsidies (grants, books and dinners)				
No. of extracurricular activities (leisure and summer camps)				
No. of health benefits (expenses not covered by social security)				
No. of nursery grants				
No. of social benefits to over 65s				
Public health				
Doctors per 1000 inhabitants				
Hospital staff per 1000 inhabitants				
Hospital beds per 1000 inhabitants				
Alcohol and drug problems				
No. alcohol deintoxifications				
No. of drug-free programmes				

Treatment with methadone
No. of syringe exchange schemes
Proportion of heroin addicts
Rate of heroin addicts between 17–40
Incidence rate of drug addiction
10 000 inhabitants

Security and citizen protection
Crime rate %
Rate of crimes reported %
No. of local police interventions
No. of national police interventions
No. of monthly police detentions
No. of local police per 1000 inhabitants
No. of national police per
1000 inhabitants
Estimated population linked to
delinquency
Prison population
Prison population rate per
1000 inhabitants
Rate of ex-prisoners per
1000 inhabitants
Citizen participation
Participation in local elections
(June 1999) %
Participation in regional elections
(October 1999) %
Participation in national elections
(March 2000) %
Participation in European elections
(July 1999) %
Urban development and housing
Surface area

Appendix 6: *(cont'd)*

Population structure	La Mina	Sant Adriá de Besós	Barcelona	Catalonia
Current land under use				
Green zone				
Occupied zone				
Industrial zone				
Facilities				
Roads				
Other uses of the land				
Housing				
Buildings constructed				
Houses				
House occupation rate				
Owner occupier %				
Council owned %				
Average surface area of houses m^2				
Substandard housing				
Overcrowding				
Houses built by their occupiers				
Shanty towns				
Industries and services				
Land occupied by industrial estates ha				
Vacant land in industrial estates ha				
Commercial premises				
Commercial premises vacant				
Transport				
Cars per 1000 inhabitants				
Lorries and vans per 1000 inhabitants				
Trailers and tractors per 1000 inhabitants				

Motorbikes and scooters per
1000 inhabitants

Culture and sport

Municipal library

No. of municipal libraries
Total documentary resources
General resources (books for adults)
Children's resources
Audiovisuals
Magazines
Local books
No. of library users
Users with respect to total population %

Theatres

No. of theatres
Theatre seats per 1000 inhabitants

Sports installations

Sports centres
Installations in state schools
Installations in private schools
Bodies with installations
Petanque fields

Environment

Surface area of green zones per m^2
Number of trees in the street
Rubbish containers (capacity)
Selective rubbish collection containers

Glass
Packets
Packets
Paper-cardboard
Paper-cardboard
Fraction organic

Appendix 6: (*cont'd*)

Population structure	La Mina	Sant Adriá de Besós	Barcelona	Catalonia
Selective rubbish collection year 2000				
Paper–cardboard kg				
Bulky kg				
Glass kg				
Light packets				

Note: *Most of the actual values of the indicators have been omitted from the table upon request by La Mina consortium.
Source: Rosique (2009).

Bibliography

Chapter 1

APUDG (2009) *Regeneration and the Recession*. All Party Urban Development Group, London.

Barton, H., Grant, M. & Guise, R. (2003) *Shaping Neighbourhoods: A Guide for Health, Sustainability and Vitality*. Spon, London.

Bevir, M. & Rhodes, R.A.W. (2003) Searching for civil society: Changing patterns of governance in Britain. *Public Administration*, **81**(1), 41–61.

Burton, E., Jenks, M. & Williams, K. (1997) *The Compact City: A Sustainable Form?* Routledge, London.

CEC (1998) *Urban Sustainable Development in the EU: A Framework for Action*, COM(98) 605 final. Commission of the European Communities, Brussels.

Cento Bull, A. & Jones, B. (2006, April) Governance and social capital in urban regeneration: A comparison between Bristol and Naples. *Urban Studies*, **43**(4), 767–786.

Clark, G. (2007) *Sustainable Development Finance for City Regions*. Greg Clark City Development Finance, London. (Retrieved March 2010 from www.citiesandregions.com).

CLG (2008) *Transforming Places; Changing Lives: A Framework for Regeneration*. Communities and Local Government, London.

CLG (2009) *Transforming Places; Changing Lives: Taking Forward the Regeneration Framework*. Communities and Local Government, London.

Colantonio, A. & Dixon, T. (2009) *Measuring Socially Sustainable Urban Regeneration in Europe: Final Report*. Oxford Institute for Sustainable Development (OISD), Oxford Brookes University, Oxford.

Dixon, T. & Marston, A. (2003) *The Role of UK Retailing in Urban Regeneration*. College of Estate Management, Reading.

Dixon, T., Raco, M., Catney, P. & Lerner, D.N. (eds) (2007) *Sustainable Brownfield Regeneration: Liveable Places from Problem Spaces*. Blackwell, Oxford.

DTZ (2009) *Retail-led Regeneration: Why it matters to our communities*. British Council of Shopping Centres (BCSC), London.

EC (2006) *Cohesion Policy and Cities: The urban Contribution to Growth and Jobs in the Regions*. European Commission (EC), Brussels.

EC (2007) *State of European Cities Report*. European Commission (EC), Brussels.

EC (2009) *Promoting Sustainable Urban Development in Europe: Achievements and Opportunities*. European Commission (EC), Brussels.

EIB (2010) *Frequently Asked Questions*. Oxford Institute for Sustainable Development, Oxford Brookes University, Oxford. (Retrieved March 2010 from: http://www.eib.org/products/technical_assistance/jessica/faq/)

EU Ministers (2007) *Leipzig Charter on Sustainable European Cities*. European Union, Leipzig.

European Institute for Urban Affairs (eds) (2007) *The COMPETE Network: Final Report – Messages for Competitive European Cities*. European Institute for Urban Affairs, Liverpool.

Florida, R. (2004) *The Rise of the Creative Classes*. Basic Books, New York.

Franke, T., Strauss, W.-C., Reimann, B. & Beckmann, K.J. (2007) *Integrated Urban Development – A Prerequisite for Urban Sustainability in Europe*. German Institute of Urban Affairs, Berlin.

Gosling, V.K. (2008) Regenerating communities: Women's experiences of urban governance in Britain. *Public Administration*, **81**(1), 41–61.

Hemphill, L., McGreal, S., Berry, J. & Watson, S. (2006) Leadership, power and multisector urban regeneration partnerships. *Urban Studies*, **43**, 59–80.

IPF (2006) *Institutional Investment in Regeneration: Necessary conditions for Effective Funding*. Investment Property Forum (IPF), London.

IPF (2009) *Urban Regeneration: Opportunities for Property Investment*. Investment Property Forum (IPF), London.

Law, C.M. (2002) *Urban Tourism: The Visitor Economy and the Growth of Large Cities*. Continuum, London & New York.

LUDA (2003) *Appraisal of Urban Rehabilitation Literature and Projects, Including a Glossary of Terms and a Preliminary Set of Indicators Characterising LUDA*. Large Scale Urban Distressed Areas (LUDA), Dresden.

Ministry of Kingdom and Interior Relations (2005) *Ministerial Meeting Urban Policy: Cities Empower Europe Conclusions – Dutch Presidency 2004* (Retrieved March 2010 from: http://www.bmvbs.de/Anlage/original_983143/Urban-Acquis-englisch-_November-2004.pdf).

ODPM (2006) *UK Presidency. EU Ministerial Informal on Sustainable Communities. European Evidence Review papers*. Office of the Deputy Prime Minister, London.

Porter, M. (1995) The competitive advantage of the inner city. *Harvard Business Review*, May–June, 55–71.

Pratt, A.C. (2009) Urban regeneration: From the arts 'feel good' factor to the cultural economy: A case study of Hoxton, London. *Urban Studies*, **46**, 1041–1061.

Raco, M. (2003) Remaking place and securitising space: Urban regeneration and the strategies, tactics and practices of policing in the UK. *Urban Studies*, **40**(9), 1869–1887.

Roberts, P. (2000) The evolution, definition and purpose of urban regeneration. In: *Urban Regeneration* (eds, P. Roberts & H. Sykes), pp. 9–36. Sage, London.

Scarpaci, J.L. (2000) Reshaping Habana Vieja: Revitalisation, historic preservation and restructuring in the socialist city. *Urban Geography*, **21**(8), 724–744.

Thomas, S. & Duncan, P. (2000) *Neighbourhood Regeneration: Resourcing Community Involvement (Area Regeneration)*. Policy Press, Bristol.

ULI (2009) *Closing the Investment Gap in Europe's Cities*. Urban Land Institute, London.

UN Habitat (2006) *State of the World's Cities*. Earthscan, London.

URBACT (2009) *Understanding Integrated Urban Development*. Urban Action. (Retrieved January 2010 from: http://urbact.eu/en/header-main/integrated-urban-development/understanding-integrated-urban-development/).

URBACT (2010) *Understanding Integrated Urban Development*. Urban Action. (Retrieved March 2010 from: http://urbact.eu/en/header-main/integrated-urban-development/understanding-integrated-urban-development/)

Chapter 2

Adler, P.S. & Kwon, S.W. (2002) Social capital: Prospects for a new concept. *Academy of Management Review*, **27**(1), 17–40.

Assefa, G. & Frostell, B. (2007) Social sustainability and social acceptance in technology assessment: A case study of energy technologies. *Technologies in Society*, **29**, 63–78.

Baines, J. & Morgan, B. (2004) Sustainability appraisal: A social perspective. In: *Sustainability Appraisal. A Review of International Experience and Practice* (eds, B. Dalal-Clayton & B, Sadler), First Draft of Work in Progress. International Institute for Environment and Development, London.

Bevir, M. & Rhodes, R.A.W. (2003) Searching for civil society: Changing patterns of governance in Britain. *Public Administration*, **81**(1), 41–61.

Biart, M. (2002) Social sustainability as part of the social agenda of the European community. In: *Soziale Nachhaltigkeit: Von der Umweltpolitik zur Nachhaltigkeit?* (ed. T. Ritt), Arbeiterkammer Wien, Informationen zur Umweltpolitik 149, Wien, pp. 5–10. (Retrieved June 2008 from http://wien.arbeiterkammer.at/pictures/importiert/Tagungsband_149.pdf)

Bramley, G., Dempsey, N., Power, S. & Brown, C. (2006) *What is 'Social Sustainability' and How do our Existing Urban Forms Perform in Nurturing it?* Paper presented at the 'Sustainable Communities and Green Futures' Conference, Bartlett School of Planning, University College London, London.

Brohman, J. (1996) *Popular Development: Rethinking the Theory and Practice of Development*. Blackwell, Oxford.

Bromley, R.D.F., Tallon, A.R. & Thomas, C.J. (2005) City centre regeneration through residential development: Contributing to sustainability. *Urban Studies*, **42**(13), 2407–2429.

Brundtland Commission (1987) *Our Common Future*. World Commission on Environment and Development, New York.

Burton, E. (2000) The compact city: Just or just compact? A preliminary analysis. *Urban Studies*, **37**(11), 1969–2001.

Butler, T. (2003) Living in the bubble: Gentrification and its 'others' in North London. *Urban Studies*, **40**, 2469–2486.

Cento Bull, A. & Jones, B. (2006, April) Governance and social capital in urban regeneration: A comparison between Bristol and Naples. *Urban Studies*, **43**(4), 767–786.

Chambers, R. & Conway, G. (1992) *Sustainable Rural Livelihoods: Practical Concepts for the 21st Century*, IDS Discussion Paper 296. IDS, Brighton.

Chiu, R.L.H. (2003) Social sustainability, sustainable development and and housing development: The experience of Hong Kong. In: *Housing and Social Change: East–West perspectives* (eds, R. Forrest & J. Lee), pp. 221–239. Routledge, London.

City of Vancouver (2005) *A Social Development Plan for the City of Vancouver: Moving Towards Social Sustainability*, Administrative Report A7, Vancouver, Canada.

Coleman, J.S. (1988) Social capital and the creation of human capital. *American Journal of Sociology*, **94**(Suppl.), S95–S120.

Coleman, J.S. (1990) *Foundations of Social Theory*. Belknap Press, Cambridge, MA.

DETR (1999) *A Better Quality of Life*. Department for Transport (DETR), London.

DFID (1999) *Sustainable Livelihoods Guidance Sheets*. Department for International Development, London.

Dixon, T. (2007) The property development industry and sustainable urban brownfield regeneration in England: An analysis of case studies in Thames Gateway and Greater Manchester. *Urban Studies*, **44**(12), 2379–2400.

Drakakis-Smith, D. (1995) Third world cities: Sustainable urban development, 1. *Urban Studies*, **32**(4–5), 659–677.

Elkington, J. (1994) Towards the sustainable corporation: Win win win business strategies for sustainable development. *California Management Review*, **36**(2, Winter 1994), 90–100.

Elkington, J. (1997) *Cannibals with Forks: The Triple Bottom Line of 21st Century Business*. Capstone, Oxford.

Freeman, L. (2001) The effects of sprawl on neighbourhood social ties. *Journal of the American Planning Association*, **67**(1), 69–77.

GVRD (Great Vancouver Regional District) (2004a) *The Social Components of Community Sustainability: A Framework*. TAC Social Issues Subcommittee, Vanvouver, Canada.

GVRD (Great Vancouver Regional District) (2004b) *The Social Components of Community Sustainability: A Framework User's Guide*. TAC Social Issues Subcommittee, Vancouver, Canada.

Hans-Böckler-Foundation (ed.) (2001) *Pathways Towards a Sustainable Future*. Setzkasten, Düsseldorf.

Hardoy, J.E., Mitlin, D. & Satterthwaite, D. (1992) *Environmental Problems in Third World Cities*. Earthscan, London.

Healey, P. (1999) Institutionalist analysis, communicative planning, and shaping places. *Journal of Planning Education And Research*, **19**(2), 111–121.

Hediger, W. (2000) Sustainable development and social welfare. *Ecological Economics*, **32**(3), 481–492.

HM Government (2005) *Securing the Future: Delivering UK Sustainable Development Strategy*. Department for Environment Food and Rural Affairs (DEFRA), London.

Hogget, P. (1997) *Contested Communities: Experiences, Struggles and Policies*. Policy Press, Bristol.

Holden, M. (2006) Urban indicators and the integrative ideals of cities. *Cities*, **23**(3), 170–183.

Kearns, A. & Turok, I. (2003) *Sustainable Communities: Dimensions and Challenges*. Liverpool John Moores University, ESRC Cities Programme and Office of the Deputy Prime Minister, London.

Layard, R. (2007) Against unhappiness. *Prospect* (online version), **137**. (Retrieved May 2008 from: www.prospectmagazine.co.uk)

Levy, M. (1996) Social and unsocial capital: A review essay on Robert Putnam's Making Democracy Work. *Politics and Society*, **24**(1), 45–55.

Littig, B. & Grießler, E. (2005) Social sustainability: A catchword between political pragmatism and social theory. *International Journal of Sustainable Development*, **8**(1–2), 65–79.

Lutzkendorf, T. & Lorenz, D. (2005) Sustainable property investment: valuing sustainable buildings through property performance assessment. *Building Research & Information*, **33**(3), 212–234.

Meadows, D.H., Meadows, D.L., Randers, J. & Behrens, W. (1972) *Limits to Growth.* Potomac, New York.

Metzner, A. (2000) *Caring Capacity and Carrying Capacity – A Social Science Perspective,* Paper presented at the INES 2000 Conference: Challenges for Science and Engineering in the 21st Century, Stockholm.

Middleton, A., Murie, A. & Groves, R. (2005) Social capital and neighbourhoods that work. *Urban Studies,* **42**(10), 1711–1738.

Nijkamp, P. & Frits, S. (1988) Ecologically sustainable development: Key issues for strategic environmental management. *International Journal of Social Economics,* **15**(3–4), 88–102.

O'Riordan, T., Cameron, J. & Jordan, A. (2001) *Reinterpreting the Precautionary Principle.* Cameron May, London.

ODPM (Office of the Deputy Prime Minister) (2003) *Sustainable Communities: Building for the Future.* HMSO, London.

ODPM (Office of the Deputy Prime Minister) (2005) *Planning for Mixed Communities.* A consultation paper on a proposed change to planning policy Guidance Note 3: Housing. HMSO, London.

ODPM (Office of the Deputy Prime Minister) (2006) *UK Presidency. EU Ministerial Informal on Sustainable Communities. European Evidence Review papers.* ODPM, London.

OECD (2001) *Analytic Report on Sustainable Development,* SG/SD(2001)1–14. Organisation for Economic Cooperation and Development, Paris.

Omann, I. & Spangenberg, J.H. (2002) *Assessing Social Sustainability. The Social Dimension of Sustainability in a Socio-Economic Scenario,* paper presented at the 7th Biennial Conference of the International Society for Ecological Economics' in Sousse (Tunisia), 6–9 March 2002.

Ormerod, P. & Johns, H. (2007) Against happiness. *Prospect* (online version), **133**. (Retrieved May 2008 from: www.prospectmagazine.co.uk)

Polese, M. & Stren, R. (eds) (2000) *The Social Sustainability of Cities: Diversity and the Management of Change.* University of Toronto Press, Toronto, Canada.

Portes, A. & Landolt, P. (1996) The downside of social capital. *American Prospect,* **26**, 18–21, 94.

Putnam, R.D. (1993) *Making Democracy Work: Civic Tradition in Modern Italy.* Princeton University Press, Princeton, NJ.

Raco, M. (2007) *Building Sustainable Communities: Spatial Development, Citizenship, and Labour Market Engineering in Post-War Britain.* Policy Press, Bristol.

Rubio, M. (1997) Perverse social capital: Some evidence from Colombia. *Journal of Economic Issues,* **31**(3), 805–816.

Rydin, Y. & Pennington, M. (2000) Public participation and local environmental planning: The collective action problem and the potential of social capital. *Local Environment,* **5**(2), 153–169.

Sachs, I. (1999) Social sustainability and whole development: Exploring the dimensions of sustainable development. In: *Sustainability and the Social Sciences: A Cross-disciplinary Approach to Integrating Environmental Considerations into Theoretical Reorientation* (eds, B. Egon & J. Thomas), pp. 25–36. Zed Books, London.

Satterthwaite, D. (1997) Sustainable cities or cities that contribute to sustainable development? *Urban Studies,* **34**(10), 1667–1691.

Sinner, J., Baines, J., Crengle, H., Salmon, G., Fenemor, A., & Tipa, G. (2004) *Sustainable development: A summary of key concepts.* Ecologic Research Report No. 2. (Retrieved June 2008 from www.ecologic.org.nz)

Talen, E. (1999) Sense of community and neighbourhood form: An assessment of the social doctrine of new urbanism. *Urban Studies*, 36(8), 1361–1379.

Temple, J. (2000) *Growth Effects of Education and Social Capital in the OECD Countries.* Economics Department, Organisation for Economic Cooperation and Development (OECD), Paris.

Thin, N., Lockhart, C. & Yaron, G. (2002) *Conceptualising Socially Sustainable Development*, A paper prepared for DFID and the World Bank, London.

Tunstall, R. & Fenton, A. (2006) *In the Mix: A Review of Research on Mixed Income, Mixed Tenure and Mixed Communities. What Do We Know?* Joseph Rowntree Foundation, York.

Uitermark, J. (2003) 'Social mixing' and the management of disadvantaged neighbourhoods: The Dutch policy of urban restructuring revisited. *Urban Studies*, 40, 531–549.

Wackernagel, M. & Rees, W.E. (1996) *Our Ecological Footprints: Reducing Human Impact on the Earth.* New Society Publishers, Gabriola Island, BC, Canada.

Wollmann, H. (2006) The fall and rise of the local community: A comparative and historical perspective. *Urban Studies*, 43(20), 1419–1438.

Chapter 3

Babb, P. (2005) *Measurement of Social Capital in the UK.* Office of National Statistics, London.

Barrow, C.J. (2000) *Social Impact Assessment: An Introduction.* Arnold, London.

Cavanagh, J.A., Frame, B.R., Fraser, M. & Gabe, G. (2007) *Experiences of Applying a Sustainability Assessment Model.* International Conference on Whole Life Urban Sustainability and its Assessment, SUE-MoT Conference Proceedings Glasgow, 27–29 June.

Coccossis, H. & Parpairis, A. (1992) Tourism and the environment: Some observations on the concept of carrying capacity. In: *Tourism and the Environment. Regional, Economic and Policy Issues* (eds H. Briassoulis & J. Van der Straaten), pp. 23–33. Kluwer Academic, Dordrecht.

Coglianese, C. (1999). The limits of consensus. The environmental protection system in transition: Toward a more desirable future. *Environment*, 41, 1–6.

Colantonio, A. & Dixon, T. (2009) *Measuring the Social Sustainability of Urban Regeneration in Europe*, EIBURS final report. Oxford Institute for Sustainable Development, Oxford.

Colantonio, A. & Potter, R.B. (2006) *Urban Tourism and Development in the Socialist State: Havana during the Special Period.* Ashgate Publishing, Aldershot, and Burlington, USA.

Dalal-Clayton, B. & Sadler, B. (2005) *Sustainability Appraisal – A Review of International Experience and Practice.* Earthscan Publications, London.

Egan, J. (2004) *The Egan Review: Skills for Sustainable Communities.* ODPM, London.

Elkington, J. (1994) Towards the sustainable corporation: Win-win-win business strategies for sustainable development. *California Management Review*, Winter, 90–100.

EC (2005) *Sustainability Impact Assessment.* European Commission, Strasburg. (Available at http://ec.europa.eu/trade/issues/global/sia/faqs.htm)

EP (2007) *The Possibilities for Success of the Sustainable Communities Approach and its Implementation.* European Parliament Study Directorate-General for Internal Policies of the Union Structural and Cohesion Policies Policy Department. European Parliament (EP), Brussels.

European Union (2003) *Evaluating Socio Economic Development, Sourcebook 2: Methods & Techniques*. Regional Policy Inforegio, Brussels.

Gasparatos, A., El-Haram, M. & Horner, M. (2007) *The Argument Against a Reductionist Approach for Assessing Sustainability*. International Conference on Whole Life Urban Sustainability and its Assessment, SUE-MoT Conference Proceedings Glasgow, 27–29 June.

Gasparatos, A., El-Haram, M. & Horner, M. (2008) A critical review of reductionist approaches for assessing the progress towards sustainability. *Environmental Impact Assessment Review*, **28**, 286–311.

George, C. (2001) Sustainability appraisal for sustainable development: Integrating everything from jobs to climate change. *Impact Assessment and Project Appraisal*, **19**(1), 95–106.

Gibson, R.B., Hassan, S., Holtz, S., Tansey, J. & Whitelaw, G. (2005) *Sustainability Assessment: Criteria, Processes and Applications*. Earthscan, London.

Glasson, J. (2001) Socio-economic impacts 1: Overview and economic impacts. In: *Methods of Environmental Impact Assessment* (eds R. Therivel & P. Morris), 2nd ed., Chapter 2. UCL, London.

Glasson, J. & Gosling, J. (2001) SEA and regional planning – overcoming the institutional constraints: Some lessons from the EU. *European Environment*, **11**(2), 89–102.

Glasson, J., Therivel, R. & Chadwick, A. (2003) *Introduction to Environmental Impact Assessment: Principles and Procedures, Process, Practice and Prospects*. London/Philadelphia, UCL Press.

Glasson, J. & Wood, G. (2008) *Urban Regeneration and Impact Assessment for Social Sustainability*. Presentation at the International Association for Impact Assessment Conference, Perth, Australia, May 4–10.

Hacking, T. & Guthrie, P. (2008) A framework for clarifying the meaning of triple bottom-line, integrated, and sustainability assessment. *Environmental Impact Assessment Review*, **28**(2–3), 73–89.

HM Government (1999) *A Better Quality of Life, a Strategy for Sustainable Development in the UK*. HMSO, London.

HM Government (2005) *Securing the Future: Delivering UK Sustainable Development Strategy*. DEFRA, London.

HM Treasury, (2005) *The Green Book*. Treasury Guidance. TSO, London.

Hughes, G. (2002) Environmental indicators. *Annals of Tourism Research*, **29**(2), 457–477.

IAIA (2003) *Social Impact Assessment International Principles*. Special Publication Series No. 2. International Association of Impact Assessment, Fargo, USA.

Imperial College Consultants (2005) *The Relationship Between the EIA and SEA Directives*. Imperial College Consultants, London.

Keirstead, J. (2007) *Selecting Sustainability Indicators for Urban Energy Systems*. International Conference on Whole Life Urban Sustainability and its Assessment, SUE-MoT Conference Proceedings Glasgow, 27–29 June.

Keogh, H.L. & Blahna, D.J. (2006) Achieving integrative, collaborative ecosystem management. *Conservation Biology*, **20**(5), 1373–1382.

Lee, N. (2002) Integrated approaches to impact assessment: Substance or make-believe? *Environmental Assessment Yearbook*, pp. 14–20. Institute of Environmental Management and Assessment/EIA Centre/University of Manchester, Manchester.

Littig, B. & Grießler, E. (2005) Social sustainability: A catchword between political pragmatism and social theory. *International Journal of Sustainable Development*, **8**(1/2), 65–79.

LUC & RTPI (2008) *Issues for the Practice of Sustainability Appraisal in Spatial Planning – A Review*. Prepared for the Sustainable Development Research Network (SDRN).

Land Use Consultants and the Royal Town Planning Institute, London. (Retrieved January 2009 from http://www.sd-research.org.uk)

ODPM (2005) *Sustainability Appraisal of Regional Spatial Strategies and Local Development Frameworks.* Office of the Deputy Prime Minister, London.

Omann, I. & Spangenberg, J.H. (2002) *Assessing Social Sustainability. The Social Dimension of Sustainability in a Socio-Economic Scenario.* Paper presented at the 7th Biennial Conference of the International Society for Ecological Economics' in Sousse, Tunisia, 6–9 March.

ONS & DEFRA (Office of National Statistics and Department for Environment Food and Rural Affairs) (2007) *Sustainable Development Indicators in Your Pocket.* Defra Publications, London.

Pope, J. (2007, January 4–7) *Sustainability Assessment as a Deliberative Learning Process,* presentation at Sustainability Conference, University of Madras, Chennai, India.

Pope, J., Annandale, D. & Morrison-Saunders, A. (2004) Conceptualising sustainability assessment. *Environmental Impact Assessment Review,* **24,** 595–616.

RCEP (2002) *Royal Commission on Environmental Pollution, 23rd Report on Environmental Planning,* Cm 5459. The Stationery Office, London.

Ruddy, T.F. & Hilty, M.L. (2008) Impact assessment and policy learning in the European Commission. *Environmental Impact Assessment Review,* **28**(2–3), 90–105.

Rydin, Y. & Pennington, M. (2000) Public participation and local environmental planning: The collective action problem and the potential of social capital. *Local Environment,* **5**(2), 153–169.

Saunders, A.M. & Therivel, R. (2006) Sustainability integration and assessment. *Journal of Environmental Assessment Policy and Management,* **8**(3), 281–298.

Schmidt, M., Glasson, J., Emmelin, L. & Helbron, H. (eds) (2008) *Standards and Thresholds for Impact Assessment.* Springer, Berlin & Heidelberg.

Scrase, J.I. & Sheate, W.R. (2002) Integration and integrated approaches to assessment: What do they mean for the environment? *Journal of Environmental Policy and Planning,* **4,** 275–294.

Sheate, W.R., Rosario do Partidario, M., Byron, H., Bina, O. & Dagg, S. (2008) Sustainability assessment of future scenarios: Methodology and application to mountain areas of Europe. *Environmental Management,* **41,** 282–299.

Shutt, J., Evans, N., Koutsoukos, S., Wishardt, M. & Littlewood, S. (2007) *The Possibilities for Success of the Sustainable Communities Approach and its Implementation.* European Parliament Study Directorate General for Internal Policies of the Union Structural and Cohesion Policies Policy Department, Brussels.

Stagl, S. (2007) *Emerging Methods for Sustainability Valuation and Appraisal* – SDRN rapid research and evidence review (pp. 1–66). Sustainable Development Research Network, London.

Stewart, M. (2001) *MMSD Life Cycle Assessment Workshop: The Application of Life Cycle Assessment to Mining, Minerals and Metals.* Centre for Risk, Environment and Systems Technology and Analysis (CRESTA) and Department of Chemical Engineering. University of Sydney for the International Institute for Environment and Development (IIED), London.

Therivel, R. (2004) *Sustainable Urban Environment-Metrics, Models and Toolkits – Analysis of Sustainability/Social Tools.* Levett–Therivel, Oxford.

Townsend, I. & Kennedy, S. (2004) *Poverty: Measures and Targets.* Research Paper 04/23, Economic Policy and Statistics Section, House of Commons Library, London.

UK Government (2004) *Planning and Compulsory Purchase Act.* HMSO, London.

UN (1992) *Earth Summit: Agenda 21, The United Nations programme of action from Rio.* United Nations, New York.

UN (2001) *Report on the Aggregation of Indicators of Sustainable Development. Background Paper for the Ninth Session of the Commission on Sustainable Development.* United Nations, New York.

UNCSD (2001) *Sustainable Development of Tourism.* United Nations Commission on Sustainable Development, Zurich.

UNEP (United Nations Environment Programme) (2004) *Assessment of Sustainability Indicators (ASI) A SCOPE/UNEP/IHDP/EEA Project.* ASI Workshop. Prague, Czech Republic, 10–14 May.

Van de Kerkhof, M. (2006) Making a difference: On the constraints of consensus building and the relevance of deliberation in stakeholder dialogues. *Policy Science*, **39**, 279–299.

Veenhoven, R. (2002) Why social policy needs subjective indicators. *Social Indicators Research*, **58**, 33–45.

Veenhoven, R. & Hagerty, M. (2006) Rising happiness in nations 1946–2004. *Social Indicators Research*, **79**, 421–436.

Chapter 4

Adair, A.S., Berry, J.N., Deddis, W.G., McGreal, W.S., Hirst, S.M., Poon, J., *et al.* (2003) *Benchmarking Urban Regeneration.* RICS Foundation, London.

APUDG (2007a) *Business Matters: Understanding the Role of Business in Regeneration.* All Party Urban Development Group, London. (Retrieved December 2009 from: http://www.allparty-urbandevelopment.org.uk/index.html)

APUDG (2007b) *Loosening the Leash: How Local Government Can Deliver Infrastructure with Private Sector Money.* All Party Urban Development Group, London. (Retrieved December 2009 from: http://www.allparty-urbandevelopment.org.uk/index.html)

APUDG (2009) *Regeneration and the Recession.* All Party Urban Development Group, London.

Ball, M. & Maginn, P.J. (2005) Urban change and conflict: Evaluating the role of partnerships in urban regeneration in the UK. *Housing Studies*, **20**(1), 9–28.

Blackman, T. (1995) *Urban Policy in Practice.* Routledge, London.

Boston Consulting Group (BCG) & Initiative for the Competitive Inner City (ICIC) (1998) *The Business Case for Pursuing Retail Opportunities in the Inner City.* Boston Consulting Group, Boston, MA.

CDVCA (2005) *Measuring Impacts Toolkit.* Community Development Venture Alliance, New York.

Clark, C., Rosenweig, W., Long, D. & Olsen, S. (2004) *Double Bottom Line Project Report, Assessing Social Impact in Double Bottom Line Ventures: Methods Catalog.* Columbia Business School, New York.

Clark, G. (2007) *Sustainable Development Finance for City Regions.* Greg Clark City Development Finance, London. (Retrieved December 2009 from www.citiesandregions.com)

CLG (2004) *Planning Policy Statement 23: Planning and Pollution Control.* Communities and Local Government (CLG), London.

CLG (2005) *Planning Policy Statement 1: Delivering Sustainable Development.* Communities and Local Government (CLG), London.

CLG (2007) *Financing Investment in Sustainable Cities and Communities in Europe – The Role of the European Investment Bank.* Communities and Local Government, London.

CLG (2008) *Transforming Places; Changing Lives: A Framework for Regeneration.* Communities and Local Government, London.

CLG (2009) *Transforming Places; Changing Lives: Taking Forward the Regeneration Framework.* Communities and Local Government, London.

Deloitte (2009) *The Northern Way: Private Investment Commission: Preparing the Ground-Private Investment in the Regions, in the Recovery Period and Beyond.* Deloitte, London.

Dixon, T. (2005, May) The role of retailing in urban regeneration. *Local Economy,* **20**(2), 168–182.

Dixon, T.J. (2006) Integrating sustainability into brownfield regeneration: Rhetoric or reality? – An analysis of the UK development industry. *Journal of Property Research,* **23**(3), 237–267.

Dixon, T. (2007) The property development industry and sustainable urban brownfield regeneration in England: An analysis of case studies in Thames Gateway and Greater Manchester. *Urban Studies,* **44**(12), 2379–2400.

Dixon, T. (2009a, December) Urban land and property ownership patterns in the UK: Trends and forces for change. *Land Policy,* **26**(Suppl. 1), S43–S53.

Dixon, T. (2009b) Sustainable commercial property. In: *Environmental Alpha: Institutional Investors and Climate Change* (ed. A. Calvello), pp. 265–296. Wiley, Hoboken, NJ.

Dixon, T. & Adams, D. (2008) Housing supply and brownfield regeneration in a post-Barker world: Is there enough brownfield land in England and Scotland? *Urban Studies,* **45**(1), 115–139.

Dixon, T., Colantonio, A. & Shiers, D. (2007a) *Socially Responsible Investment (SRI), Responsible Property Investment (RPI) and Urban Regeneration in the UK and Europe: Partnership Models and Social Impact Assessment.* Measuring Social Sustainability: Best Practice from Urban Renewal in the EU 2007/02: EIBURS Working Paper Series, September, Oxford Brookes University, Oxford.

Dixon, T., Raco, M., Catney, P. & Lerner, D.N. (eds) (2007b) *Sustainable Brownfield Regeneration: Liveable Places from Problem Spaces.* Blackwell, Oxford.

DoE (1977) *White Paper: Policy for the Inner Cities (Cmnd. 6845).* Department of Environment, London.

EIB (2005) *Sustainable Urban Renewal.* European Investment Bank (EIB), Luxembourg.

EIB (2007) *Conclusions and Recommendations of Expert Working Group on EIB Loan Finance for Building Sustainable Cities and Communities.* European Investment Bank (EIB), Luxembourg.

EIB (2009) *EIB and London Development Agency Join Forces for a Sustainable London Area* [Press Release]. European Investment Bank (EIB), Luxembourg.

Elkington, J. (1997) *Cannibals with Forks: The Triple Bottom Line of 21st Century Business.* Oxford, Capstone.

EU (2007a) *State of European Cities Report.* Commission of the European Communities, Brussels.

EU (2007b) *Territorial Agenda of the European Union: Towards a More Competitive and Sustainable Europe of Diverse Regions.* Informal Ministerial Meeting on Urban Development and Territorial Cohesion. Leipzig, 24–25 May.

European Commission (2003) *Guidelines for Successful Public–Private Partnerships. Directorate-General Regional Policy.* EC, Brussels.

European Commission (2004) *ABC of the Main Instruments of CSR.* EC, Brussels.

European Commission (2007) *JESSICA: Sustainable Development for Urban Areas.* EC, Brussels. (Retrieved December 2009 from http://ec.europa.eu/regional_policy/funds/2007/jjj/jessica_en.htm)

Frankental, P. (2001) Corporate Social Responsibility – A PR Invention? *Corporate Communications: An International Journal*, **6**(1), 18–23.

Gershon, P. (2004) *Releasing Resources to the Front Line – Independent Review of Public Sector Efficiency*. HM Treasury, London.

GLA Economics (2008) *Credit Crunch and the Property Market*. GLA Economics, London.

Global Legal Group (2007) *The International Comparative Legal Guide to PFI/PPP Projects 2007*. International Comparative Legal Guides, London.

Hackett, P. (ed.) (2009) *Regeneration in Downturn: What Needs to Change?* The Smith Institute, London.

Hagerman, L.A., Clark, G.L. & Hebb, T. (2007) Investment intermediaries in economic development: Linking public pension funds to urban revitalisation. *Community Development Investment Review*, **3**(1), 45–65.

HM Government (2005) *Securing the Future: Delivering UK Sustainable Development Strategy*. DEFRA, London.

IPD (2007) *IPD Regeneration Index*, Summer 2007. Investment Property Databank, London.

IPD (2009) *IPD Regeneration Index: Autumn*. Investment Property Databank, London.

IPF (2006) *Institutional Investment in Regeneration: Necessary conditions for Effective Funding*. Investment Property Forum (IPF), London.

IPF (2009) *Urban Regeneration: Opportunities for Property Investment*. Investment Property Forum (IPF), London.

Kinder, P.D. (2005) *Socially Responsible Investing: An Evolving Concept in a Changing World*. KLD Analytics, Boston, MA.

King Sturge (2009a) *Short Term JESSICA Consultancy Study: Final Report*. King Sturge, Bristol.

King Sturge (2009b) *JESSICA Preliminary Study for Wales: Final Report*. King Sturge, Bristol.

Lyons, M. (2004) *Towards Better Management of Public Sector Assets: Report to the Chancellor of the Exchequer*. HM Treasury, London.

Macdonald, S. (2007) Grow money, grow. *Regenerate*, February, 16–18.

McNamara, P. (2005) *Socially Responsible Investment in Property – Making a Proper Contribution*. Professorial Lecture, Oxford Brookes University, 27th April.

Mills, R. & Atherton, M. (2005) Financing urban regeneration – the case for PPPs. In: *Financing the Future* (ed. P. Hackett), pp. 56–65. Smith Institute, London.

Minton, A. (2002) *Building Balanced Communities: The US and UK Compared*. RICS, London.

NAO (2007) *The Thames Gateway: Laying the Foundations*. National Audit Office, London.

Parkinson, M. (2009) *The Credit Crunch and Regeneration: Impact and Implications*. Communities and Local Government (CLG), London.

Pivo, G. & McNamara, P. (2005) Responsible property investing. *International Real Estate Review*, **8**(Issue 1), 128–143.

Pivo, G. & McNamara, P. (2008) Sustainable and Responsible Property Investing. In: *Sustainable Investing: The Art of Long Term Performance* (eds C. Krosinsky & N. Robins), pp. 117–128. Earthscan, London.

Porter, M. (1995) The competitive advantage of the inner city. *Harvard Business Review*, May–June, 55–71.

Power, A. (2007, February) Living neighbourhoods. *Search Magazine (Joseph Rowntree Foundation)*, **45**, 4–7.

Power, A. & Houghton, J. (2007) *Jigsaw Cities: Big Places, Small Spaces*. Policy Press, Bristol.

Rapson, D., Shiers, D. & Roberts, C. (2007) Socially Responsible Property Investment (SRPI): An analysis of the relationship between equities SRI and UK property investment activities. *Journal of Property Investment and Finance*, **25**(4), 342–358.

RICS (2007) *A Green Profession? RICS Members and the Sustainability Agenda*. Royal Institution of Chartered Surveyors, London.

Roberts, C., Rapson, D. & Shiers, D. (2007) Social responsibility: Key terms and their uses in property investment. *Journal of Property Investment and Finance*, **25**(4), 388–400.

Roberts, P. (2000) The evolution, definition and purpose of urban regeneration. In: *Urban Regeneration: A Handbook* (eds P. Roberts & H. Sykes), pp. 9–36. Sage Publications, London.

Savills (2005) *Mixed Use Issues: Advance of the Mixed Use Phenomena*. Savills Research, London.

SIF (2006) *2005 Report on Socially Responsible Investing Trends in the United States*. Social Investment Forum, Washington, DC.

Sorrell, S. & Hothi, K. (2007, June–August) Approaching regeneration in partnership: Models for private and public sector collaboration. *Journal of Urban Regeneration and Renewal*, **1**(1), 37–43.

Trache, H. & Green, H. (2001) Partenariat Public-Privé, Les Cahiers Pratiques du Renouvellement Urbain. *Caisse des Dépôts et Consignations*, **1**, 1–80.

Trache, H. & Green, H. (2006) *Partners 4 Action: Public Private Partnership in Urban Regeneration*. URBACT. (Retrieved December 2009 from: http://urbact.eu/fileadmin/subsites/partner4action/pdf/Baseline_Report_(Final_Version_Mar_06).pdf)

ULI (2009) *Closing the Investment Gap in Europe's Cities*. Urban Land Institute, London.

UNEPFI (2007) *Responsible Property Investment: Property Workstream*. United Nations Environment Programme Finance Initiative, Nairobi, Kenya. (Retrieved December 2009 from: http://www.unepfi.org/work_streams/property/responsible_property_investment/index.html)

URBACT (2006) *Public Private Partnership in Urban Regeneration: A Guide to Opportunities and Practice*. URBACT, Paris.

Von Boxmeer, B. & Van Beckhoven, E. (2005, April) Public–private partnership in urban regeneration: A comparison of Dutch and Spanish PPPs. *European Journal of Housing Policy*, **5**(1), 1–16.

Webber, C. & Marshall, A. (2007, June–August) Bridging the gap: Delivering infrastructure investment in Britain's cities. *Journal of Urban Regeneration and Renewal*, **1**(1), 7–21.

World Economic Forum (2005) *Mainstreaming Responsible Investment*, WEF, Geneva.

Chapter 5

Atkinson, R. (2000) Combating social exclusion in Europe: The new urban policy challenge. *Urban Studies*, **37**(5–6), 1037–1055.

Atkinson, R. (2007) *EU Urban Policy, European Urban Policies and the Neighbourhood: An overview of concepts, programmes and strategies*. Paper presented at the EURA Conference: The Vital City, Glasgow, 12–14 September.

Barca, F. (2009) *An Agenda for a Reformed Cohesion Policy: A Place-based Approach to Meeting European Union Challenges and Expectations*. Commission of the European Communities, Brussels.

Berg, L. van den, Braun, E. & Meer, J. van den (eds) (1998) *National Urban Policies in the European Union: Responses to Urban Issues in the Fifteen Member States.* Ashgate Publishing Ltd, Aldershot.

Boddy, M. & Parkinson, M. (2004) *City Matters: Competitiveness, Cohesion and Urban Governance.* Policy Press, Bristol.

Buck, N., Gordon, I., Harding, A. & Turok, I. (eds) (2005) *Changing Cities: Rethinking Urban Competitiveness, Cohesion and Governance.* Palgrave, Basingstoke.

Carley, M., Chapman, M., Hastings, A., Kirk, K. & Young, R. (2000) *Urban Regeneration Through Partnership: A Study in Nine Urban Regions in England, Scotland and Wales.* Area Regeneration Series, Policy Press, Bristol.

Carpenter, J. (2006) Addressing Europe's urban challenges: Lessons from the EU URBAN Community Initiative. *Urban Studies,* **43**(12), 2145–2162.

CEC (1994) *Laying Down Guidelines for Operational Programmes which Member States are Invited to Establish in the Framework of a Community Initiative Concerning Urban Areas.* Decision 94/C 180/02, 15th June 1994, Notice to Member States. Commission of the European Communities, Brussels.

CEC (1997) *Towards an Urban Agenda in the European Union,* COM(97)197 final, 06.05.1997. Commission of the European Communities, Brussels.

CEC (1998) *Urban Sustainable Development in the EU: A Framework for Action,* COM(98) 605 final. Commission of the European Communities, Brussels.

CEC (1999) *European Spatial Development Perspective.* Commission of the European Communities, Brussels.

CEC (2001a) *European Governance: A White Paper,* CEC (2001) 428 final. Commission of the European Communities, Luxembourg.

CEC (2001b) *A sustainable European for a Better World: A European Union Strategy for Sustainable Development,* COM(2001)264 final. Commission of the European Communities, Brussels.

CEC (2003a) *Partnership with the Cities: The URBAN Community Initiative.* Commission of the European Communities, Brussels.

CEC (2003b) *Regions in Action, a Country on the Move: A Selection of Successful Projects Supported by the Structural Funds in Greece.* Commission of the European Communities, Brussels.

CEC (2004) *A New Partnership for Cohesion: Convergence, Competitiveness, Cooperation.* Third Report on Economic and Social Cohesion. Commission of the European Communities, Luxembourg.

CEC (2006) *Cohesion Policy and Cities: The Urban Contribution to Growth and Jobs in the Regions.* Communication from the Commission to the Council and Parliament, July 2006. Commission of the European Communities, Office for Official Publications of the European Communities, Luxembourg.

CEC (2007) *State of European Cities Report.* Commission of the European Communities, Brussels.

Chorianopoulous, I. & Iosifides, T. (2006) The neoliberal framework of EU urban policy in action: Supporting competitiveness and reaping disparities. *Local Economy,* **21**(4), 409–422.

Council of European Communities (1988) Council Regulation (EEC) No. 2052/88 of 24 June 1988. *Official Journal of the European Communities,* **L185**, 15/7/88, 9–20.

Council of European Communities (1993) Council Regulation (EEC) No. 2081/93 of 20 July 1993. *Official Journal of the European Communities,* **L193**, 31/7/93, 5–19.

Council of European Communities (1999) Council Regulation (EEC) No. 1260/1999 of 21 June 1999 laying down general provision on the Structural Funds. *Official Journal of the European Communities,* **L161**, 26/6/99, 1–42.

DTZ Pieda Consulting (2005) *URBAN II Programme – Updated Mid Term Evaluation.* Office of the Deputy Prime Minister, London.

ECOTEC, ECORYS-NEI, MCRIT, Nordregio, OIR & SDRU (2004) *Territorial Effects of the Structural Funds in Urban Areas* – ESPON Action 2.2.3: A final report to the ESPON Coordination Unit. ECOTEC, Birmingham. (Available at: http://www.espon.eu/export/sites/default/Documents/Projects/ESPON2006Projects/PolicyImpactProjects/StructuralFunds/fr-2.2.3-full.pdf)

ECOTEC-ECORYS (2009) *European Evaluation of the URBAN II and URBACT Programmes: Presentation on the Findings to Date.* (Retrieved February 2010 from: ec.europa.eu/regional_policy/sources/docgener/evaluation/expost_reaction_en.htm)

Ekins, P. & Medhurst, J. (2006) The European Structural Funds and sustainable development: A methodology and indicator framework for evaluation. *Evaluation*, **12**, 474–495.

EPRC & Nordregio (2001a) *The Spatial and Urban Dimensions in the 2000–06 Objective 2 Programmes.* Report to the CEC, DG Regio, Brussels.

EPRC & Nordregio (2001b) *The Spatial and Urban Dimensions in the 2000–06 Objective 1 Programmes.* Report to the CEC, DG Regio, Brussels.

EU Ministers (2007) *Leipzig Charter on Sustainable European Cities*, 24 May 2007.

GHK (2003) *The Ex-Post Evaluation of the URBAN Community Initiative 1994–1999*, Final Report to CEC. DG Regio, Brussels.

GHK, PSI, IEEP & Cambridge Econometrics (2002) *The Contribution of the Structural Funds to Sustainable Development*, Final Report to CEC. DG Regio, Brussels.

Lawless, P. (2004) Locating and explaining area-based urban initiatives: New Deal for Communities in England. *Environment and Planning C*, **22**(3), 383–399.

Lisbon European Council (2000) *Presidency Conclusions*, 23 and 24 March 2000.

ODPM (2003, February) *Sustainable Communities: Building for the Future.* Office of the DeputyPrime Minister, London.

ODPM (2005) *Bristol Accord: Conclusions of Ministerial Informal on Sustainable Communities in Europe.* Office of the DeputyPrime Minister, London.

ODPM (2006) *UK Presidency. EU Ministerial Informal on Sustainable Communities. European Evidence Review Papers.* Office of the DeputyPrime Minister, London.

Parkinson, M. (1998) *Combating Social Exclusion: Lessons from Area-Based Programmes in Europe.* The Policy Press, Bristol/Joseph Rowntree Foundation, York.

Putnam, R. (1993) *Making Democracy Work: Civic Traditions in Modern Italy.* Princeton University Press, Princeton, NJ.

Simmie, J. (2001) *Innovative Cities.* Spon, London.

Tavistock Institute (1999) *The Thematic Evaluation of the Partnership Principle, Final Synthesis Report*, February 1999. Report to the CEC. Tavistock Institute, London. (Available at: http://ec.europa.eu/regional_policy/sources/docgener/evaluation/rathe_en.htm)

Chapter 6

Bell, S. & Morse, S. (2008) *Sustainability Indicators: Measuring the Unmeasurable.* Earthscan, London.

CBDC (1987) *Corporate Plan (Annual).* Cardiff Bay Development Corporation, Cardiff.

CBDC (2000) *Renaissance.* Cardiff Bay Development Corporation, Cardiff.

Cardiff Council (2005) *Cardiff Bay.* Cardiff Council, Cardiff.

Cardiff Council (2007) *Competitive Capital: The Cardiff Economic Strategy (2007–2012).* Cardiff Council, Cardiff.

Colantonio, A. & Dixon, T. (2009) *Measuring Socially Sustainable Urban Regeneration in Europe: Final Report*. Oxford Institute for Sustainable Development (OISD), Oxford Brookes University, Oxford.

Davies, J. (2002) *Cardiff: A Pocket Guide*. University of Wales Press/Western Mail, Cardiff.

European Institute for Urban Affairs (2007) *The COMPETE Network: Final Report – Messages for Competitive European Cities*. European Institute for Urban Affairs, Liverpool John Moores University, Liverpool.

EUROSIF (2008) *European SRI Study*. EUROSIF, Paris.

Francis, L. & Thomas, H. (2006) Evaluating property-led initiatives in urban regeneration: Tracing vacancy chains in Cardiff Bay. *Local Economy*, **21**(1), 49–64.

Hooper, A. (2006) From 'coal metropolis' to 'capital Cardiff'. In: *Capital Cardiff 1975–2020: Regeneration, Competitiveness and the Urban Environment* (eds A. Hooper & J. Punter), pp. 1–16. University of Wales Press, Cardiff.

igloo (2010) *footprint™*. (Retrieved January 2010 from: http://www.igloo.uk.net/sustainable-investment)

igloo/DEGW (2008) *Roath Basin Southside*. igloo/DEGW, London.

LDA DESIGN (2006) *Roath Basin South: Public Realm Strategy and Guidelines*. LDA DESIGN, London.

Locum Destination Review (2000) Born again: the resurrection of Cardiff Bay. *Locum Destination Review*, **2**, 2000.

ODPM (2006) *Devolving Decision-Making: Meeting the Regional Challenge – The Importance of Cities to Regional Growth*. Office of the Deputy Prime Minister, London.

Parkinson, M. & Karecha, J. (2006) *Cardiff: A Competitive European City*. European Institute for Urban Affairs, Liverpool.

Punter, J. (2006a) A city centre for a European capital? In: *Capital Cardiff 1975–2020: Regeneration, Competitiveness and the Urban Environment* (eds A. Hooper & J. Punter), pp. 122–148. University of Wales Press, Cardiff.

Punter, J. (2006b) Cardiff Bay: An exemplar of design-led regeneration? In: *Capital Cardiff 1975–2020: Regeneration, Competitiveness and the Urban Environment* (eds A. Hooper & J. Punter), pp. 149–178. University of Wales Press, Cardiff.

Punter, J. (2007) Design-led regeneration? Evaluating the design outcomes of Cardiff Bay and their implications for future regeneration and design. *Journal of Urban Design*, **12**(3), 375–405.

Punter, J. (2008) *'Slum of the future' fear for Bay*. Interview with Mark Hannaby, BBC News, 8 June 2008. (Retrieved January 2010 from http://news.bbc.co.uk/1/hi/wales/7442388.stm)

Rakodi, C. (2009) *The Politics of Urban Regeneration in Cardiff, UK: Case Study Prepared for Revisiting Urban Planning: Global report on Human Settlements*. (Retrieved January 2010 from http://www.unhabitat.org)

Robert Huggins Associates (2005) *The World Knowledge Competitiveness Index*. Robert Huggins Associates, Pontypridd, Wales.

Storper, M. (1997) *The Regional World: Territorial Development in a Global Economy*. Guilford Press, New York.

Stren, R. & Polese, M. (2000) Understanding the new sociocultural dynamics of cities: Comparative urban policy in a global context. In: *The Social Sustainability of Cities. Diversity and the Management of Change* (eds M. Polese & R. Stren), pp. 3–38. University of Toronto Press, Toronto.

Thomas, H. (1999a) Regenerating Cardiff Bay: The first steps in their historical and policy contexts. *Planning Research*, **170**. Cardiff University, Cardiff.

Thomas, H. (1999b) Spatial restructuring in the capital: Struggles to shape Cardiff's built environment. In: *Nation, Identity and Social Theory: Perspectives from Wales* (eds R. Fevre & A. Thompson), pp. 168–188. University of Wales Press, Cardiff.

Thomas, H. (2003) *Discovering Cities: Cardiff*. Geographical Association, Sheffield.

Thomas, H. (2004) Identity building and cultural projects in Butetown, Cardiff. *City*, **8**(2), 274–278.

Thomas, H. & Imrie, R. (1999) Urban policy, modernisation, and the regeneration of Cardiff Bay. In: *British Urban Policy: An Evaluation of Urban Development Corporations* (eds R. Imrie & H. Thomas), 2nd edn, pp. 106–127. Sage, London.

Williams, P. (2006) The governance of sustainable development in Wales. *Local Environment*, **11**(3), 253–267.

Chapter 7

Ajuntament de Sant Adriá de Besós (1996) *Proposta d'Actuacio' al Barri de la Mina*. Sant Adriá de Besós.

Borja, J. & Fiori, M. (2004) El cas de La Mina: alguns aspectes de la seva transformació urbanistico-social. In: *Urbanisme i barris en dificultats: El cas de la Mina* (Fundació Carles Pi i Sunyer d'Estudis Autonòmics i Locals), Jornada-Seminari Urbanisme i barris en dificultats. El cas de La Mina, 26 de setembre de 2003, Barcelona.

CCCB (2008) *Dossier de Premsa*. Centre De Cultura Contemporanea De Barcelona, Barcelona.

CIREM-GES-TRS (1997) *Pla de Transformacio del Barri de la Mina*. Ler Document, Ajuntament de Sant Adriá de Besós.

CIVITAS (2007) *CIVITAS: A Regional Approach: An Added Value for Urban Regeneration. Executive Summary* [online]. (Retrieved June 2009 from: www.urbact.eu/fileadmin/general_library/CIVITASOKdef3.pdf)

Consorci del Barri de La Mina (2007) *Plan de Transformación del Barrio de La Mina*. Consorcio del barrio de La Mina, Sant Adriá de Besós.

Consorci del Barri de La Mina (2009) [online]. (Retrieved December 2009 from: www.barrimina.org)

Consorcio del Barrio de La Mina (2008) *Memoria de actuaciones. Plan de transformacion del barrio de La Mina*. Consorcio del barrio de La Mina, Sant Adriá de Besós.

EC (2004) *A New Partnership for Cohesion Convergence Competitiveness Cooperation. Third Report on Economic and Social Cohesion*. Office for Official Publications of the European Communities, Luxembourg [online]. (Retrieved January 2010 from: www.ec.europa.eu/regional_policy/sources/docoffic/official/reports/pdf/cohesion3/cohesion3_toc_en.pdf)

Evans, G. (2009) From cultural quarters to creative clusters – creative spaces in the new city economy. In: *The Sustainability and Development of Cultural Quarters: International Perspectives* (ed. M. Legner), pp. 32–59. Institute of Urban History, Stockholm.

Generalitat de Catalunya (2004) *Llei 2/2004, de 4 de juny, de millora de barris, áreas urbanes I viles que requereixen una atenció especial* [online]. (Retrieved January 2010 from: www10.gencat.cat/ptop/AppJava/cat/documentacio/normativa/ciutat/arquitectura/llei22004.jsp)

Generalitat de Catalunya (2006) *Llei de millora de barris, arees urbanes I viles que requereixen una atencio especial*. Barris, Barcelona.

Gutiérrez Palomero, A. (2005) *La Unión Europea y la intervención integral en barrios en crisis: el caso URBAN II – La Mina.* VIII Coloquio y jornadas de campo de Geografía Urbana [online]. (Retrieved January 2010 from: www.uib.es/ggu/ACTAS%20VIII%20 COLOQUIO/P1CO6%20Gutiérrez.pdf)

IDPM (1998) *The Integrated Development Plan for La Mina.* (Retrieved February 2010 from: http://www.gencat.cat/diari_c/4180/04201003.htm a)

Ine (2008) *Instituto Nacional de Estadística* [online]. (Retrieved December 2009 from: www.ine.es)

Inforegio (2009) *URBAN II Sant Adriá de Besós* [online]. (Retrieved December 2009 from: www.ec.europa.eu/regional_policy/country/prordn/details.cfm?gv_OBJ=6&gv_ PAY=ES&gv_reg=ALL&gv_THE=6&gv_PGM=331&LAN=8&gv_PER=1&gv_defL=9)

Majoor, S. (2009) The disconnected innovation of new urbanity in Zuidas Amsterdam, Orestad Copenhagen and Forum Barcelona. *European Planning Studies,* **17**(9), 1379–1403.

Majoor, S. & Salet, W. (2008) The enlargement of local power in trans-scalar strategies of planning: Recent tendencies in two European cases. *Geojournal,* **72**, 91–103.

Miranda, L. (2006) *It's Illegal to Be Ugly and Do Anything That Isn't Profitable: Policing Public Space in Contemporary Barcelona.* University of California International and Area Studies, Berkeley, CA. (Retrieved March 2010 from www.escholarship.org/item/ uc/item/4gc9n3s2)

Nelo, O. (2008) *Contra la segregación urbana y por la cohesión social: la ley de barrios de Cataluña* [online]. (Retrieved January 2010 from: www.colcpis.org/files/documents/92_ material.pdf)

Pareja Eastaway, M. (1999) *The Metropolitan Region of Barcelona as an Example of Urban Network. An Analysis Regarding Residential Migrations and the Housing Market.* University of Barcelona.

Pareja Eastaway, M. (2009) The Barcelona metropolitan region: From non-existence to fame. *Built Environment,* **35**(2), 212–219.

Project for Public Spaces (2010) *Hall of Shame: Diagonal Mar.* (Retrieved March 2010 from http://www.pps.org/great_public_spaces/one?public_place_id=623)

UN-Habitat (2006) *Best Practices Database* [online]. (Retrieved December 2009 from: www.unhabitat.org/bestpractices/2006/mainview04.asp?BPID=1716)

Van Boxmeer, B. & Van Beckhoven, E. (2005) Public–private partnership in urban regeneration: A comparison of Dutch and Spanish PPPs. *European Journal of Housing Policy,* **5**(1), 1–16.

Viure, S.A. (2009, August) *Bulleti Municipal,* **134**. (Retrieved November 2009 from: www. sant-adria.net)

Walliser, A. (2004) A place in the world: Barcelona's quest to become a global knowledge city. *Built Environment,* **30**(3), 213–224.

Chapter 8

Avedano, L. (2007) *Porta Palazzo Flea Market – The Gate Project.* European Week of Regions and Cities, Brussels, 8–11 October 2007.

Balducci, A., Calvaresi, C. & Procacci, F. (2003) *Participation, Leadership, and Urban Sustainability: PLUS. The Italian National Case Study.* (Retrieved September 2009 from: http://www.eura.org/plus-eura/public%20pdf%20files/italian_country_ report.pdf)

Bricocoli, M. & Savoldi, P. (2005) *Call for Policies? Local Government and Housing Programs, Competitions and Project-Driven Attitudes in Recent Italian Experiences.* Paper presented at the Aesop Association of European Schools of Planning Congress, Vienna, July 2005.

Canestri, S. & Leonarduzzi, D. (2006) *Sécurité et régénération urbaine: politiques intégrées à Turin.* Susanna Canestri & Danila Leonarduzzi. City of Turin.

Cicsene (2002) *Relazione Sulle Trasformazioni Dell' Area di Porta Palazzo 1996/2001.* Turin. (Retrieved September 2009 from: www.comune.torino.it/portapalazzo/bancadati/pdf/cicsene.pdf)

Curti, I. (2007) *Progetto The Gate – Porta Palazzo.* Presentation at REGENERA final Conference, Lyon, 15 January 2007.

Essex, S. & Chalkley, B. (2007) Olympic Games: Catalyst of urban change. In: *Leisure Studies: Critical Concepts in the Social Sciences, Vol. 2: Leisure, Space and Place* (eds S. Page & J. Connell), pp.309–330. Routledge, London.

GMF (2008) *Case Study: The Gate.* German Marshall Fund of United States of America, Washington, DC. (Retrieved June 2009 from: http://www.gmfus.org/template/page.cfm?page_id=515)

ISTAT (1997) *I sistemi locali del lavoro 1991.* Argomenti 10, Rome.

ISTAT (2009) *Popolazione Comune di Torino.* Istitituto Nazionale di Statistica, Italy. (Retrieved January 2010 from: http://www.demo.istat.it/bilmens2009gen/index.html)

Janin Rivolin, U. (2004) *European Spatial Planning e le innovazioni dell' Urbanistica.* La Pianificazione Territoriale in Europa, International Seminar, Venice, 13 November 2004.

Maggi, M. & Piperno, S. (1999) *Turin: The Vain Search For Gargantua.* Ires, Turin.

Magnano, G. (2007) *Abitare Sociale Rigenerazione Urbana e Accompagnamento Sociale* [unpublished]. Citta' di Torino, Italy.

Poggesi, S. (2007) *Public-Private Partenership for Urban Regeneration: The Case of the Urban Transformation Companies.* Paper presented at The Eleventh International Research Symposium on Public Management, Potsdam University, 2–4 April 2007.

Ricci, A. (2009) *Approach to Financing and Monitoring Housing Projects.* Presentation at OISD–EIB Workshop on Social Sustainability and Urban Regeneration in EU Cities, 19–20 Feb 2009, Oxford Institute for Sustainable Development (OISD), Oxford Brookes University, Oxford.

Roland Berger Strategy Consultants (2005) *Modelli di Partenariato Pubblico-Privato per il Finanziamento delle Strutture – Sintesi Direzionale del Rapporto di Ricerca.* Munich. (Retrieved November 2009 from: www.funzionepubblica.it)

Rosso, E. (2004) *Torino: Policies and Actions at a Metropolitan Level.* Paper given at the conference La Gouvernance Metropolitaine: Recherche de coherence dans la compléxité. Montréal, 7–8 October 2004.

Salone, C. (2006) *The Strategic Plan of Torino and the Re-development of the Metropolitan Area.* Paper presented at International City Development Policy Conference, Alexandria, 20–21 March 2006.

Tedesco, C. (2006) *Beyond URBAN. The Difficult Attempt to Mainstream the 'URBAN Approach' in the Apulia Region, Southern Italy.* European Urban Policy and URBAN Researchers Workshop, Humboldt University, Berlin, 6–7 April 2006.

Torino Internazionale (2000) *Il Piano Strategico della Città.* Torino Internazionale, Torino.

Turin City Council (2001) *Torino negli ultimi 100 anni.* (Retrieved February 2010 from: http://www.comune.torino.it/ucstampa/2001/torino100anni.html)

Turin City Council (2007) *Periferie. Il Cuore della Città. Progetto Speciale Periferie: Le Aree di Intervento.* TCC, Turin.

Winkler, A. (2007) *Torino City Report*, CASE report 41. CASE, London School of Economics, London.

Chapter 9

Acioly, C., Ruijsink, S., Huysman, M. & Geurts, E. (2007) *Making Cities Safer: How Different Approaches and Instruments Succeed in Cities Worldwide*. Report prepared for World Habitat Day Report, 2 October 2007, Rotterdam.

Aedes (2007) *Dutch Social Housing in a Nutshell*. Aedes vereniging van woningcorporaties, Hilversum, May 2007.

Cadell, C., Falk, N. & King, F. (2008) *Regeneration in European Cities: Making Connections*. Report prepared for Joseph Rowntree Foundation, London.

Couch, C. (2003) Rotterdam: Structure, change and the port. In: *Urban Regeneration in Europe* (eds C. Couch, C. Fraser & S. Percy), pp. 109–125. Blackwell Publishing, Oxford.

Dekker, K. & van Kempen, R. (2004) Urban governance within the Big Cities Policy: Ideals and practice in Den Haag. *Cities*, **21**(2), 109–117.

ESPON (2007) *ESPON Project 1.4.3 Study on Urban Functions, Final Report* [online]. (Retrieved January 2010 from: www.espon.eu/mmp/online/website/content/projects/261/420/index_EN.html)

Federal Ministry of Transport, Building and Urban Affairs (2007) *Strengthening the Local Economy and the Local Labour Market in Deprived Urban Areas*. Bundesministerium fur Verkehr Bau aund Stadtentwicklung (BMVBS), Berlin.

Gemeente Rotterdam (2007) *Stadsvisie Rotterdam. Spatial Development Strategy 2030*. City of Rotterdam.

Gemeente Rotterdam (2008) *Rotterdam sociaal gemeten.1e meting door de Sociale Index*. City of Rotterdam Publishing, Rotterdam.

Gemeente Rotterdam (2009a) *Reisgids*. City of Rotterdam Publishing, Rotterdam.

Gemeente Rotterdam (2009b) *Opportunity Zones After 4 Years*. Rotterdam City Development Corporation, Rotterdam.

Gemeente Rotterdam (2009c) *Klushuizen (DIY homes): From Experiment to Instrument*. Rotterdam. (Retrieved February 2010 from: http://www.rotterdam.nl/169huizen)

Koppelaar, P. (2009) *Sociale Index: A Social Monitor for the Municipality of Rotterdam*. Presentation at the Urban Regeneration and Social Sustainability Workshop, Oxford Institute for Sustainable Development, Oxford Brookes University, 19–20 February 2009.

Legnani, F. (1996) L'intervento Kop van zuid a Rotterdam. In: *L'ecosistema urbano: sviluppo razionale ed utilizzo delle aree dismesse* (ed. G. Righetto), pp. 166–176. Studio interdisciplinare, Piccin Nuova Libraria, S.p.A., Padova, Italy.

Leidelmeijer, K., van Iersel, J. & den Herder, N. (2007) *Sociale Index Rotterdam Bijlagenrapport*. Unpublished, RIGO Research en Advies BV, Amsterdam.

OECD (2007) *Competitive Cities in the Global Economy*, OECD Territorial Reviews. Organisation for Economic Cooperation and Development (OECD) Publishing [online]. (Retrieved January 2010 from: http://www.oecd.org/document/2/0,3343,en_2649_3373 5_37801602_1_1_1,00.html)

Pact op Zuid, (2006) *Intentieovereenkomst van de Partners binnen het Pact op Zuid*. Unpublished Rotterdam City.

Pact op Zuid (2007) *The Rotterdam South Pact*. Rotterdam City, The Netherlands

Pact op Zuid (2008a) *Annual Programme*. Rotterdam City.

Pact op Zuid (2008b) *The Rotterdam South Pact, A Summary*. Rotterdam City.

Pact op Zuid (2008c), *Pact op Zuid, 2008 Guidebook, Establishing the baseline*. Uitgeverij Ijzer, Utrecht.

Priemus, H., Boelhouwer, P. & Kruythoff, H. (2002) Dutch urban policy: A promising perspective for the big cities. *International Journal of Urban and Regional Research*, **21**(4), 677–690.

Ramsden, P. (2010) *Kansenzones*. (Retrieved March 2010 from: http://www.wikipreneurship.eu/index.php5?title=Kansenzones)

RIGO (2007) *Sociale Index Rotterdam Bijlagenrapport*. RIGO Research en Advies BV, Amsterdam.

URBED (Urban & Economic Development) & van Hoek, M. (2007) *Regeneration in European Cities: Making Connections. Case Study of Kop van Zuid, Rotterdam (The Netherlands)*, [online]. (Retrieved January 2010 from: www.urbed.com/cgi-bin/get_binary_doc_object.cgi?doc_id=277&fname=extra_pdf_4.pdf)

Van Boxmeer, B. & Van Beckhoven, E. (2005) Public-Private Partnership in Urban Regeneration: A Comparison of Dutch and Spanish PPPs. *European Journal of Housing Policy*, **5**(1), 1–16.

Chapter 10

Battis, U., Krautzberger, M. & Löhr, R.-P. (2007) *Commentary on the Federal Building Code*. Beck, Munich.

BMVBS (ed.) (2008) *Status Report, The Programme 'Social City' (Soziale Stadt) Summary*. Bundesministerium für Verkehr Bau und Stadtentwicklung, Berlin.

BMVBS & Stadt Leipzig (eds) (2008) *Broschüre 5 Jahre Lokales Kapital für soziale Zwecke 2004–2008*. Bundesministerium für Verkehr Bau und Stadtentwicklung, Berlin/Leipzig.

DIFU (ed.) (2002) Conference *Integrative Action for Social Development of Urban Quarters*. Working Papers for the Programme 'Socially Integrative City'. Deutsches Institut für Urbanistik, Berlin.

DIFU (2003) *Strategien für die Soziale Stadt, Endbericht der Programmbegleitung*. Deutsches Institut für Urbanistik, Berlin.

DIFU (2006a) *Dritter Fachpolitischer Dialog zur Sozialen Stadt: Praxiserfahrungen und Perspektiven, Auswertungsbericht*. Deutsches Institut für Urbanistik, Berlin, Germany

DIFU (2006b) *Verstetigungsansätze zum Programm Soziale Stadt*. Deutsches Institut für Urbanistik, Berlin.

DIFU (2007) *Vierter Fachpolitischer Dialog zur Sozialen Stadt: Integration von Zuwanderern vor Ort, Auswertungsbericht*. Deutsches Institut für Urbanistik, Berlin.

DIFU (2008) *Statusbericht zum Programm Soziale Stadt, im Auftrag des Bundesministeriums für Verkehr, Bau und Stadtentwicklung (BMVBS) vertreten durch das Bundesamt für Bauwesen und Raumordnung (BBR)*. Deutsches Institut für Urbanistik, Berlin.

Jacoby, Ch., Univ. der Bundeswehr München, Institut für Verkehrswesen und Raumplanung, Neubiberg (eds) (2008) *Konversionsflächenmanagement zur nachhaltigen Wiedernutzung freigegebener militärischer Liegenschaften* (REFINA-KoM). Schlussbericht Konzeptionsphase, Neubiberg, 2008.

Jones, G.A. (2007) Assessing the success of the sale of social housing in the UK. *Journal of Social Welfare and Family Law*, **29**(2), 135–150.

Stadt Leipzig (ed.) (2007) *Abschlussbericht zum Forschungsprojekt Kleinräumiges Monitoring des Stadtumbaus in Leipzig.* Leipzig.
Stadt Leipzig (ed.) (2008a) *Das Bewertungssystem für Maßnahmen der Stadterneuerung, Die Produktbeschreibung.* Leipzig.
Stadt Leipzig (ed.) (2008b) *EFRE-Fördergebiet Leipziger Osten – Dokumentation 2000–2007.* Leipzig.
Stadt Leipzig (ed.) (2008c) *Monitoringbericht 2007.* Leipzig.

Legal texts

Baugesetzbuch (BauGB) in der Fassung der Bekanntmachung vom 23. September 2004 (BGBl. I S. 2414), zuletzt geändert durch Artikel 4 des Gesetzes vom 31. Juli 2009 (BGBl. I S. 2585)
Städtebauförderungsgesetz (StBauFG), 27.07.1971.
Verwaltungsvorschrift des Sächsischen Staatsministeriums des Innern über die Förderung der Städtebaulichen Erneuerung im Freistaat Sachsen (Verwaltungsvorschrift Städtebauliche Erneuerung – VwV StBauE) SächsABl. Jg. 2008 Bl.-Nr. 32 S. 1018 Gkv-Nr.: 5532-V08.3 Fassung gültig ab: 08.08.2008.

Chapter 11

Chambers, R. (1992) Rural appraisal: Rapid, relaxed and participatory. *IDS Discussion Paper*, **311**, 69–84.
Chan, E. & Lee, G.K.L. (2008) Critical factors for improving social sustainability of urban renewal projects. *Social Indicators Research*, **85**(2), 243–256.
Colantonio, A. & Dixon, T. (2009) *Measuring Socially Sustainable Urban Regeneration in Europe.* Oxford Institute for Sustainable Development (OISD), Oxford Brookes University, Oxford.
Coleman, J.S. (1988) Social capital and the creation of human capital. *American Journal of Sociology*, **94**(Suppl.), S95–S120.
Dixon, T. (2009) Sustainable commercial property. In: *Environmental Alpha: Institutional Investors and Climate Change* (ed. A. Calvello), pp. 265–296. Wiley, Hoboken, NJ.
Dixon, T., Colantonio, A. & Shiers, D. (2007) *Measuring Social Sustainability: Best Practice from Urban Renewal in the EU 2007/02.* EIBURS Working Paper Series. Oxford Institute for Sustainable Development (OISD), Oxford Brookes University, Oxford.
East Thames Housing Association (2006) *East Thames High Density Toolkit.* ETHA, London. (Retrieved January 2009 from: http://www.east-thames.co.uk/highdensity)
Egan, J. (2004) *The Egan Review: Skills for Sustainable Communities* ODPM, London.
Elkington, J. (1994) Towards the sustainable corporation: Win-win-win business strategies for sustainable development. *California Management Review*, **Winter**, 90–100.
EP (2007) *The Possibilities for Success of the Sustainable Communities Approach and its Implementation.* European Parliament Study Directorate-General for Internal Policies of the Union Structural and Cohesion Policies Policy Department. European Parliament (EP), Brussels.
Eurostat (2001) *Sustainable Development Indicators.* Eurostat, Brussels.
Hammer, J. (2009) *Draft Social Bottom Line Framework.* College of Urban and Public Affairs, Portland State University, OR. (Retrieved August 2009 from: http://www.pdx.edu/sites/www.pdx.edu.cupa/files/media_assets/SBL%20Draft%20Framework.pdf)

Healey, P. (1992) Planning through debate: The communicative turn in planning theory. *Town Planning Review*, **63**(2), 143–162.

Hemphill, L., Berry, J. & McGreal, S. (2004) An indicator-based approach to measuring sustainable urban regeneration performance: Part 1, conceptual foundations and methodological framework. *Urban Studies*, **41**(4), 725–755.

igloo (2010a) *igloo Factsheet*. igloo, London. (Retrieved January 2010 from: http://www.igloo.uk.net/)

igloo (2010b) *footprint™*. igloo, London. (Retrieved January 2010 from: http://www.igloo.uk.net/sustainable-investment)

IPF (2009) *Urban Regeneration: Opportunities for Property Investment*. Investment Property Forum, London.

King Sturge (2009) *JESSICA Preliminary Study for Wales: Final Report*. King Sturge, Bristol.

Layard, R. (2005) *Happiness: Lessons From a New Science*. Penguin, New York.

Loorbach, D. & Rotmans, J. (2006) Managing transitions for sustainable development. In: *Understanding Industrial Transformation: Views from Different Disciplines* (eds X. Olshoorn & A.J. Wieczorek), pp. 187–206. Springer, Dordrecht.

NEF (2007) *Measuring Real Value: A DIY Guide to Social Return on Investment*. New Economic Foundation, London.

Newell, G. (2008) The Strategic Significance of Environmental Sustainability by Australian-listed Property Trusts. *Journal of Property Investment and Finance*, **26**(6), 522–540.

Nussbaum, M. & Glover, J. (eds) (1995) *Women, Culture, and Development: A Study of Human Capabilities*, pp. 360–395. Oxford University Press, New York.

Putnam, R.D. (1993) *Making Democracy Work: Civic Tradition in Modern Italy*. Princeton University Press, Princeton, NJ.

Rotmans, J., Kemp, R. & van Asselt, M. (2001) More evolution than revolution: Transition management in public policy. *Foresight*, **3**(1), 1–17.

Sachs, I. (1999) Social sustainability and whole development: Exploring the dimensions of sustainable development. In: *Sustainability and the Social Sciences: A Cross-disciplinary Approach to Integrating Environmental Considerations into Theoretical Reorientation* (eds B. Egon & J. Thomas), pp. 25–36. Zed Books, London.

Sen, A K. (1985) *Commodities and Capabilities*. Oxford University Press, Oxford.

Sen, A K. (1992) *Inequality Re-examined*. Clarendon Press, Oxford.

Sen, A.K. (1993, March) Capability and well-being. *The Quality of Life*, **25**, 30–54.

Tobias, L. (2007) Green builds a head of steam. *IPE Real Estate*, **June**, 44–46.

UKGBC (2008) *UK Green Building Council Consultation: Code for Sustainable Buildings Task Group*. UK Green Building Council, London.

UNEPFI (2008) *Responsible Property Investing: What the Leaders are Doing*. United Nations Environment Programme Finance Initiative, Geneva.

UNEPFI (2009) *Sustainable Investment in Real Estate … Your Fiduciary Duty*. United Nations Environment Programme Finance Initiative, Geneva.

Wackernagel, M. & Rees, W.E. (1996) *Our Ecological Footprints: Reducing Human Impact on the Earth*. New Society Publishers, Gabriola Island, BC, Canada.

Chapter 12

APUDG (2010) *Next Steps: A Regeneration Agenda for the Next Government*. All Party Urban Development Group, London.

Bell, S. & Morse, S. (2008) *Sustainability Indicators: Measuring the Immeasurable?* 2nd edn. Earthscan, London.

Cadell, C., Falk, N. & King, F. (2008) *Regeneration in European Cities: Making Connections.* Joseph Rowntree Foundation, York.

Clark, G. (2009) *Recession, Recovery and Reinvestment: The Role of Local Economic Leadership in a Global Crisis.* Organisation for Economic Cooperation and Development (OECD), Paris.

EC (2008) *Regions 2020: An Assessment of Future Challenges for EU Regions.* European Commission, Brussels.

EC (2009) *Promoting Sustainable Urban Development in Europe: Achievements and Opportunities.* European Commission, Brussels.

EIB (2010) *Frequently Asked Questions.* (Retrieved March 2010 from: http://www.eib.org/products/technical_assistance/jessica/faq/)

Emerson, J. (2003) *The Blended Value Map: Tracking the Intersects and Opportunities of Economic, Social and Environmental Value Creation.* (Retrieved March 2010 from: http://www.blendedvalue.org/)

EU Ministers (2007) *Leipzig Charter on Sustainable European Cities.* Leipzig, 24 May 2007.

Evans, J., Jones, P. & Krueger, R. (2009, August) Organic regeneration and sustainability, or can the credit crunch save our cities? *Local Environment,* **14**(7), 683–698.

Fisher, J. (2010, February) Delivering a sustainable masterplan. *Town and Country Planning,* 91–93.

Franke, T., Strauss, W.-C., Reimann, B. & Beckmann, K.J. (2007) *Integrated Urban development – A Prerequisite for Urban Sustainability in Europe.* German Institute of Urban Affairs, Berlin.

igloo (2010) *footprint™.* (Retrieved January 2010 from: http://www.igloo.uk.net/sustainable-investment)

Jacquier, C. (2005) *Can Distressed Urban Areas Become Poles of Growth?* Organisation for Economic Cooperation and Development (OECD), Paris.

Jacquier, C., Bienvenue, S. & Schlappa, H. (2007) *REGENERA: Urban Regeneration of Deprived Areas across Europe.* Grandlyon, Lyon, France.

Kazmierczak, A., Curwell, S.R. & Turner, J.C. (2007) Assessment methods and tools for regeneration of large urban distressed areas. In: *Proceedings of the International Conference on Whole Life Urban Sustainability and its Assessment,* Glasgow. (Retrieved March 2010 from: http://download.sue-mot.org/Conference-2007/Papers/Kazmierczak.pdf)

LUDA (2003) *Appraisal of Urban Rehabilitation Literature and Projects.* Large Urban Distressed Areas (LUDA), Dresden.

LUDA (2006) *E-compendium: Handbook E2 – Understanding Large Urban Distressed Areas.* Large Urban Distressed Areas (LUDA), Dresden.

Marcuse, P. (1985) Gentrification, abandonment and displacement: Connections, causes and policy responses in New York City. *Journal of Contemporary Law,* **28**, 195–240.

Ministry of Kingdom and Interior Relations (2005) *Ministerial Meeting Urban Policy: Cities Empower Europe Conclusions – Dutch Presidency 2004.* (Retrieved March 2010 from: http://www.bmvbs.de/Anlage/original_983143/Urban-Acquis-englisch-_November-2004.pdf)

Murray, R. (2009) *Danger and Opportunity: Crisis and the New Social Economy.* National Endowment for Science, Technology and the Arts (NESTA), London.

NEF (2010) *Good Foundations: Towards a Low Carbon, High Well-being Built Environment.* New Economics Foundation, London.

OECD (1998) *Integrating Distressed Urban Areas.* Organisation for Economic Cooperation and Development, Paris.

OECD (2009) *Competitive Cities and Climate Change.* Organisation for Economic Cooperation and Development, Paris.

Rubio, E. (2009) *Social Europe and the Crisis: Defining a New Agenda.* Notre Europe, Paris.

Sato, P. (2010) *Cities and Deprived Neighbourhoods in the Crisis: How Can they Contribute to the Recovery?* (Retrieved March 2010 from: http://urbact.eu/fileadmin/general_library/Paul_Soto_article_EN.doc)

Shaw, K. (2009) Rising to a challenge. In: *Whose Urban Renaissance? An International Comparison of Urban Regeneration Strategies* (eds L. Porter & K. Shaw), pp. 253–260. Routledge, Abingdon.

Swyngedouw, E. (2007) Impossible 'sustainability' and the post-political condition. In: *The Sustainable Development Paradox: Urban Political Economy in the United States and Europe* (eds R. Krueger & D. Gibbs), pp. 13–40. Guilford Press, London.

UCLG (2009) *The Impact of the Global Crisis on Local Governments.* United Cities and Local Governments, Barcelona.

URBACT (2010) *Understanding Integrated Urban Development.* (Retrieved March 2010 from: http://urbact.eu/en/header-main/integrated-urban-development/understanding-integrated-urban-development/)

Warren, R.L. (1963) *The Community in America.* Rand McNally, Chicago, IL.

Work Foundation (2009) *Recession and Recovery: The Role of Local Economic Leaders.* Work Foundation, London.

Young Foundation (2009a) *Fixing the Future: Innovating More Effective Responses to the Recession.* Young Foundation, London.

Young Foundation (2009b) *Breakthrough Cities: How Cities Can Mobilise Creativity and Knowledge to Tackle Compelling Social Challenges.* British Council, London.

Appendices

Baxter, T., Bebbington, J. & Cutteridge, D. (2002) *The Sustainability Assessment Model (SAM).* Proceedings of the SPE International Conference on Health, Safety and Environment in Oil and Gas Exploration and Production, 20–22 March 2002, Malaysia.

City of Vancouver (2005) *A Social Development Plan for the City of Vancouver: Moving Towards Social Sustainability,* Administrative Report A7, Vancouver, Canada.

Future 500 (2007) *Sustainability Tool Kit for Corporate Professionals.* (Available from: http://www.future500.org/custom/26/)

igloo (2010) *footprint™.* (Retrieved January 2010 from: http://www.igloo.uk.net/sustainable-investment)

RICS (2007) *A Green Profession? RICS Members and the Sustainability Agenda.* Royal Institution of Chartered Surveyors, London.

Rosique, J.L. (2009) *Diversifying Funding Strategy and EU URBAN Monitoring Indicators.* Oxford Institute for Sustainable Development (OISD), Oxford Brookes University, Oxford. (Retrieved December 2009 from: http://www.brookes.ac.uk/schools/be/oisd/workshops/urss/index.html)

The Accounting for Sustainability Group (2006) *Accounting for Sustainability.* (Retrieved May 2008 from: http://www.accountingforsustainability.org/)

UNCSD (2001) *Indicators of Sustainable Development: Framework and Methodologies,* ninth session. United Nation Commission on Sustainable Development, New York.

Index

Page numbers in *italics* denote figures and tables.